The ambassador is a symbol of the foreign state and personifies international relations. This volume, the first of its kind written by an Indian scholar–diplomat, provides an insider's view of this institution. Looking back at the traditional functions of the ambassador, it examines the direction in which this is being constantly redefined, to the point where the envoy now functions as a public affairs entrepreneur. It also looks at how Indian diplomacy has evolved in recent years.

The introduction explores the history of ambassadors, the changing context of international relations, and related gender issues. The book's thematic concerns are four-fold—the greater functional necessity of envoys in the volatility of contemporary international relations, the potential for more productive use of diplomatic services by developing nations, the pivotal role of the diplomatic machinery in advancing national interests, and the study of diplomacy as a profession.

Praise for *The 21st Century Ambassador*

'*The 21st Century Ambassador* reminds us that diplomacy is not only about politics and society, but increasingly in a global world about economic relations, how we can further these to build a global community... [Rana's] book is well-researched and sprinkled generously with wisdom, insight and experience...'

Sunil Kant Munjal, President, Confederation of Indian Industry

'I was very impressed to read Ambassador Rana's book...As ambassadors and high commissioners we don't work for the foreign ministry anymore, we work for the government as a whole...[and] at least fifty per cent of my time and the effort of my staff goes into business in the widest sense of the word...this book goes very much to that...'

Sir Michael Arthur, British High Commissioner in India

'Mr Rana's book is very refreshing...It points out what is very obvious but not apparent to all of us...The concept of the CEO ambassador mentioned in this book is very important...'

Chak Mun See, Singapore High Commissioner in India

'Kishan S. Rana's book...focuses on the ambassador as an institution that continues to represent the cutting edge of the international diplomatic system, and considers ways in which that institution's functioning can be optimized in today's environment...Rana's own career...combined with extensive research, gives this book credibility...the sheer breadth of coverage is impressive in itself...*The 21st Century Ambassador* could serve very well as preparatory text...or even for new senior political appointees... The book has much to say and provides much thoughtful guidance on how to do effective diplomacy in today and tomorrow's world.'

Edward Marks, Former US Ambassador, Foreign Service Journal, *Washington DC, June 2004*

The 21st Century Ambassador
Plenipotentiary to Chief Executive

Kishan S. Rana

OXFORD
UNIVERSITY PRESS

YMCA Library Building, Jai Singh Road, New Delhi 110001

Oxford University Press is a department of the University of Oxford. It furthers the
University's objective of excellence in research, scholarship, and education
by publishing worldwide in

Oxford   New York
Auckland   Cape Town   Dar es Salaam   Hong Kong   Karachi
Kuala Lumpur   Madrid   Melbourne   Mexico City   Nairobi
New Delhi   Shanghai   Taipei   Toronto

With offices in
Argentina   Austria   Brazil   Chile   Czech Republic   France   Greece
Guatemala   Hungary   Italy   Japan   Poland   Portugal   Singapore
South Korea   Switzerland   Thailand   Turkey   Ukraine   Vietnam

Oxford is a registered trademark of Oxford University Press
in the UK and in certain other countries

Published in India
by Oxford University Press, New Delhi

© Kishan S. Rana 2005

The moral rights of the author have been asserted
Database right Oxford University Press (maker)

First published by DiploFoundation, Malta and Geneva, 2004

This edition is reprinted with permission from DiploFoundation

First published 2005
Second impression 2006
Oxford India Paperbacks 2010

All rights reserved. No part of this publication may be reproduced,
or transmitted in any form or by any means, electronic or mechanical,
including photocopying, recording or by any infomation storage and
retrieval system, without permission in writing from Oxford University Press.
Enquiries concerning reproduction outside the scope of the above should be
sent to the Rights Department, Oxford University Press, at the address above

You must not circulate this book in any other binding or cover
and you must impose this same condition on any acquirer

ISBN 13: 978-019-806966-9
ISBN 10: 019-806966-9

Typeset in Dante MT 11.5/13 by Eleven Arts, New Delhi 110 035
Printed in India by De Unique, New Delhi 110 018
Published by Oxford University Press
YMCA Library Building, Jai Singh Road, New Delhi 110 001

For

Mimi,

Ajit and Deepika, Priya,

Suneira and Karnavir

CONTENTS

Preface to the Paperback Edition	x
Preface to the Indian Edition	xii
Acknowledgements	xxvii
List of Abbreviations	xxix
Introduction	1
Evolution	2
The Diplomatic Process and Developing Countries	3
The Context	8
Gender Issues	18
1. The Transformed Plenipotentiary	20
Who is the Ambassador?	23
Theory and Practice	26
Empirical Evidence	30
New Responsibilities	33
Bilateral and Multilateral Envoys	37
2. Ritual and Form	39
Protocol and Ceremonial	39

Non-Career Appointments 47
The Diplomatic Corps 52
Privilege and Immunity 55
Operational Modalities: Duration, Channels and Withdrawal 57
Personal Security 62

3. **Partners and Techniques** 64
Official Interlocutors 64
Non-State Partners 74
Principal Functions: Negotiation, Promotion and Outreach 76
Feedback 88
Management 91
Servicing 92

4. **The Multilateral Ambassador** 96
Multilateral and Bilateral Work 97
Form and Substance 100
Methods and Goals 104
Work Procedures 108
Regional Diplomacy 112
The Home Base 115
A Downside? 117

5. **The Domestic Dimension** 121
The Home Context 123
Performance Management 129
Foreign Ministry Interface 133
Official Partners 136
Political Masters 136
Non-State Agencies and Public Diplomacy 138
Latitude and Innovation 141

6. Leadership in the Embassy 143
   The Ship's Captain 144
   The Embassy Team 146
   Intelligence, Defense and Other Specialists 151
   Consuls—Career and Honorary 154
   Country Team 156
   Mission Size and Management 157
   The Spouse and Families 158
   The Residence and Entertainment 160

7. Human Resources 165
   Training and Conferences 165
   Personal Qualities 168
   Professional Skills 170
   Language and Other Expertise 172
   Career Management 174
   The Ethical Dimension 177
   Rogue Ambassadors 180
   Reward and Sanction 184
   In Retirement 186

8. The Future 190
   EU Experience 190
   The Entrepreneur-Ambassador 192
   Power and Influence 196
   Globalized Diplomacy 198

Notes 205
Select Bibliography 248
Index 252

PREFACE TO THE PAPERBACK EDITION

The issue of this paperback edition from Oxford University Press, New Delhi, gives me an opportunity to update some developments concerning the modern envoy. Let me mention three issues: professionalism, performance monitoring and training.

Many countries, some in the developing world, are preoccupied with a need to reinforce professional standards in diplomatic services, including the selection and functioning of envoys abroad. In countries as varied as Argentina and Kenya, there is concern over a need to reduce political appointments of ambassadors, especially if those selected are not public figures of standing, but are instead beneficiaries of unwarranted largesse. Yet, despite recognition that the inculcation of professional qualities suffers with such appointments, in many developing states, especially in African and Latin American countries, very many envoys continue to hold office through grace and favor.

Another trend is wider application of performance norms, borrowed from the corporate world, ranging from 'key performance indicators' and 'balanced scorecards' for embassies, to 'performance contracts' for envoys. In Africa, Botswana and Kenya are two countries where I have observed and assisted with the application of these processes.

Training is another area that has seen major developments. In 2008, the Indian government mandated training courses for all officials at mid-career levels, as a precondition for promotion to ranks of director and joint secretary (that is, officials with about 16 to 23 years of service). The Ministry of External Affairs has taken an easy way out, outsourcing this training to one of the country's top management institutes at Hyderabad. Alas, that does not help, nearly as much as a dedicated course at the Foreign Service Institute might. This is largely because management institutes are fine at training those handling public-service projects and development tasks, but have little interest in, or knowledge of, diplomacy. In contrast, diplomatic academies at places like Kenya and Malaysia have developed their own special training programs for envoys. We can count on mid-career and senior-level training to expand in the years ahead.

Foreign ministries would benefit from mutually sharing experience in relation to all such activities.

PREFACE TO THE INDIAN EDITION

The evolution of the institution of the ambassador in India, sheds light on how several generations of envoys have served this country in nearly six decades since Independence. It also offers insight into the issues typically faced by developing countries, as also the post-Cold War transition states.[1] Among its international peers India is regarded as an active diplomacy practitioner, one that has mobilized its institutional apparatus in a sustained manner, advancing its foreign policy goals.

Before Independence, India's experiment with diplomacy developed along two tracks, the colonial and the nationalist. As a colony India was projected in world affairs as early as 1919, at a time when partial, hesitant evolution of India's 'dominion status' commenced. Britain registered India as one of the founders of the League of Nations. India opened its diplomatic representation abroad at the next stage of constitutional evolution, the passage of the India Act of 1935. An Indian High Commission was established in London in 1935, not as a real diplomatic mission, but as the colony's liaison office in the imperial capital. It worked under the shadow of the Office of the Secretary of State for India, handling the day-to-day issues of detail, such as recruitment of British officials sent to India, payment of pensions to Britons who had served in the Indian Army, and a myriad of details of collaboration with the metropolitan power. A major component of this High Commission was a 'Stores Department' that handled the procurement of goods and services needed by different official agencies in New Delhi. Later this entity came to be known as the 'Supply Wing', run by officials from the 'Ministry of Supply'. In proof of Parkinson's Law, this anachronistic outpost survived in London, and in Washington DC, all the way till the late-1980s; it took a decisive Rajiv Gandhi to close these large 'diplomatic' appendages.²

Predating even the High Commission in London, special missions of the colonial era were set up in Ceylon, Malaya and South Africa, for the protection of Indians. These were run by the Overseas Indians Department, which handled the emigration of Indian labor to these and other colonies, and sought to safeguard their work and living conditions.

One of the major colonial agencies in New Delhi was the Political Department, staffed by both the Indian Civil Service (ICS) and the special cadre of this Department, working as an embryonic foreign ministry, focused primarily on the frontier regions of British India, especially the North-West, given Britain's obsession with the threat from Russia and the interplay of conflicting interests in Central Asia that came to be known as the 'Great Game'. In 1946, on the eve of the transfer of power, when the Provisional Government headed by Jawaharlal Nehru took office, it reshaped itself as the External Affairs Department. The Overseas Indians Department had already become the Commonwealth Department, and in 1947 it was merged into a single Ministry of External Affairs (MEA).

The second trajectory of pre-Independence development was the evolution of an autonomous international policy. The very first session of the Indian National Congress in 1885 passed a resolution criticizing the annexation of Upper Burma, while the second one a year later referred to the disturbed conditions of Europe, and the role that India could play in assisting Britain, if it was given a role under the self-rule formula. Mahatma Gandhi's return to India from South Africa in 1914 marked a further awakening of the nationalist movement to global affairs. The Congress sessions of 1922 and 1923 supported the Arab cause in Palestine. Visiting Ceylon in 1927, Gandhiji urged the Indians settled there to work for that country's independence. Foreign policy gained further impetus in 1927 when

Jawaharlal Nehru assumed charge of this activity in the Congress Party, and its foreign affairs department was established. That year Nehru had attended the International Congress Against Imperialism and was elected one of the five honorary presidents.[3] In 1938, on the eve of the outbreak of World War II, Nehru traveled to Prague to express solidarity with the Czech people threatened by Nazi Germany; he denounced the Munich Pact as 'shameful betrayal and dishonor'. 1939 found him in Chungking, and he was forced to cut short his trip owing to the outbreak of the World War, dropping his plan to visit Mao Tse-tung in his revolutionary base at Yennan. This visionary independence movement read well the larger international cause.

Indian Envoys Over the Years

The evolution of Indian diplomacy can be traced through several stages, illustrated with exemplars. These individuals have been outstanding, but many others could be named for each vintage.

Before 1947

Sir Girija Shankar Bajpai (1891–1954), one of the stars of the Indian Civil Service, attended the Round Table Conferences on Indian constitutional change in 1930–31, and served as a Member of the Viceroy's Executive Council in 1935–36 and in 1940–41. He established the quasi-diplomatic mission in Washington DC in 1941, serving there until 1946, called an 'Agent-General'.[4] When the Nehru-led Provisional Government assumed office in New Delhi in preparation for the transfer of power, he was re-designated as the Indian Chargé d'Affaires. He returned to New Delhi in 1947, heading MEA as its Secretary General for the first five years. In 1952 he was appointed Governor of Bombay province. It was a tribute to both the professionalism and the innate nationalism of these ICS officials—'the steel frame'—that Bajpai and his senior counterparts heading the administration in the ministries made that transition, from serving a fading alien Empire, to Independent India, with exemplary felicity, gaining credibility as public servants of the new Republic. Bajpai is also remembered as the man of prescience who urged Nehru in 1953 to resolve the issue of an imprecise boundary with China as a matter of urgent priority, in the negotiations that led up to the 1954 Border Trade Agreement, advice that went unheeded because Panditji was fixated on a different strategy.

1947–62

The first Indian ambassadors sent out were drawn from diverse sources, many of them 'political' appointees, ranging from eminent historian K.M. Pannikar in China and Egypt, Nehru's sister Vijayalakshmi Pandit to Moscow, Washington DC and London, and the acerbic Krishna Menon to London and as Permanent Representative in New York—and others mentioned in this book.[5] In those years Indian envoys operated in rarified high political diplomacy, in consonance with Nehru's assertive global foreign policy. India successfully projected itself as a builder of accommodation between the Cold Warriors. The Korea armistice in 1953, as well as the first Indo-China peace accord negotiated at Geneva two years later, were both products of that phase of mediatory diplomacy. The memoirs of those stalwarts are fascinating, describing their roles as interlocutors, often dealing directly with the principal international leaders, handling major issues with fluid ease, enjoying considerable autonomy of action.[6]

An archetype was the cerebral G. Parthasarathy (1912–95). Starting his career as a journalist, swiftly rising to the Chief Editorship of the country's principal press agency PTI, he was sent on his first overseas assignment to Cambodia (1955), to head the International Control Commission. Thereafter, between 1957 and 1965, he served as India's ambassador to Indonesia, China and Pakistan, then as the Permanent Representative in New York (1965–68). Returning home, he became the first Vice-Chancellor of the Jawaharlal Nehru University, New Delhi, followed some years later as the Deputy Chairman of the Planning Commission. When Indira Gandhi returned to power in 1980, he served as her foreign policy adviser, till her assassination in 1984. 'G.P.' as he was popularly known, personified quiet diplomacy, his incisive mind generating an analytical understanding of world affairs that became a base for policy.

1962–73

The crisis in relations with China, culminating in an armed conflict along the entire Himalayan frontier in September–October 1962, marked a watershed for Indian foreign policy. Pushed onto the backfoot, Indian diplomacy struggled to regain momentum. These were hard years, with other landmark events: the India–Pakistan War of 1965; the 1966–67 food crisis that required massive imports from the US (under its PL-480 law) and left the legacy of a huge Rupee debt overhang; and the Bangladesh crisis, culminating in the triumph of the December 1971 War. Operating within limited options, Indian diplomacy navigated a cautious path, focused on narrow national objectives, working for its space between the two superpowers, while preserving the core of its non-aligned status.

Eric Gonsalves (1928–) joined the IFS in 1949, and has been among the high achievers of that first post-Independence generation. He served as ambassador to Japan (1975–78) and to Belgium and to the EEC (1982–86), but one should include among his ambassadorial hats his time in Washington DC as the Deputy Chief of Mission (1972–75), when he played a major role in negotiating the bilateral agreement that dealt with the Rupee food imports debt. Others of that generation had gained their ambassadorships a little earlier, beginning with M.K. Rasgotra, sent to Morocco in 1967, and N. Krishnan as permanent representative to Geneva in that same year. Over their careers, these individuals and others like them materially transformed the bilateral and multilateral relationships handled by them.

1973–91

The 1973 'oil shock', that sudden quadrupling in the global price of crude oil, coincided with a fading of the euphoria of the Bangladesh victory, and a domestic economic resource scarcity engendered partly by the sharp rise in defence spending after 1962. That produced the internal political crisis culminating in Indira Gandhi's 'Emergency Rule' of 1975–77, her defeat in the 1977 elections, and the country's first non-Congress government. These domestic developments did not produce a marked alteration in the substance of the country's foreign policy, though the syntax changed, and clichés like 'genuine' non-alignment and the pursuit of 'beneficial bilateralism' gained currency. Beyond these, Indian diplomacy underwent a quiet metamorphosis.

Economic diplomacy became the highest priority, driven by the need to earn more through exports to pay for expensive oil. New embassies were opened in the Gulf region, and envoys were exhorted to become commercial warriors, to win project and construction contracts, and seek foreign placement for Indian engineers, skilled workers, and the like. MEA shifted to an innovative phase, and the Economic Division gained importance and inspirational leadership, first under Bimal Sanyal, followed by Romesh Bhandari. Diplomats with barely 15 years experience, holding substantive ranks of counselor, were sent as ambassadors to the oil-rich states of the region, and for the great part this worked rather well.[7] The nearly four million Indian professionals and skilled workers in the Gulf, and the wide-ranging economic cooperation established in that and other regions, are a testimony to the initiatives of that era.

These events in India coincided with the emergence of developing countries as a new vocal bloc at the UN, the G–77, demanding a just, equitable international order. Indian diplomacy played a substantial role in that evolution, and several of its brightest provided intellectual inputs into the 'development decades' that took shape in the years that followed, plus the demands for 'new international orders' in trade, development finance, information and the rest. This became the era of declaratory diplomacy, and elaboration of the North–South divide. While it absorbed vast multilateral diplomatic energy, it proved to be a chimera in the real value it delivered.

A model of that generation is Hamid Ansari (1937–), Arabic scholar. He has played a key role in forging new bilateral economic and political partnerships across the Gulf region. His first ambassadorship was in the UAE (1976–80); he then headed the missions in Canberra, Kabul, and Tehran (later heading the Permanent Mission in New York (1993–96); on the eve of retirement he was sent as Ambassador to Saudi Arabia for four years). He has been highly effective at both economic and political diplomacy, bilateral and multilateral.

After 1991

India's Economic Reforms of 1991, unleashing the country's creative potential, represent the single most important event in the country's post-Independence policy. These Reforms resulted from two partly connected events: externally, the end of the Cold War and the collapse of the Soviet Union, and domestically, an acute financial crisis that forced India to sell part of its gold reserves. That story is well-known, how that crisis produced a new set of options for two leaders produced by circumstance, Prime Minister P.V. Narasimha Rao and Finance Minister Manmohan Singh. The force of necessity led them to undertake the unthinkable, to shed India's self-imposed shackles of a failed *dirigiste* economic system, moving rapidly from de-licensing to market economics. External policy proceeded to draw inspiration from these Reforms, and adapted itself to the paradigm shift in the global system.

The foreign policy-diplomacy response took the shape of an intensified international relationship building, extending to virtually every region. The consequences were incremental for the great part, but of colossal value in sum. In South-East Asia it produced the 'Look East' policy, articulated by Narasimha Rao in Singapore in 1993. In Central Asia it led to the opening of new embassies led by envoys that have seen their task in holistic terms of producing innovative new connections across the gamut of emerging possibilities. In Africa it gave a new push to economics-driven partnerships.[8] In Latin America it generated a search for congruities in the trade, technology and investment sectors. With the major powers, the quality of engagement deepened markedly, to become more productive than at any time in the past. Though the Indian nuclear tests of May 1998 produced a setback with the US, Japan and Germany, this was later overcome and produced closer mutual understanding.

In South Asia, the realization has emerged among the smaller neighbors that India is 'the region's economic locomotive'.[9] In parallel, India has rethought its trade policy, embracing the concept of regional free trade agreements (FTAs) with the zeal of a new convert; the two-way success of the India-Sri Lanka FTA of 2000 has produced a rash of new agreements, signed and under finalization. In doing this, India has shed its earlier 'ideological' stance that it would work only for universal trade accords, in the GATT-WTO framework. In a word, in external economics as in politics, rigid doctrinism has been replaced by flexible response, and tactical suppleness.

Shyam Saran (1946–) was appointed Foreign Secretary in August 2004, by the Manmohan Singh government that had assumed office two months earlier; it is said that he was also the choice of the outgoing government, a rare meeting of minds of political adversaries. He is the first head of the Foreign Service who has never served in a major Western capital,[10] and to have superceded, without serious demur, nearly a dozen of his senior colleagues. He exemplifies the post-Reform breed of savvy envoys. He served as High Commissioner to Mauritius in 1992, and successively thereafter as ambassador to Myanmar, Indonesia and Nepal. At each place, he was responsible for an accretion in the bilateral relations.

An envoy who merits special mention is J.N. Dixit (1935–2005), unmatched in his assignments in neighboring countries, starting with Dacca, where he opened India's mission in January 1972 immediately after the Bangladesh War (staying an as Deputy High Commissioner). He later served in Afghanistan, Sri Lanka and Pakistan, where he handed over charge in 1992 to take over as Foreign Secretary. Dixit gained unique recognition as a strategic thinker and a forceful patriot, narrating his experiences in nine books (a record in the Service), until his untimely demise in January 2005 while serving as National Security Adviser.

A missing element in Indian diplomatic history is the relative absence of personal narratives; rather few retired diplomats have penned their own memoirs. Coupled with de facto closed archives, despite an obligation on paper to open classified documents to the public after 30 years, it has meant that the real accounting of achievements—and of failures as well—remains shrouded. Nor is there any comprehensive set of oral history record that scholars and others can access, other than a limited set of such material at the Nehru Library. Five of the six ambassadors mentioned above have not authored their memoirs, though three of them could yet do so.

What qualities distinguish the above individuals, and many others of their ilk, not named here for reasons of space? A subjective response: an abiding sense of service, a commitment to public purpose, larger than one's self. Add to that: integrity of the understated kind, used not as an instrument of career advancement, but forming the core of personal values; professionalism that holds firm to the national interest, across the changes in political masters at home; the ability to lead by personal example, inspiring others and mentoring the next generation; a capacity to adapt to the circumstances of each assignment and multilateral setting, as well as absorb the customary vicissitudes of one's career. As diplomatic actors, they have left a unique imprint in the countries where they have served.[11]

Of course there have been Indian envoys of pedestrian achievement, those who have gone with the flow, seldom taking initiative or face the risk implicit in new actions. Others have golfed, cavorted, or metaphorically slept through their assignments, or spent their time in alcoholic amnesia. Worse have been the few cases of errant behavior, surfacing occasionally in the public gaze. Such problems are compounded by tolerant attitudes, a kind of 'don't-ask-don't-tell' policy, instead of tough disciplinary enforcement. Diplomatic services, like all establishments, do not advertise their human failures, so as with icebergs, beneath the few visible instances lie buried the figurative skeletons of other sinners. Rather than pursue such instances (and risk libel!), it is more profitable to look at the institution's strong and weak points.

Characteristics and Style

The vast majority of Indian ambassadors are career professionals, serving members of the IFS. Successive prime ministers (the appointing authority in the Indian system) have upheld Pandit Nehru's tradition of just a small handful of 'political' appointees.

At any point in time, non-career envoys number eight or ten, out of a total of around 115; some among them are retired Foreign Service officials.

One major shift has been in the issues handled by the envoys, from political concerns to economics, from high to low diplomacy, where 'soft' areas such as culture, media management, image promotion, education, science and technology, and relations with ethnic communities crowd their daily agenda. This is also the experience of other diplomatic services. Indian diplomats have been ahead of their peers on the learning curve for the new skills, after exclusive concern with political diplomacy was shed, the mid-1960s onwards. This is also true of cultural, education and science diplomacy, but in the arena of external media management, the performance has been uneven.

Another revealing dimension is the location preference of the ambassadors, and the regional distribution of the senior-most envoys. As with foreign policy, the 'developing country focus' of IFS personnel was weak in the early years, owing to a strong West bias. How else can one explain the fact that at different times in the 1970s and 1980s, not a single envoy in Grade I (out of a total of 15 assigned abroad, now grown to 22), could be found in Africa south of the Sahara? Yet, capitals of relatively secondary importance, be it Berne, Copenhagen or The Hague, have seldom been peopled by any other than those in that Grade. This has now partly changed; more of the senior officials are to be found in Africa and Asia. The Service's best and the brightest now vie to serve in the hard, challenging posts—not just the ambassadors but the younger diplomats as well—this is visible in the assignment 'bidding' process that MEA has introduced in recent years.

Take another aspect of the work of ambassadors abroad, the domestic dimension, especially the entanglements of home politics. Unlike its sister entity, the Indian Administrative Service (IAS), the IFS for long remained insulated from domestic pressures. Even today, the extent to which ambassadors have to deal with political parties, or accommodate demands of individual politicians, remains minimal, mainly as these actors have little interest in external affairs. One growth area is the politicization of overseas Indians, and their enlistment in home politics, as narrated in this book. Another source of political entanglement—in a rising trend—is when IFS officials themselves enlist the support of politicians, on the basis of their own regional and other affiliations, or professed political inclination, in pursuit of assignments, promotions and extensions in service. Despite this, for the great part the Service remains apolitical.

Two other sets of domestic interactions deserve attention. Relations between MEA and the other branches of government began on the wrong foot in the early years of Independence, since MEA was Panditji's own Ministry, and its officials at different levels routinely dealt with the Prime Minister. This, coupled with the typical airs that diplomatic services often assume with home counterparts, produced resentment. Very few institutional networking arrangements were established with other official agencies, though in recent years, the situation has improved a little. For instance, the Foreign Secretary and the Defence Secretary have a dialogue mechanism of their own, and in 2000, for the first time, a couple of defense experts were brought into the division dealing with disarmament and security affairs. And yet, the in-placement of officials from other agencies into MEA remains anathema, though at any point in time 15-odd MEA officials are to be found on out-placement in the Ministries of Finance, Commerce, Defence and others. In this situation, Indian ambassadors have played a role in extending outreach, since the expanded subject heterogeneity of their work mandates such broad interface.

With the other domestic constituency segment, the non-official actors on the foreign affairs stage, MEA has a better record of open dialogue, though it depends on individual initiatives, not institutionalized arrangements. For instance, despite its leadership role in economic diplomacy, work that now hinges on public-private partnership, MEA has no advisory body of experts from chambers of commerce, export entities, and others. Again it is the ambassadors and their teams that are key in this process, since industry associations, export bodies and individual enterprises are all their natural partners in pursuit of external economic goals.

Embassy teams have also improved their interaction with other home agencies, the media, academia, and think tanks, though as seen by the latter set of actors, the picture is less reassuring. Unlike the business chambers and companies that acknowledge a more customer-friendly response from envoys, both in major capitals, as also the far outposts (which generally extend a warm welcome to the relatively few visitors from home), the non-economic actors still speak of instances of neglect. In part this is an image issue, and underscores a need for better marketing at home. Few Indian envoys deal with NGOs and other civil society advocates, while MEA has no unit for such contacts, or for public diplomacy.

Take the societal background of the envoys. The rigorous process of selection to high civil services ensures that those who qualify are talented individuals, in a word, the elites.[12] What has changed dramatically is that new IFS entrants now come from far wider regional, income and educational backgrounds than before. Long-standing urban middle-class bias remains, but it is moderated by the presence of some from rural backgrounds, and those educated in the interior of the country, not just the products of the famous metropolitan institutions. In varying degrees, we see the same phenomenon of greater diversity and plurality in operation in other countries.[13] In gender representation, the Indian record compares moderately well with others, in that women diplomats do not face impediments in career advancement, but the numbers of women entering the Service each year are stuck at around 10 to 15%, with no rising trend.

India has never held a conference of all its ambassadors, something that is an annual routine in China, Japan and Germany. Ambassadors to major countries are called to Delhi once in eight or ten years, though regional conferences are held in rotation once or twice a year, when this can be accommodated by the External Affairs Minister or the Prime Minister in the midst of an overseas trip. This misses out on the implicit re-orientation, even quasi-training, dimension that the others build into their conferences. Senior-level training is not conducted, of the kind now gaining currency elsewhere. This is part of a bigger issue of inadequate in-service training, though MEA re-launched its first mid-career program in 2004, after a break of many years.

A big weakness is the lack of any systemic guidance to envoys on the changing parameters of their work, re-training and institutional supervision. Performance management concepts that are increasingly in vogue in other diplomatic systems and in the public services of other countries are absent, with the exception of annual plans prepared by embassies, which are seldom monitored by MEA.[14] An 'inspectorate' has often been considered, but does not exist. The envoys that shine are self-motivated, but the system does little to encourage and guide. The reasons are weak leadership, over-worked senior officials at headquarters with no time for supervision, and a lack of systemic controls. As in other agencies, individuals make up our system, not an organized method.

To sum up, the best Indian ambassadors have been outstanding, inspiring others to perform their best. The average level is also high, as professionals of other services know, and sometimes acknowledge. What is missing is institutionalized support, and a systemic enforcement of standards, of the kind that other comparable diplomatic networks treat as mandatory, described in this book.

Notes

1. For a detailed analysis of the Indian system, see Kishan S. Rana, *Inside Diplomacy* (Manas, New Delhi, 2000 and 2002).
2. Indian embassies in Berlin, London, Paris and Washington DC still house 'railway wings', equally anachronistic equipment and services procurement entities that have managed to survive.
3. The other four honorary presidents were Einstein, Romain Rolland, Madame Sun Yat Sen and George Lansbury.
4. The diaries of Leo Amery, Secretary of State for India in the Churchill government of World War II that was in power from May 1940 to August 1945, reveal that even the issue of raising G.S. Bajpai's status to the diplomatic rank of 'minister', occupied the attention of the British Cabinet. Amery brought up the proposal twice during 1943 and 1944, but Winston Churchill, then in the depths of his aversion for all things Indian (as Amery records almost in every second or third entry relating to Cabinet meetings), turned down the proposal (source: Churchill Archives, Cambridge).

5. The Indian Foreign Service (IFS) was formed in 1946, composed of ICS officials (many from the erstwhile Political Department), plus ad hoc recruits from varied sources, including the armed forces, a few young princes from the former ruling states, journalists and others. The first direct recruitment into the IFS took place in 1948, through the Union Public Services Commission.
6. Notable accounts among them are: K.P.S. Menon, *Many Worlds: An Autobiography* (Oxford University Press, Bombay, 1965); Badr-Ud-Din Tyabji, *Memories of an Egoist* (Roli, New Delhi, 1988), and *More Memories of an Egoist* (Har-Anand, New Delhi, 1994); Y.D. Gundevia, *Outside the Archives* (Sangam, Hyderabad, 1984); M.R.A. Baig, *In Different Saddles* (Asia, Bombay, 1967).
7. This was the only time when ambassadors were sent in Grade IV, equivalent to the home rank of director (the other three grades are the equivalent of the home civil service ranks of 'secretary to the government of India', additional secretary and joint secretary). The author was among the fortunate appointees of that time, sent to Algeria. His exhilarating experiences with economic diplomacy and the efforts of those days to project an India 'brand', are narrated in *Inside Diplomacy* (Manas, New Delhi, 2000 and 2002).
8. For example, the 'Team Nine Initiative' of 2002, focused on Francophone West Africa, neglected in the past.
9. This term was used in a BBC interview by a leading Pakistani businessman attending the annual 'India Summit' meeting organized by the World Economic Forum and the Confederation of Indian Industry in December 2004.
10. Shyam Saran served as a First Secretary in Geneva in his younger days, and was the Deputy Chief of Mission in Tokyo in 1986–89. In Mauritius, he was the author's direct successor; Mauritian friends have testified to his winning manner and success.
11. Apa Saheb Pant served for about four years as India's first Commissioner to East Africa, 1947 onwards; see pages 30–1. During my Kenya assignment (1984–86), on the two occasions that he visited Nairobi I saw the respect that he inspired, three decades after his service in that country. One also learnt that when Pant had visited Nairobi in 1964 as a senior official accompanying the External Affairs Minister of State of the time, a year after Kenya became independent, President Jomo Kenyatta invited him to dinner at the State House; when Pant requested the Indian Minister's inclusion at the dinner, he was told that the dinner was in his honor, but at his suggestion

the Minister would also be invited. At the dinner, in the presence of the entire Cabinet, Kenyatta paid a warm tribute to Pant's exceptional service.

12. In the 1960s, some 20,000 candidates competed in the elaborate annual written examination conducted by the Union Public Services Commission, which winnowed the number to around 600 that were called for interviews and appointed to the total of around 300 vacancies in all the civil services. The annual IFS intake has varied between eight to twenty. Today, around 300,000 sit for the two-stage written examination, and around 10,000 qualify for the second set of written papers, followed by interviews for the chosen few.
13. Source: Hocking, *Foreign Ministries* (see bibliography), and the author's research.
14. See Kishan S. Rana, *Performance Management in Foreign Ministries*, 'Studies in Diplomacy' series of papers, Clingendael, July 2004, available at the website: *http://www.clingendael.nl/cli/publ/diplomacy/pdf/issue93.pdf*.

ACKNOWLEDGEMENTS

This book began as an idea at the end of 2000, suggested by Professor G.R. Berridge, acclaimed teacher of diplomacy and kind friend, while I was in Windhoek, on a six-month Commonwealth assignment advising the Namibian Foreign Ministry. The impressions of Africa gathered during that period (and those accumulated during four previous assignments in different parts of that continent), reinforced my experience of the Indian diplomatic system, that while developing countries have learnt well the forms of international discourse, they have had less success in fully harnessing the diplomatic process in the pursuit of their national interests. Published material on the operation of diplomatic services in developing countries is relatively scarce, and the same is true of comparative studies on foreign ministries. Nor are there many internal studies in these states looking to the best practices of others, or attempts to benchmark against them.

Over the past three years, I conducted 40 interviews while collecting data for the book. Among the interviewees, 29 were ambassadors, serving and former, four were diplomats of other rank, and seven were from outside the profession, belonging to the international affairs community. They came from 16 countries around the world. Information collected in the course of other concurrent studies, including a survey of the diplomatic process in Asian and some other countries, was of considerable help. I am very grateful to all of them, for generously offering their experiences and insights, which provided vital direction for this work.

My special thanks to Professor Stephen Cohen and the Brookings Institution at Washington DC, for informal use of their unique facilities in mid-2001. I am also grateful to Foreign Service colleagues Hamid Ansari, Kamal Bakshi, Ranjit Gupta, and Amar Ram, among others, for their unstinted help with reading some of the chapters, and for their advice, comments and criticism.

Above all my profound thanks to my family for their constant support, to my wife Mimi, son Ajit and his wife Deepika and their lovely children Suneira and Karnavir, and daughter Priya, my editor and ally who has helped in so many ways.

KISHAN S. RANA

ABBREVIATIONS

APEC	Asia Pacific Economic Cooperation
ARF	ASEAN Regional Forum
ASEAN	Association of South-East Asian Nations
BIMST-EC	Bangladesh, India, Myanmar, Sri Lanka, Thailand Economic Cooperation (Bhutan and Nepal have also joined this group)
Caricom	Caribbean Community (comprising 16 member-countries, mainly small island states).
Cd'A	chargé d'affaires
CEO	chief executive officer
CFSP	Common Foreign and Security Policy (of the EU)
DCM	deputy chief of mission
ECOWAS	Economic Cooperation for West African States agreement
EP groups	eminent person groups
EU	European Union
FAO	Food and Agricultural Organization
FTA	free trade agreement
GATT	General Agreement on Trade and Tariffs
GCC	Gulf Cooperation Council
IAEA	International Atomic Energy Agency
ILO	International Labor Office
IR theory	international relations theory

IT	information technology
MFA	foreign ministry
NATO	North Atlantic Treaty Organization
NODIS	no distribution (a classification used in the US for cipher messages that have limited distribution)
NGO	non-governmental organization
OAU	Organization of the African Union (formerly Organization of African Unity)
PR	permanent representative
SAARC	South Asian Association of Regional Cooperation
UN	United Nations
UNESCO	UN Educational Scientific and Cultural Organization
WIPO	World Intellectual Property Agreement
WTO	World Trade Organization

INTRODUCTION

In 2003, Thailand announced a 'CEO ambassador policy' as part of the reform of the public sector, under which Thai ambassadors were to '... act as chief executive officers in their assigned countries, taking a strong lead to promote Thailand overseas both politically and economically, with representatives of other agencies serving as members of the team's executive board. They are also expected to be the persons to be held accountable in the first place for the implementation of the Government's strategies abroad'.[1] A pilot project was implemented in April involving the Thai ambassadors to the US, Japan, Belgium, China, India and Laos; later the Thai Foreign Ministry decided to progressively convert all its ambassadors to CEO-style management. This is but one instance of the application of business management concepts and methods to diplomacy, which can be identified as one of the defining changes of our times.[2]

Resident ambassadors and their embassy teams represent the cutting edge of the diplomatic system. The paradigm change in international affairs since the end of the Cold War, evolving globalization, and the 'internalization' of external policy that most countries have witnessed, not only compel an adaptation in foreign policy, but also in the process through which that policy is implemented. This book examines the ambassador as an institution, and considers the ways in which his functioning can be optimized.

Evolution

The *Arthashastra*, composed by Kautilya (also known as Chanakya) around 300 BC, was handed down in an oral tradition as a comprehensive treatise on statecraft.[3] Kautilya is credited with helping Chandragupta Maurya to win the throne of Magadha, in the heart of the Gangetic plain. Some have doubted if it is Kautilya's work, suggesting that it may have been composed a few centuries later, in the version known to us. More relevant for our purpose is the context: a time of warring states, a checkerboard of shifting alliances and rivalries, demanding high governance skills, in strategy and tactics. Describing the attributes of good kingship, including the maintenance of law and order, an efficient administration, and economic policy to sustain prosperity, the treatise also covers relations between states, and the dispatch of emissaries. This makes it one of the oldest documents on the work of envoys, sent by one king to another, for negotiation, observation, the procurement of materials, the release of hostages and other missions.

It is clear from the *Arthashastra* and other evidence that the institution of the resident envoy was yet to be invented, but situations of a relatively lengthy stay of envoys in foreign courts were well known. Kautilya's advice was pragmatic, founded on *realpolitik*. The envoy's tasks were to send information to his king, 'uphold the king's honor', acquire allies for him, and 'instigate dissension among the friends of the enemy'. On presenting himself to the other king, he was to deliver the message exactly as it was 'given to him, even if he apprehends danger to his life'.[4] The assumption was that adversarial relations existed among kingdoms, as well as the absence of an overarching system of mutual accommodation or of a dominant empire that enforced peace. But the short references to envoys are studded with practical advice, that envoys should not let honors go to their head, avoid women and liquor, and 'sleep alone'.

The practice of sending permanent envoys to other states began in medieval Italy in the 15th century, and by the time of the Treaty of Westphalia in 1648, it became customary in much of Europe. But even prior to this, the institution of the resident consul was known in the Mediterranean. The first comprehensive study of the real work of the envoy is by the Dutch diplomat and scholar Abraham de Wicquefort, whose book *The Embassador and his Functions*, published in 1681, was translated into English by John Digby in 1716.[5] Since then, the resident ambassador has been the theme of many works, some listed in the bibliography.

In historical evolution, resident ambassadors preceded the institution of the foreign ministry by a couple of centuries. It was in Paris that a dedicated agency of the government was created in 1626 to manage the system of envoys based abroad. The other classic functions of the foreign ministry came later. While the modern foreign ministry serves several functions that are not directly related to the network of envoys based abroad, it is this network that is its *raison d'être*. This ministry and the embassies it supervises constitute the intertwined diplomatic system.

The Diplomatic Process and Developing Countries

The foreign policy of a state depends on its attributes, its capacity to engage in relations with other countries, and its international goals. The tools and technique through which different countries implement their foreign policy are for the great part similar, almost identical. Thus, there exists a 'diplomatic process' that is shared between countries, with a methodology routinely practiced by the diplomatic services of different states. Of course, there is potential in the system for change and innovation as well, but most of these are transportable, capable of emulation and adaptation. This makes comparative diplomatic studies rather interesting.

I am indebted to Canadian scholar Justin Robertson[6] for the realization that foreign ministries and diplomatic services in developing countries—and by the same token, those in the transition states as well—are not traditionally seen as potential recipients for assistance in 'capacity building'. And yet, in point of fact, they have the same requirement to be assisted in building up their organizations and methods, as also their human resources, as the other institutions of governance working in domestic affairs, to which external donors and international organizations provide considerable technical and other assistance. The obvious reason is, of course, that a country's diplomatic institutions constitute the very mechanism through which international communication takes place, and it is indiscreet for donors to advise that the diplomatic institutions need upgrading or improvement. It is even harder for the recipient states to seek this foreign assistance, even when they realize the need for this. We are then left with self-improvement as a viable model for carrying out change.

There is another way of looking at the diplomatic process. Ensuring that the country has the best possible mechanism for advancing its external interests is a 'public good', and a factor of basic good governance. It does not suffice that a country should have a foreign policy that best serves its interests. It must also have the optimal ground mechanism to implement this policy and to build and operate the external relationships that best serve its interests. This is a complicated way of saying that the process is almost as important as the policy. Yet, in our discussions of national affairs in different countries, how little attention is devoted to process issues?

The diplomatic system works as a delivery mechanism of foreign policy, the process through which a country's external policy is implemented. It may appear as a one-way relationship, with policy driving the process, but since the diplomatic machine delivers the responses and assessments that become policy determinants, this feedback loop interrelates the two. Moreover, in the real world, the implementation of policy often becomes part of policy itself. Thus, policy and process are intertwined, virtually inseparable.

When we examine the diplomatic process, it is easy to see the importance of the institution of the ambassador, in bilateral and multilateral roles, as a central element of the entire diplomatic system. With the foreign ministry functioning as the core or hub, the ambassador and the team he or she heads at the embassy are the field units, each vitally dependent on the other. This study examines the contemporary role and the future of the ambassador, as a component of the international system.

The principal thesis of this book is that today there is a greater functional necessity for the resident ambassador than at any previous time, since Italy launched this innovative institution in the 15th

century. Some may view this with skepticism, accustomed as they may be to a refrain that ambassadors are marginalized by technology and instant communications. Moreover, critics might add that a direct dialogue between principals even bypasses foreign ministries, and that the technicalities of international discourse also makes the generalist envoy rather irrelevant, or of secondary value, at best.

True, the operational ethos of international relations has been transformed over the years. The ambassador is today seldom a contributor in the determination of war and peace between states, though he still has a role to play in the reduction of tensions, often at multilateral instances where his country may have only an indirect interest. There are other elements to be taken into account.

The central tasks of the ambassador are less dramatic, and even less obvious—the advancement of his country's interests in a world of complex interdependence, where issues in the external dialogue are interwoven. In the entire government machinery, he is the one who has the best overview, in real time, of the current shape and content of the bilateral relationship entrusted to his charge. This produces an opportunity for bargaining, linkage and tradeoffs, across the full panorama of issues, political, technical, and cross-disciplinary, in which the countries concerned are engaged. In the volatility of contemporary international relations, states are continually searching for convergence with other countries, to build issue-specific coalitions. In all these activities, the ambassador ideally integrates near-seamlessly into the structures of the home establishment, especially the foreign ministry, and becomes a participant in the policy making and decision process, relying on instant communications to overcome distance and the traditional barriers of 'missions and headquarters' mindsets.

Does this happen in practice? Yes, in the relatively few countries that have seized the blending of technology with necessity. Many more are yet to realize the possibilities that are open to them, for deriving better value from the entire diplomatic process. Indirectly, this book offers a blueprint of the attainable in one specific area—optimizing the work of the ambassador.

A second theme of the book is that there are very many countries, most of them unfortunately of the developing world, that have remained mired in the forms and symbols of diplomatic usage, without seizing the substance. In such cases, the ambassador and the system of external representation that he heads have not been used to the full potential. The irony is that improving this delivery system of diplomacy involves neither additional sums of money nor a radical change in systems. In contrast to these countries, some of the new actors on the international stage, the states of Eastern Europe and Central Asia that are variously described as 'emerging' or 'in transition', are innovatively reforming their diplomatic systems to better meet new expectations. The lament of 'capacity enhancement' that the countries of the South frequently put forth at gatherings of the World Trade Organization (WTO), refers to real problems. But here is one arena where capacity amelioration involves a straightforward reform of organizations and methods, within the existing capacities, not the mastering of new technical subjects.

A third and related theme is good governance. Many countries now have 'citizen's charters' for the foreign ministry, spelling out the services that this ministry and the ambassadors abroad are expected and mandated to provide. But the notion that citizens have a right to a good foreign policy and effective implementation of that policy by the diplomatic establishment is not directly acknowledged. It is overlooked that ambassadors and others on their staff are catalysts and instruments in the advancement of national interests, and that an effective diplomatic machine is in itself a major contributor to achieving national goals abroad, be it directly in expanded exports, stronger inflows of investments and technology, and foreign tourists, or in the indirect areas of building a good image for the country and sustaining a web of beneficial foreign relationships.

The final theme of this study is that diplomacy is a profession; the ambassador is a master craftsman, whose skills have been accumulated and shaped over time. For every John Kenneth Galbraith[7] or Madeleine Albright,[8] there are hordes of non-career envoys of forgettable performance. The increasing complexity of contemporary professional demands also requires much better re-training and a constant process of renewal. Similarly, the chasm that exists between the theorists of international relations and diplomacy studies and the practitioners in the field also needs to be addressed.

The bulk of the work of ambassadors and their staff relates to 'low diplomacy', the ordinary business of managing relations with single countries bilaterally, or handling undramatic conference work in international and regional organizations. In a typical career, there are moments of high diplomacy too, where the envoy is a spectator or even an actor. But to string together a narrative of the ambassador's work that consists of selected events that have occurred over time and geography, is both misleading and a distortion of the real content of diplomacy as it is practiced on the ground. Therefore, the examples offered do relate to singular events, but the flow of the narrative and the description of the ambassador's role is necessarily more pedestrian. Taken individually or in the collective, this is nevertheless vital in the projection and promotion of the external interests of one's country.

The ambassador we study in this book is typically at a place of medium importance, where the opportunity exists to build new cooperation frameworks, as well as sustain and extend the ones that exist. He thus has the capacity to deliver real value for both the sending and the receiving country. It would be unrealistic to focus exclusively on the capitals of the highest importance, fascinating as these places are, because this would convey an unrealistic flavor of the tasks performed. But a reference to these places will occur, as needed, to create a realistic setting and to underscore special challenges at the world's powerful capitals. Equally, our envoy represents a country of medium or moderate importance, because a study focused exclusively on the activities of great power representatives would not be representative of the profession.

A developing country perspective is often offered in this study. I am more familiar with that environment than any other. Given the relative paucity of this genre of diplomacy literature, I hope that this is of interest to those located outside the developing world. A normative purpose, or a hope, is that some ideas offered might evoke reactions and help both developing and transition states to think of ways that better order their diplomacy and optimize the tools. We can agree that the ambassador as an institution must serve national purposes in the best way possible.

The book incorporates the author's experience in a 35-year career, plus data gathered in research, dialogue, and 40 interviews with current and former ambassadors from 16 countries, and others involved with foreign affairs.

The Context

Let us provisionally accept the hypothesis that the ambassador remains relevant to the implementation of foreign policy, and to the advancement of the country's external interests. We will come back to this issue at the end of the book. How have internal developments within countries, and changes on the international canvas, affected the role of ambassadors? Diplomacy is a living craft, practiced around the world in the dynamic situations of the day. It is a truism that it adapts continually. Some changes are incremental, often unremarked, and there are others of the more dramatic kind, attracting comment. What are the contextual elements that we should take into account?

The framework of international relations has undergone a paradigm transformation after 1990, at the end of the Cold War, after the collapse of the Soviet Union and the Marxist doctrine, and a wide acceptance of market capitalism and democracy as the dominant global governance concepts, even while these are implemented around the world in varied and divergent ways so that we are far from a single universal model. We also live in a time of exceptional fluidity in international relations. More than a decade after the Cold War, the world is still in a transitional phase. The US is unchallenged as the dominant locus of military power. The only surviving defense alliance, NATO, has reinvented itself as a co-opted enforcer of peace, no longer limiting actions to its home region. Other global power centers vie for attention, and assert their differentiation on soft issues, even if we are quite far from a truly multipolar world.

In such times of uncertainty and rapid change, countries exert themselves to maximize their foreign policy options, applying the core calculus of self-interest. This gives a centrality to diplomacy, in the continual search for an external matrix that optimizes the advantage for one's country. This is visible in global affairs, with many states searching for innovative partnership formulae. Regional diplomacy is strongly practiced, taking the shape of preferential trade groupings, resource pooling and shared development strategies, sometimes using economics as a basis for collective security. For instance, the ASEAN Regional Forum (ARF) method of using networking diplomacy to engender stronger security has inspired others, like the Gulf Cooperation Council (GCC). Another feature of regionalization is the search for cooperative structures across geographic regions. Some like APEC, straddling continents on the logic of the 'Pacific rim' and focused on trade, are visibly successful. Others like the Ganga–Mekong Basin group (attempting a link between several countries of South and South-East Asia) or the World Bank-led 'Nile Basin Initiative' (looking for a solution to interrelated problems among nine states, some of which are political adversaries), represent innovative attempts to cobble commonalities. The driving force is a win-win external partnership.

What are the contextual factors to be considered?

One. The foreign ministry (MFA) is no longer the exclusive, and sometimes not even the dominant, channel of international contacts. Virtually every ministry or agency of government has its direct foreign contacts, via the participation in international and regional conferences, dialogue with overseas counterparts and the pursuit of aid cooperation agreements. Even a 'centralist' foreign ministry like Japan's *Gaimusho*, renowned for tight control over external contacts, has given up its insistence that officials lead all delegations at foreign negotiations. They rationalize this change on the ground that officials are now available in other ministries with sufficient English language mastery to handle delegation leadership.[9] This is true, but the real reason for change is the relative ascendancy of functional ministry specialists gaining over the MFA generalists.

In developing countries, the finance ministry or the planning ministry is usually the arbiter on foreign aid issues, and the MFA is often a spectator.[10] The finance ministry often unilaterally handles the dialogue with multilateral institutions like the World Bank and the IMF. This is also to some extent the situation in some of the developed countries.[11] There is an identical situation with regard to WTO affairs, where ministries of foreign trade or commerce call the shots. The impact of these elements is portrayed in a fascinating collection of essays on foreign ministries edited by Brian Hocking. He speaks cogently of the new 'coordination role' that MFAs have to carve out for themselves if they are to remain relevant.[12] But in many countries the actual situation in external relations is more akin to unregulated *laissez faire* than any kind of orderly MFA-led harmonization.[13] This is not a sudden development, but one that has been accentuated in recent years. For instance, the agenda of pre-1994 GATT was not nearly as politically or economically charged as that of its successor, the World Trade Organization (WTO).

Another level of complexity is the external role that sub-state entities have developed, whether they are provinces or regions of countries, or major cities. We see this best in West Europe where the process of EU integration has been accompanied by a counter-trend for regions to establish their own direct contacts in neighboring countries and others—summed up in the word 'disintermediation'. Often, the regional cultural identity of a sub-state is the driving force, compounded by economics, a search for markets and inward investment. ASEAN has its 'growth triangles and quadrilaterals' that imaginatively unite neighboring regions of member-countries. Similar trends are visible in large federal countries like Australia, India and the US.

These developments place the ambassador in a dilemma, both at the place of assignment and in relation to his home country. He is the representative of the entire government, with the MFA as his direct master, and the MFA sometimes resents his initiatives with other ministries. At the same time, he finds a new opportunity to carve out a constructive role for himself, by developing his own contact network with all the official agencies that are engaged in bilateral, regional and multilateral relations, both at home and abroad. He is able to make a unique contribution, as a value provider. As Kingman Brewster has written: 'The ambassador is more important than when only the (State) Department was engaged in foreign relations.'[14]

Two. In like fashion, non-state actors are increasingly active on the international stage.[15] Globalization has ensured that 'the accepted notion of which actor operates in which environment erodes' and this blurs 'public–private distinction in the management of international policy', as Hocking argued in a case study covering Swiss banks, and their handling of Nazi gold.[16] He shows that these banks faced severe criticism in the US, and Swiss diplomacy made critical errors in handling US public opinion; Hocking concludes that the banks found themselves abandoned by home officials and eventually dependent on intervention by the US State Department.

Governments find it essential to co-opt non-state agencies as partners in handling foreign relationships, bilateral and multilateral. For instance, it is now common practice to take business delegations to accompany heads of state and government—and even foreign ministers or other ministers—involving them in the economic dialogue.[17] At the meetings of the G-15 group of developing countries (a kind of counter-point to the G-8, established in 1989), a parallel business forum attempts to create new linkages among the countries, to solidify South–South cooperation. Similar business fora accompany other international summits. Delegations to multilateral meetings like those of WTO now routinely include representatives of apex bodies of industry and business and other social sectors, as more and more countries realize that complex economic issues demand inputs that government officials are unable to furnish. Such non-official participation is also essential for building domestic consensus. When nations are faced with adverse external developments, they sometimes find home allies among non-official agencies, to help argue their case with foreign partners. For instance, facing pressure in the US and Europe over software services outsourced to India, the industry and the government work in partnership, each tackling the interlocutors where it best carries conviction.[18] Some countries have institutionalized such public–private partnerships, while others rely on flexible ad hoc arrangements.

Not all interventions by domestic non-state actors are to the liking of their governments. Civil society agencies and NGOs play external affairs roles that flow from their own agendas or tele-guided by external sponsorship.[19] Sometimes they defy the country's official stand. Examples from the US: the activities of ordinary citizens at places like Iraq before the war of April 2003, or earlier in the former Yugoslav states. Sometimes they create situations of embarrassment to the home country, for instance, when they join foreign NGOs to criticize their own government on human rights issues. Some observers argue that 'the era of the ordinary person has finally arrived in international relations.... Citizen diplomats want to bypass professionals. They are more altruistic, autonomous agents.'[20] Non-state agencies believe that they have a better long-term perspective of the national interest than governments, while in fact they are special interest minority groups, often projecting their agendas via ethical principles.

Especially relevant in international affairs are the 'track two' dialogue initiatives by non-official agents. Sometimes governments use them for trial balloons or deniable soundings; at other times they autonomously anticipate or prepare the way, if official dialogue faces an impasse through blocked, antagonistic positions. The virtue of non-state activities in conflict resolution is flexibility and tension-reduction. Yet, these non-official agents need some connection with governments, such as a reporting channel, to valorize their activities.

Communication with domestic non-state bodies is mainly handled by home agencies, while embassies concentrate on non-state entities in the country of assignment. The ambassador cultivates non-state sectors because they occupy a part of the foreign affairs *espace*, especially when they possess credibility in their areas of speciality. Understanding them is part of his 'outreach' to the movers and shakers of the receiving country. An instance where an envoy used such contacts to strengthen his message to the host country is narrated in Chapter 3. Ambassadors sometimes develop these contacts in attempts to neutralize their influence on issues of serious divergences, though such interventions are not easy and can backfire.[21]

Three. Issues on the international agenda have multiplied, and are more complex, intertwined and technical than ever before. This is a manifestation of globalization and the increased interdependence among nations. The ambassador and other diplomats find themselves interacting with a diversity of specialists, one day dealing with subjects relating to gene pools or climate change, and the next day with the impact of financial derivative trading on the velocity of short-term capital flows. The ambassador has to deal with many kinds of specialists from a policy or coordination perspective. For example, the daily 'prayer' or coordination meeting at a major EU permanent mission at Brussels may bring together some 200 or more officials, many of them engaged in highly technical dialogue with EU counterparts or the European Commission. The permanent representative to the EU, who has on his team one or more deputies of ambassador rank, may not have the time to discuss more than a few of the day's subjects that need local decision, or give direction on the tactics to be pursued in the committees and working groups.[22] This calls for an ability to master diversity and complexity. Some have also called this 'broad-band' ability, and high 'learnability'. These are the new requirements for the ambassador.

Four. The pace of bilateral and multilateral encounters among heads of state and governments has multiplied. Up to 1930, the total number of foreign heads who had visited the US was about 30; today a larger number visit Washington DC in any quarter of the year. The exchange of visits among smaller countries is no less intense. Besides traditional 'state' visits, there are frequent 'working' as well as 'unofficial' and 'routine' visits, and even 'stopover' encounters between high dignitaries. In these innovations, the focus is on intensive consultations among leaders, devoid of protocol frills. The peregrinations of foreign ministers are no less hectic; keeping them company are the ministers dealing with economic issues and others. Add to this the demands of regional diplomacy, also producing frequent encounters. At the UN General Assembly, a new trend is the transformation of the first days of the traditional opening in late September into a global summit, under one rubric or another, attracting leaders from around the world. There is no dearth of special UN summits and other episodic gatherings, like the St Petersburg tercentenary in May 2003, assembling the leaders of 40 countries. Dean Rusk was prophetic when he wrote: 'Summit diplomacy is to be approached with the wariness with which a prudent physician prescribes a habit-forming drug.'[23]

These personal contacts among leaders are supplemented with

phone calls and direct messages that may bypass MFAs and ambassadors. The practice of such direct diplomacy is not confined to political leaders. Senior officials based at home too have shed traditional inhibitions and pursue direct contacts of their own. Records of such direct diplomacy are not always maintained. Sometimes the ambassador who learns that his leader has spoken to his counterpart in the country of assignment finds it easier to obtain a summary of the issues discussed, and the follow-up that he aught to undertake, from local friendly sources within the receiving country—usually the aides in the offices of the high personalities—rather than from the home country.[24]

Such multiple and sometimes unrecorded contacts have several consequences. It makes it harder to capture a precise overview of what is happening in relationships. This is a greater problem for the MFA than for the ambassador. For one thing, the MFA at home lacks the local informal, multiple resources of the envoy. Further, varied contact channels, operating in real time across different subjects and locations, produce a kaleidoscopic pattern that the MFA has neither the energy nor the means to follow.

At first sight, it reduces the role of the ambassador in terms of his direct participation. But in most situations it actually adds to his coordination responsibility. It is the task of the resident embassy to piece bits of information together to produce the nearest approximation to the full picture in a particular country. An experienced European diplomat has written that it is an illusion that direct dialogue and concordance at the top can resolve issues. All the work of preparation, communication at multiple levels in the partner country, and follow-up to produce sustainable result also has to be carried out, and this falls on the resident envoy. He sums up this vital support work: 'The ambassador is there to check, channel, patch up, temporize, catalyze, buffer.'[25]

Five. The spread of the Internet and the availability of vast amounts of information on websites, has led to a kind of 'commodification' of information. When anyone can get hold of information, control over it is seldom the lever. If from the comfort of one's office or home one can scan the principal news stories, feature articles and editorials from almost any newspaper or journal in the world, geography does not matter, and the diplomat's location abroad is no longer so exclusive. Similarly, the MFA does not depend on the embassy as its prime external resource. The embassy team now concentrates on the analysis and information synthesis of issues that are not addressed by the media, or lie in sectors that the general public interest does not cover, but are valuable for MFAs and others at home. Thus the tasks for analysis and data collection are reoriented.

The other consequence is that the velocity at which one has to respond has accelerated, and the mission–MFA communication has to be continuous and rapid. For instance the 'official spokesperson' of a foreign ministry cannot hide behind his inability to comment on fast-breaking news, because this leaves the terrain open to others to present their own slant. The political officer and the ambassador have to be tuned to the way developments in their country of assignment are playing at home, and move with alacrity to provide the MFA with vital material or angles, from the perspective of the home country. A book on the work of ambassadors in Washington DC quotes the Egyptian envoy as saying: 'CNN is the enemy of today's ambassador. We are always behind. Often I am awakened in the middle of the night with a call from home. I turn to CNN immediately to see what's happened while I was sleeping.'[26]

Six. Good governance concepts have entered the political lexicon. Around the world, there is a concern with governments delivering value to citizens. Public opinion holds governments accountable. This means value-for-money in all activities that use public funds, and a transparency in action and documentation. For instance, most democracies have legislation that upholds the public right to information, typically enacted in the past decade or less. Countries in Africa are extending 'citizen charter' principles to the MFA and to embassies.[27] In a few countries, such accountability concepts are now being extended to the foreign affairs establishment.

In the UK, under the impetus first given by Prime Minister Margaret Thatcher two decades back, the British Foreign Office and other departments publish detailed documents on policy goals and actual performance in meeting predetermined targets; for the great part these are quantified and enumerated.[28] Australia and New Zealand have carried out similar open narrations of the objectives and outcomes of their own diplomatic process. In France a new organic fiscal law mandates the publication of performance norms.

This too impacts on the ambassador, who finds that his activities are under closer scrutiny, by the government and the public. His performance is measured against pre-set norms. This works best in a tangible area like the delivery of consular services, the one activity that brings diplomatic and consular offices closest to ordinary members of the public. Some techniques are borrowed from business management. These notions are anathema to diplomacy traditionalists, but the way an ambassador should run his embassy is in principle no way different from how the regional chief executive of a transnational enterprise operates a country office. The product handled by the envoy is mainly intangible, but so is the portfolio of some comparable commercial offices, for example the brand equity value safeguarded by international product manufacturers, or the intellectual property they own. Similarly, standard human resource management techniques are now widely used in MFAs, applied to assessments of individual performance, promotions as also the selection of career envoys. Performance management is reviewed further in the Chapter 5.

Seven. We have considered the revolution in information technology and communications moving to a convergence of these sectors. We realize that the image of the ambassador as a messenger at the end of a telephone or data modem, executing instructions from the home, is a caricature. What may not be immediately apparent is that technology has in fact enhanced the envoy's role. Distinguished US diplomat Ellsworth Bunker had written a decade earlier: '[It is] more feasible than it used to be for the ambassador to be part of the policy-formulation process.'[29] It is now far easier to consult him instantaneously, and obtain his inputs into the policy process, before the high decision makers are presented with options, of a tactical or strategic character. Communication convenience anchors the ambassador more firmly into the policy loop. One interlocutor pithily declared during an interview: 'No ambassador should receive instructions that he has not helped to draft!'[30]

This is not to say that the ambassador was not consulted earlier. After all, policy advice has been a classic responsibility. Besides the advice routed via cipher telegrams and dispatches, foreign ministries call envoys at key assignments to headquarters for consultations, at least a couple of times a year, sometimes often as two months or less, as in the case of envoys to neighboring countries. Most foreign ministries hold documents that cannot be sent out from headquarters, and face-to-face dialogue is often indispensable. The change is that Internet-based 'intranets' and similar communication protocols now make it everyday routine for the envoy to interact with colleagues belonging to different departments and ministries at headquarters, and get a sense of the way thinking is evolving.[31] This permits the envoy to make his input in a more decisive and result-oriented manner than was ever possible without this facility, going by the remarks of several interlocutors during this study.[32]

Canada is one country that has moved fast in the application of state-of-the-art communications and information technology in its diplomatic establishment. One of the conclusions of a workshop held in Ottawa in June 1997 was: 'New IT will not replace missions abroad, but the work conducted at missions has evolved and the number of people posted abroad has declined as some work is centralized at Ottawa.'[33] Around the world, countries are upgrading their diplomatic communication systems; this invariably enhances the quality of the dialogue between the ambassador and his team, and headquarters.

Eight. With the involvement of many ministries and government agencies in external affairs, many of their representatives are to be found within the embassy. One study notes that the percentage of personnel within US embassies from the State Department has varied over the years between 15% and 23%.[34] There are US embassies that accommodate representatives of up to 30 different departments. Other countries do not witness the same numerical proliferation or diversity, but there is comparable growth in the range of representatives housed within the mission. A rule of thumb: the larger the embassy, the greater the diversity and the smaller the representation of the diplomatic service. In contrast, small missions often consist exclusively of MFA officials.

For the ambassador, diversity translates into serious management problems, plus a difficulty in imposing a unified approach, as we examine in Chapter 6. It should not be surprising that the US, faced with an acute diversity challenge, has tried to impose coordination and discipline through a strong official mandate for the ambassador. Another problem with embassy diversity is that officials may not speak with one voice to the agencies of the receiving country. There is also a lack of uniformity in assessments sent to the home country. This is not a bad thing in itself, since a single perspective can miss out other valid angles that should be addressed. But the direct communication between agency representatives and their own headquarters often do not factor in the ambassador's perspective; this can lead to distorted feedback.

Nine. A certain 'class' of entrants, in terms of educational background, plus social and family background, earlier dominated the old diplomatic services. Virtually all countries now witness a democratization of their services. In the UK, this has meant an end to the domination by 'Oxbridge'. In several other European countries, the preeminence of law graduates has ended. Similarly, in Thailand, the past concentration of aristocratic families is diluted. In China, the new entrants come from a wider spectrum of educational institutions. Across South Asia, beyond the urban elite, the net is now cast much wider: young people with rural backgrounds join the foreign services, reflecting also greater regional diversity, and a wider range of disciplines studied.[35]

This means that a greater variety of ambassadors are being appointed, today and tomorrow. Elite values, or 'service standards' do not dominate as before. One consequence is a need for better cultural understanding when diplomats treat with one another. Cross-cultural studies should figure prominently in the training curriculum. Training will also need to be more intensive, focused especially on the mid-career stages, on the analogy of advanced management training for senior business executives, or war colleges for armed force officers of command rank, even if many foreign ministries do not recognize this as yet (Chapter 7).

Gender Issues

Gender disparity is a striking fact in diplomatic services, as in other branches of civil services in most countries. In the majority of countries, the percentage of women ambassadors is between 5% and 10%. At the UN headquarters in New York, out of 190 permanent representatives, barely ten or twelve on average are women, a situation that one female envoy formerly stationed there characterized as 'shocking'.[36] The situation is a little better in the presence of women in diplomatic services as a whole, with an average that hovers around 15% to 20%, while numbers in Scandinavia and East and Central Europe are much higher. Until the early 1970s, countries such as the UK and India, even required women officers to resign on marriage. Around the world, more women now enter diplomatic services, and this must translate into a larger numbers of female ambassadors.

For reasons of family obligations, personal choice and perceived discrimination as well, the attrition rate among women tends to be higher than among male counterparts in most foreign services. Countries of Scandinavia, East Europe and Latin America are the trend leaders. For instance, Copenhagen is renowned as especially welcoming female envoys, and consistently ranks as the diplomatic capital with the largest number. In a number of diplomatic services—in Central Europe, Scandinavia, Singapore and China, among others—some 40% to 50% of new entrants are women, which holds the promise that gender equations will change dramatically.

This book uses the pronoun 'he' for the ambassador, simply in recognition of an overwhelming reality, without implying that male envoys are superior or preferable to female counterparts. Both personal experience and the evidence gathered from others amply demonstrate that the performance of many female ambassadors is outstanding. They have the advantage of natural grace in a profession where to some degree image is also the substance. Given that women envoys reconcile their careers with frequently heavy demands of family life, like many other female professionals, we should admire them even more. Diplomacy is one profession where the male does not start with any special advantage. The clear trend in most countries is towards a redressal of a gender imbalance, and an elevation to a high rank is therefore welcome.[37] This too is one of the changes afoot in diplomacy.

1

♦

THE TRANSFORMED PLENIPOTENTIARY

An outstanding Indian diplomat of the first generation, K.P.S. Menon, who served as ambassador to the Soviet Union from 1952 to 1961, has written of a conversation with an old woman during his visit to the town of Novogrod. The lady asked his interpreter who he was; hoping that she would be impressed, the interpreter explained that 'his excellency' was the Indian ambassador. She responded impatiently: 'Yes, yes, I know he is ambassador. What does he do?' Menon adds: '[This is] a question which, for the good of my soul, I have often asked myself.'[1]

Does the ambassador have a role to play in today's globalized world? What value is delivered to the nation-state by what appears to be largely a conspicuously extravagant apparatus of flag-flying permanent diplomatic representation abroad? Can the tasks and services the envoy performs be handled in other, more economical ways?

During post-World War II decolonization, the international system underwent rapid expansion. The mere 50 states that signed the UN Charter at San Francisco in 1945 had tripled in 25 years. For these new states, establishing their representatives abroad and receiving foreign envoys at home was a high priority, an expression of their international personality. Those years were the final phase of classic diplomacy, comprising almost exclusively of privileged dialogue among official agents, far from the public gaze. Ambassadors routinely enjoyed direct personal access to heads of state and government in the receiving state, and handled weighty political issues with authority.[2] Trade seldom engaged these ambassadors.[3] Matters like investment mobilization and technology access were not even on the ambassador's horizon. Culture did figure in his agenda, but only the grander events. Issues relating to the media, science or other functional fields seldom intruded on his day-to-day activities. It was still the age of high diplomacy.

This pluralization of international relations reacted with other alterations in the diplomatic process, and since about the 1970s, other change elements have come into play, leading to a substantial transformation. The ambassador may still be engaged in high diplomacy, but only during fleeting moments. It is the principals at home, the presidents, prime ministers and foreign ministers, who rule over the elevated political dialogue. The ambassador—working together with his home counterparts at the foreign ministry—has become the facilitator, the handler of detail, the remover of obstacles, the master of logistics, the specialist of follow-up, the resident trouble-shooter, and the one who sometimes handles the fallout if there are problems, to put back on track a derailed relationship. In opportune situations he may also have the role of a catalyst. He spans a bewildering array of functional areas and subjects, and deals with multiple players, both abroad and at home. Almost nothing is excluded from his action arena. He thus finds himself deeply engaged in low diplomacy, much of it unglamorous, but representing the very stuff of contemporary international life.

The termination of the Cold War in 1990 ended the stable framework of international relations that had anchored the foreign policy and diplomacy of most countries. Those that belonged to the West or the East had operated in the certitude of bloc dynamics, with its pre-determined relationships. For the countries of the South, non-alignment and its economic variant, G-77, broadly provided a fixed set of compass points, within which each navigated its own set of policies. The global terrain was familiar and predictable. It provided the setting for the great issues of détente, disarmament and development that dominated the international discourse.

We have since moved into times that are unpredictable,

characterized by transformation occurring at an unprecedented velocity. The fluidity of the international system produces a renaissance of diplomacy, where each country seeks to build a web of diversified relationships that supports its external objectives, and maximizes its policy options. Countries give priority to developing beneficial partnerships with as wide a range of countries as possible, through intensive bilateral diplomacy, as well as coalition building, often of an issue-specific nature. Regional diplomacy is a major growth industry, with states attempting to combine geography and economics, not leaving out history, culture and ethnicity, to intensify mutually advantageous cooperation in their neighborhood, and create a support net of political affinity as well. Multilateral diplomacy is a high priority, sometimes even at the cost of other forms of diplomacy.

These circumstances make it worthwhile to re-examine the instruments through which states deal with one another—prominent among which is the ambassador. In particular we need to ask if latent potential in the system of external representation can be optimized. As we see, the envoy no longer monopolizes external representation. But the very plurality of actors has increased his responsibility as the constant element in the multiform dialogue between states. Our generic examination of the envoy is pertinent because many foreign ministries have carried out reform and restructuring since 1990, but there is little published information or any thorough new study of the contemporary role of the ambassador, other than a German review of 2000, the Paschke report on embassies in the European Union.[4]

While diplomacy is in its renaissance, paradoxically, foreign ministries and their apparatus are increasingly queried for their *raison d'être*, particularly in Europe, where the EU integration process has created a new governance terrain that is neither domestic nor foreign. Foreign ministries jostle for credible roles in this shared *espace*, continually challenged by functional ministries that were earlier circumscribed in their domestic competencies.[5] Diplomatic services face intensive scrutiny over their performance and even their value.[6]

Robert D. Kaplan wrote in 1996: 'The embassy may not survive beyond a few more decades.'[7] The profession has its pessimists too. A US Consul in Moscow who resigned in 1980 asserted: 'We do not need an ambassador in Moscow...he has nothing to do.'[8] Some years back there was an abundance of dismissive caustic comments on this theme from former US National Security Adviser Frank Carlucci;[9] Henry Kissinger once remarked: 'Ambassadors don't count anymore.'[10]

These are among the issues this study attempts to address. It postulates an ideal yet completely practical action arena that is available to the ambassador. We assume that the ambassador has the motivation to deliver his best for the country he represents, and that the ambassador and the system of overseas representation he heads are vital to promoting the external interests. Further, in our age of globalization, interdependence and multi-form dialogue between states, the work of the ambassador has increased. This applies to the bilateral as well as the multilateral arena. In the real world not all the players live up to their challenges, and this is especially true of the bureaucracy. The account that is offered in this study is both descriptive and normative.

Who is the Ambassador?

For many, the ambassador is the personification of international relations between states. He is a visible symbol of foreign relationships, even more than his direct master, the foreign minister and the official apparatus that the minister heads—called variously the ministry of foreign affairs, the foreign office, the external affairs ministry, the department of state, *et al*, abbreviated for convenience as the MFA. The ambassador serves in the frontline, in foreign capitals, and comes to notice especially in periods of difficulty in relationships, when he becomes a symbol of national honor. A *Dictionary of Diplomacy* calls him 'a diplomatic agent of the highest rank...head of a diplomatic mission to a foreign state'.[11] He is also the one often held responsible when things go wrong in a bilateral relationship or at a multilateral institution.

After the decolonization wave that started in 1945, the newly independent nations gave high priority to installing their envoys abroad and receiving embassies from foreign states. These envoy exchanges were perceived as a powerful symbol of the new sovereign personality, even the legitimacy of the state. One visible manifestation of this receptivity to envoys from abroad was the allocation of prime land to foreign diplomatic missions in the capitals of new states.[12] Countries, large and small, also invested sizable resources—always scarce, facing competing needs at home—in bedecking their ambassadors abroad with the paraphernalia of high office. This has included a large residence with ample space for holding receptions and other representational functions, chauffeured limousines and other material resources, plus a hierarchy of support personnel of diplomatic and non-diplomatic rank. For some newly independent states, projecting a favorable and distinctive image of the home country abroad became a greater priority than the concrete work of building relationships.[13] For the older states of Europe and others too, the symbolism of the ambassador and his representational role has been no less important. These states have also extended their diplomatic reach far and wide, even more than the developing states.

The past thirty years have witnessed a clear global trend towards a reduction of ceremonial and ritual, for instance in summit diplomacy and foreign visits by leaders. But the image endures of the ambassador as a member of an elite grouping, the diplomatic corps, hobnobbing with the most prominent of the host country's national political and official personalities, plus the leaders of society, the *glitterati*. An abundance of local social journals and gossip columns burnish this otherworldly image, even in small capitals. This glamour is a legacy of the days when the foreign envoy was a member of a royal court, representing one sovereign to another. An obstinately cherished set of diplomatic ceremonials evoking the past, also refuses to die out. It starts with the extravagant language of the 'letter of credential', with which the sending head of state entrusts to a brother foreign head of state the execution of the ambassador's duties. Another apparent legacy is the whole panoply of real-life privileges and immunities that the ambassador enjoys, and the classification of envoys and their ranking codified by the Vienna Congress of 1815. In fact, inviolability of the envoy's person harks back much further, to the very oldest days of exchange of *ad hoc* emissaries in different civilizations for which record is available to us—one of the oldest of which are the Amarna archives of Middle Egypt in the second millennium BC. As we see later, these immunities serve a vital purpose even today.

The vast majority of ambassadors are resident envoys charged with representing the sending country in one single receiving country. In addition, there are the ambassadors who head permanent missions to international organizations, engaging in multilateral work that is qualitatively different from that of the bilateral envoy. Then there are other individuals who bear the title but perform varied tasks, or simply use the title as an honorific. It is useful to distinguish between the different kinds of ambassadors; this is detailed in an extended endnote.[14]

Another point to be considered as we look at the ambassador's actual role and work parameters: where is he assigned? His tasks, priorities, methods, working style and operational environment, hinge on the importance of the country of his location *as perceived by his own country*. Given the differences among nations in power, economic capability and the role they play on the international stage, it is this subjective judgment of the sending state that determines the order of importance of envoys sent abroad.

There are several parallel criteria that determine the relative international hierarchy for each country. The countries of one's own region are usually ranked high in importance on the basis of the classic SWOT formula: strength, weakness, opportunity and threat. Then are the 'problem' countries that endanger one's security or vital interests, or control vital resources or access routes. The great powers, on the basis of their influence in one's own region, their capacity to pose a real threat, or the potential they offer for productive partnership are as vital.[15] Other countries are ranked by several interrelated factors: the density of relationships (measured in trade and investments, cultural and educational contacts, other cooperation arenas, diaspora settlements, etc.); future potential for developing cooperation; historical, linguistic, religious or ethnic affinities, and special elements as mutually perceived.

Using such a matrix of concurrent and dynamic calculations, a priority map can be drawn for each nation. Most countries have a formal or informal internal system of ranking their own ambassadors, in grades or categories. For example the US has three effective grades, as do Germany and India. Only a few countries, such as Kenya, Thailand and Turkey, appoint ambassadors in a single grade. In the majority of diplomatic services, the ambassador carries his own grade to the assigned post; an ambassador in grade I at say, Tokyo, might be succeeded by another in grade II—the internal rankings naturally do not affect his status for the receiving country. There are a few countries like Germany and China that attach ranks to capitals; for instance, only a German ambassador in the highest grade can serve in Tokyo, or at any of the other 12 assignments reserved for this rank.[16] China ensures that only envoys with the personal rank of vice-minister are sent to the seven locations abroad that it deems as the most vital.

Theory and Practice

International relations (IR) theory is divided into several broad streams, but none of these directly touch on the role of the ambassador.[17] In some ways the ambassador may feel close to the 'agency' theory advocates. For one thing, he is conscious of his own action arena, for advancing his country's interests. Given the work that he undertakes, the ambassador tends to be a pragmatist, aware that save in exceptional situations, he will accomplish incremental gain, or at best open up a new activity segment, often to be developed further by a successor. He learns quickly enough that what is attainable, is often not the best or the ideal. Negotiation and dialogue involve compromise, generally settling for less than the full cake. The envoy realizes that he is an artisan engaged in a long-term endeavor, working in a continuum like the builder of the past engaged on a major cathedral or temple project, indebted to his predecessors, and conscious that it is his successors who must carry forward the labors.

Some scholars challenge the rigidity of IR theory constructs, especially the dominant neo-realist ideas, which over-emphasize the political-security dimension in international relations at the cost of economic, cultural and the other soft forms of diplomacy.[18] A pursuit of this discussion involves too large a digression from our theme, but suffice it to say that practice-determined analysis of diplomacy, from times past to the present day, tends to suggest that these non-political dimensions of diplomacy are more dominant in external relations, and govern the actual work content, than most IR theorists would have us believe. The typical work domain of envoys and other diplomacy practitioners is better understood through empirical research than abstract theory.

A peculiarity of diplomacy studies is the gulf between practitioners on the ground and academic theorists. Former Israeli Foreign Minister Abba Eban has called this an 'intrinsic antagonism', adding that diplomacy 'is not as yet plugged into any recognized science' and that 'it does not hide behind an inaccessible vocabulary'.[19] Distinguished theorist Richard Langhorne has noted the confusion on whether 'diplomacy is an expertise in its own right or a collection of skills'.[20] Another study notes: 'The value of a diplomat lay not in any specialist knowledge he might possess, but in his ability to communicate, negotiate and persuade.'[21] This begs the question: why is diplomacy not acceptable more universally as a specialist skill?

A consequence of the theorist–practitioner distance and incertitude about the profession is that few working diplomats study the concepts or theoretical structures offered by academics. In return, the latter seem disjointed from the practical field where their ideas can be tested and refined. This situation is not unique, but there may not be many disciplines offering more spectacular divergence.

This leads to misjudgments. An instance: the speculation some years back on the relevance and utility of the ambassador. In the early 1990s it became a fashionable theme in academia that the resident envoy had outlived his utility, and was reduced to providing services as an inn-keeper, travel agent and greeter and receiver of visiting high personalities and delegations from the home country. His plenipotentiary powers had long been rendered irrelevant; he simply acted to implement instructions sent to him from home, via instant communication methods. 24-hour TV news networks and the print media overtook his role as providers of information. Heads of state and foreign ministers talked directly to one another, as did senior officials from their capitals. Consequently, the resident envoy had become more or less irrelevant, bereft of value.[22] It became customary to ask students in academic diplomatic studies if the traditional embassy 'has not outlived its usefulness'. Another scholar asked a bit plaintively: 'How can we explain the persistence of the ambassador?'[23] A good catalogue is provided in a section entitled 'The Case for Euthanasia' in a fine textbook by G.R. Berridge, who goes on to elaborate a 'Case for Reprieve' as well.[24] A counter-trend produced a whole set of writings that asserted the continuing vitality of the resident envoy, often couched in defensive terms.[25]

While this debate raged, in the real world the networks of resident diplomatic representation continued to grow. The end of the Cold War and the break-up of the Soviet Union and Yugoslavia increased the number of sovereign states, and changed the matrix of strategic calculations. Many countries found it vital to develop relationships with this expanded set of international partners, and widen their external options. In the other direction, cutbacks in government spending produced a counter-trend, of closing down missions in places of marginal interest. On balance, an expansionary trend has outweighed the cutbacks in the past ten years. There have been some other interesting developments.

Following the unification of Germany in 1991, the German Parliament decided to shift the capital from Bonn to Berlin, with a sizable minority of government agencies remaining behind in Bonn. This set in motion an event unique in modern times, the near-total relocation of the government of a major power.[26] The capital transfer was implemented in 1999, when the new Federal Chancellery building opened in Berlin and the Parliament moved into the rebuilt *Reichstag*. Diplomatic missions were forced to acquire new embassy premises in the very expensive new capital, or refurbish old buildings if they were lucky enough to own something from the past.[27] They had to decide on the size of embassies they needed for the future, based on a realistic calculation. Virtually every country has opted for bigger chancery premises, reflecting a uniform calculation of high-profile diplomatic representation. An exception has been the US that has implemented a downsizing of its mission, mainly as a result of the end of the residual post-WWII arrangements that became irrelevant in unified Germany. Between 1991 and 1996, US-based embassy and consulates staff was cut by one third.[28]

The other development in Germany as a member of the EU has been the Paschke Report (September 2000), which examined the role of the bilateral embassy among EU states. The report notes that member-country ministry personnel communicate directly with their opposite numbers and many ministries have liaison officers from partner governments; joint committees and the like have created dense exchange networks and huge flows of information. It adds that:

...certain functions of traditional diplomacy have become superfluous. Ambassadors in Europe no longer need to negotiate with host country governments or handover letters; formal démarches also tend to be rare, if only because bilateral problems between EU members are also a rarity. However, the number of themes and issues which are the common concern of all partners is constantly increasing...

The fact that political leaders know each other well...have resulted in a situation where communication between governments usually takes place without the intervention and often even the knowledge of embassies.

Nevertheless, embassies in Europe have not become obsolete.

Among our 14 partner governments there is not a single one that would support such a view. The opposite is in fact the case. Almost all partners agree that Europe has imposed new tasks on their embassies. Some have increased their embassy staffs in EU countries...others have decided to open embassies in countries where they have hitherto had no presence.[29]

The Paschke Report lists three tasks that embassies no longer need to perform: conducting formal negotiations with the host government, briefing home governments, and trade promotion, which are now the tasks of other actors. The list of the 'new challenges' is much longer, namely: 'public diplomacy', i.e. explaining to the wider public in partner countries what Germany is trying to achieve in the European integration process; 'promoting Germany as an attractive place in which to invest and do business'; 'keeping an overall view of the whole spectrum of relations with our respective partners'; 'coordinating individual aspects and analysing political developments'; consular services; cultural contacts; and promoting the German language and interest in higher education in Germany. It is not surprising that the Paschke report has produced an impact in other countries as well.

Empirical Evidence

Every diplomatic service has its envoy exemplars. For the erstwhile Soviet Union, Anatoly Dobrynin was one such, for twenty-four years their point man in Washington DC, enjoying access to presidents and secretaries of state, who for a while even had a special parking spot in the State Department garage! In the first years of the Cold War the US had George Kennan in Moscow, widely acknowledged as a giant figure in the shaping of policy, author of the famous 'long telegram', a cipher message that shaped the US policy of containment towards the Soviet Union. These names are well documented in diplomatic history.[30]

There are less renowned but equally persuasive models. In the early 1980s, the Bulgarian Ambassador in Delhi was one Tocho Tochev, unique for the access he enjoyed across the official spectrum, from Prime Minister Indira Gandhi to the junior-most of desk officers. Then there was Singapore's Ambassador in Bonn in the period 1990–94, Tony Siddique, who used a combination of exceptional German language ability, networking finesse and single-minded application of eco-political diplomacy to build strong connections for the benefit of his city-state, and for ASEAN. He transformed the Asia-Pacific group of ambassadors in Germany into a proactive force for joint region marketing, reaching out to different Federal States, major cities and leading corporates.

India had a remarkable envoy in Apa Saheb Pant, the scion of a small princely ruler in Maharashtra, sent on his first assignment as India's Commissioner to East Africa, reaching Nairobi on 15 August 1947, the day India became independent. With his exceptional integrity and passion, in four years he built such a network of influence with the leaders of the independence movement in the region, including Jomo Kenyatta, the father of Kenya's liberation, that the British colonial administration was compelled to seek his discreet withdrawal. At Nairobi and subsequent ambassadorships at Jakarta, Oslo, Cairo, Rome and London, Apa Saheb combined deep faith in his mission, and personal credibility built on transparent actions, which won him acceptance in the host country and strong confidence of the home authorities, a balance that is hard to sustain in practice. In the multilateral arena there have been envoys like Singapore's Tommy Koh, and India's Rikhy Jaipal, who too gained singular acclaim among their hard-boiled contemporaries at the U.N. Headquarters in New York, and advanced the vital interests of their countries. A generation earlier, there was India's Arthur Lall, who chaired the international conference in Vienna that framed the 1961 Convention on Diplomatic Relations, and went on to become the Permanent Representative in New York, a distinguished professor at Columbia University and author of several important books.

One of the strangest stories concerns Indian non-career envoy Kushak Bakula, who represented India in Mongolia from 1989 till 1999. Bakula is the head monk of the important Buddhist monastery Sankar, located in Ladakh, and is much revered as a religious leader. After a low-profile six-year term as a member of the Rajya Sabha (the upper house of the Indian parliament), he went on his solitary overseas assignment to Mongolia, at a time when the global collapse of communist rule and that country's search for identity created a unique juncture of circumstance. He was an instant success in Ulan Bator, accepted by the state hierarchy and by ordinary Mongols as a religious mentor, who effectively helped them towards a reawakening of their Buddhist faith. Each day people thronged in queues a kilometer long, for his *darshan* (i.e. invocation of his blessings). Though his activities bore little resemblance to normal diplomatic representation, he also advanced bilateral cooperation to new levels.[31] His unique role in the revival of Buddhism in Mongolia owes little to the professional edicts of Nicolson, but harks back much further in Indian history, recalling the emissaries sent by Emperor Ashoka of the Maurya dynasty (270–230 BC) to Sri Lanka and South-East Asia to promote the Buddhist religion.

Each singular success of an envoy, in circumstance extraordinary or banal, occurs at the intersection of a distinctive context and an individual with the vision and tenacity to grasp the offered opportunity. The human agent is a powerful force for change.

Evidence is available from the history of different countries that the right envoy at the appropriate location has played a critical role in transforming and enriching bilateral relations, or advancing national interests on the international stage. This is visible in the manner in which an ambassador is sometimes especially effective, much beyond the norm or average. At his best, he is an active agent of change. There are those who seize windows of opportunity, to advance national interests in the political, economic and other fields in a tangible way, with measurable results. These are the envoys remembered much after their time. It should be the goal of a good diplomatic system to offer opportunities for excellence and leadership for their envoys.

Inevitably, there are instances of the opposite kind—surely more in number—of ambassadors who have performed in a routine fashion, unimaginatively following instructions and procedures, opting for the path of least resistance. They do not offer instruction. When initiatives are not taken, or where the envoy has functioned in a reactive manner, one can only estimate the missed opportunities hypothetically, since one lacks viable evidence. This book sketches the work environment that is theirs as well. The challenge for every diplomatic service and for the other public services as well, is to create conditions where average performance is raised, and those who tend to be reactive, learn the proactive way.

One of the goals of this book is to identify success methods, and to see if these are capable of being emulated and replicated. With the exception of the European Union, which has extended the foreign policy integration process to include regular dialogue among MFA heads of administration, there is a limited sharing of experiences, or of emulation, in the diplomatic profession. One result of this study might be to awaken interest in different countries in such a comparative analysis of the diplomatic process.

We should not ignore the envoys who commit transgressions of a personal character, or more rarely, of a professional nature. Interestingly, experience shows that the damage that results from such incidents seldom endures for long. Host countries are generally relieved at the end of an episode involving inappropriate conduct by a foreign envoy, and seldom perceive or find deliberate design in such incidents. That said, very exceptional situations also occur, where offensive behavior by an envoy is used as an instrument of policy. Such rarities take place when there are problems or a conflict between states.

New Responsibilities

Subsequent chapters look in detail at the work of the ambassador, his partners, the operational sectors, his role within the embassy and *vis-à-vis* the home authorities, and the need for training. For the present, let us depict in broad brush-strokes the consequences of the major trends narrated above. What is their collective impact on the essential role of the ambassador?

As far back as 1970, a US State Department memo had talked of diplomacy needing 'a new breed of diplomat–managers'.[32] The ambassador has now grown in vocation as the 'relationship manager' in the country of assignment, even if this is not fully understood as yet. He emerges as the country's best resource, in terms of the totality of the concerned bilateral relationship. No territorial division or bureau in the MFA—or 'country director'—is able to keep track of sectoral activity or the actions of functional ministries and the non-state actors in the target country. Further, the MFA lacks the inclination, manpower and information sources to engage in this kind of micro-management—though one would prefer to call it mastery of detail and visualization of the grand mosaic. The MFA has to be satisfied if other ministries and official agencies keep it in the picture in relation to major developments and actions undertaken by them, and if it is able to coordinate with them their principal actions. The MFA overview of the activities of non-official actors is even less comprehensive. Consequently, the embassy becomes the single best provider, in real time, of total activity in the target country. We presuppose that the ambassador and his team are on the ball, and have cultivated the essential outreach, in the receiving country and at home, to perform this role. I have presented this thesis over the past three years in other writings, and found in mid-2002 that the German Paschke Report comes to almost an identical set of conclusions.[33]

Personal trust and credibility are the vital assets in the envoy's armory which govern his contacts at all levels. They give access to networking contacts, information, a persuasive presentation of his own viewpoints, plus application of linkages, trade-offs and leverage. A person is believed if he or she has a reputation for straight dealing. Often, the interlocutor has a margin of action, to act as the envoy asks, and there is always some kind of risk in doing so. That is where credibility and trust help to swing the balance. It is only the resident envoy who has the possibility of developing the requisite relationships, and taking advantage of transitory opportunities, as elaborated subsequently.

Several consequences follow. The ambassador becomes the best adviser on not just local developments in the country of assignment, but for providing a holistic perspective of the complete bilateral relationship, taking into account the official and non-state levels, at both ends of the game. It becomes vital for the diplomatic system to consult him on all aspects of policy and tactics. Modern communications technology makes this permanent consultation feasible in a way that previous generations of envoys could not have dreamt. In particular, with his 'integrated' perspective, the ambassador is able to suggest to his government the areas in which trade-offs, inducements and leverage are available, and indicate the ways in which these can be used, in dealing with a partner country. He has other advantages as well. On the ground it is easier for him to cross-check with local non-MFA partners, or obtain bits of corroborating information, feeding in this information to the home foreign ministry. Finally, the presence of other ministries from home in the large embassy also enhances the coordination role, provided the ambassador has established sound working relationships within his entire team. He does this not by 'right' or status, but through winning their confidence. It follows that this kind of integrated role is more feasible at a larger mission than in a smaller one, which generally corresponds to the level of bilateral engagement with foreign countries.

In earlier writings I had likened the ambassador to a 'systems engineer', a professional who is not necessarily the master of every process that is in play, but like the systems engineer in a complex petro-chemical plant (which is an agglomeration of dozens of separate units and sub-units, with different processes functioning in a continuous chain), he understands the relationship of each to the other.[34] He is able to take an overview and help make the entire system function optimally. That is his role in relationship management, interrelating discrete components, tying them together and producing maximum value.

This breadth of knowledge also makes him a 'catalyst', as some have described this function.[35] He is a potential source of innovative ideas, perhaps the best one in the system. His colleagues at the MFA are generally over-preoccupied with classic headquarter functions, (typically covering the examination of day-to-day issues, the application and interpretation of policy, the brief preparation for ministers, digestion of reports, and responses to demands for briefings, inter-agency coordination, parliamentary work and the like). They lack the ambassador's single-focus or tunnel vision, honed on the bilateral relationship.

This mono-focus also produces its drawbacks. There are problems of excessive concern with one's own parish, which can develop into a full-blown case of what is called 'localitis'—a conviction that one's place of assignment is the center of the universe. It is precisely for these reasons that the ambassador and his team function continually under close supervision of the MFA, with the territorial division acting as the lead or 'parent' agency. This supervision needs to be effective, especially to monitor performance. The goal of headquarters should not be to judge or to apply sanctions—though this is a byproduct of the monitoring process, in any event. The deeper aim is to raise performance levels of ambassadors and their teams, and to improve the delivery capacity at the median level. The envoy too has to continually cultivate balance and sound judgment that provides the foundation of his credibility at home.

Where does this leave the ambassador in his historical legacy?

Among the leading diplomacy states, the US has a special tradition of ambassadors drawn from public life. After all, of the very first eight presidents, five had once headed US diplomatic missions in Europe. This demonstrates the origin of the system of non-professional appointments that has partly degenerated into a crude spoils system of rewarding contributors to political campaigns. It may be this public policy origin that has led the US to have higher expectations of the ambassador than elsewhere. A 1981 Senate report on 'The Ambassador in US Foreign Policy' examined the notion that he had become an anachronism, and stated: '[He] no longer plays a meaningful role in developing or even managing American foreign policy...he is seen merely as the tool for its implementation, and is told via satellite [encoded cables] what is expected of him.'[36] Most countries do not traditionally expect the ambassador to play a sizable role in developing foreign policy in any event, and regard him as one who implements instructions, and may see nothing wrong with the way he has been described above. But as this study argues, the reality is quite different.

The ambassador's 'plenipotentiary powers' have long withered away. It can be argued that the quasi-autonomous role implied in that phrase was seldom reality anyway, once new communications developed more than a century ago, i.e. the telegraph and radio links that made it possible to instantaneously transmit instructions and receive reports. This abolished the earlier penumbra zone of suspended animation, the transit delay in two-way communication, which gave the envoy some local autonomy. Today, the more apt analogy for the envoy is with the chief executive of a country unit of a transnational enterprise. Like this corporate leader, the ambassador enjoys a mastery of the local scene, an authority over the country team, and an ability to function as the best adviser to the headquarters or the holding company. His true value is that of a principal adviser on the overall policy that should apply at that location, within the framework of headquarters vision and strategy. He also executes approved policy on the ground and manages that delivery process, being held accountable for results.

The chief executive analogy is also suitable as it sheds the baggage of pomp and concentrates on the promotion, outreach, negotiation, feedback, management and servicing functions (these six are the principal functions of contemporary diplomacy, as elaborated in

Chapter 3). The envoy is not the master of the entire enterprise, if we relate him to the full foreign policy and diplomacy apparatus of the country. One could argue that even the foreign minister does not play that role, since the head of government is almost always more directly involved in external affairs than before. Be as it may, for our purpose the ambassador is the first one responsible for a particular bilateral relationship, and is comparable to the chief manager or the country CEO.

Bilateral and Multilateral Envoys

The great majority of ambassadors on full-time assignment resident abroad engage in classic diplomacy, at bilateral posts, representing the sending state in a foreign country. In 1999 there were about 7700 of them, an average of 41 ambassadors in each of the world's capitals.[37] The figure is always a little fluid, but is not subject to large variation. There are places where embassies lie closed on account of war, major local upheaval or breakdown in law and order (as has happened recently in Afghanistan, Iraq, Somalia and Sudan, but resident embassies have gradually reopened at each places). In East Timor, after its independence in May 2002, just a few states have established embassies. We ignore the usually temporary situation where some embassies are headed by a chargé d' affaires *ad interim*, at any point in time. We also ignore 'concurrent representation', where one ambassador also handles representation in one or more neighboring countries. Roving ambassadors are actually like heads of task forces, charged with particular functional issues. Like 'non-resident ambassadors' described elsewhere, they generally operate from the home country capital.

The other kind of ambassador is the multilateral envoy, customarily called a permanent representative (PR), accredited to the UN or a specialized agencies or some international organization. New York has 190 of them, one virtually for every member-country; at the other major UN center Geneva, the number is about 130. We should also take into account the full-time permanent representatives to agencies such as UNESCO and OECD in Paris, FAO in Rome, IAEA in Vienna and others. Factor in also the full-time permanent representatives like the ones to the EU and NATO at Brussels, and we come to a figure of about 600 multilateral ambassadors. (Some countries give a personal rank of ambassador to deputy permanent representatives, but it is the PR who is the head of mission.)

Some ambassadors handle both bilateral and multilateral work, if a country has a single mission abroad that deals both with the host country and any international agency located there. They may concentrate on bilateral work; treating the other responsibility as secondary. This happens typically at Nairobi, in relation to multilateral work at UNEP and HABITAT, or in Rome in relation to FAO. But at Vienna, IAEA and UNIDO responsibilities have overtaken bilateral work for many that have combined missions. At Brussels, EU work takes precedence over bilateral accreditation to the Belgian government, for those that have combined missions.[38]

The ambassador we study in this book is primarily a bilateral envoy responsible for advancing the home country's interests in a single foreign country. The work of the multilateral ambassador, whether handled by a full-time permanent representative or by one who puts on that hat as needed, is sufficiently distinct to warrant separate examination (Chapter 4). We will also consider in that case if multilateral work is to be recognized as a specialized variant of the genre.

2

♦

RITUAL AND FORM

In diplomacy, appearance is inseparable from function. The public face and image are among the tools the ambassador uses to reach his objectives. For instance, the professional access that he or she enjoys is as much dependent on the glamour and attractiveness of his receptions or dinners, as to his diplomatic skills.[1] At capitals like London, Paris or Washington DC, each with a massive diplomatic corps of 150 to 170 resident embassies, leading to intense mutual competition for access to the powerful, such an aura of style and *savoir faire* produces result. Success, in a word, breeds success. At the more remote locations too, the public image that the ambassador projects is a source of influence, with tactics tailored to the situation.

Protocol and Ceremonial

Protocol is defined as the 'rules of diplomatic procedure'.[2] It evolved as a set of customary practices enforcing standards and the uniform treatment for envoys sent abroad by states, large and small, as personal representatives of their monarchs and presidents. The Vienna Congress of 1815 laid down the principle of equality among them. Precedence among foreign ambassadors in any capital is determined exclusively by the date of the presentation of credentials—with the single exception noted below. Reciprocity is the principle that underpins both protocol and the immunities and privileges enjoyed by ambassadors and their staff—treat me right and I will do the same for you!

For the rest, protocol covers ceremonial at state functions, hierarchies among officials and other personalities, and guidelines for proper conduct. Some protocol customs are arcane, but for the most part they are based on courtesy and good sense.[3] For instance, each country enforces its own 'warrant' or listing of precedence, setting out the ranking of holders of high offices, reflecting a national tradition. Ambassadors customarily rank after cabinet ministers of the receiving state, together with high officials. But there are a few countries that equate foreign ambassadors with cabinet ministers.[4] Protocol procedures may appear tiresome to outsiders (burnishing what Americans call the 'striped pants and cookie-pusher' image), but for an experienced ambassador, compliance with protocol comes fairly naturally. It entails common-sense application of easily understood principles. For instance, at a formal dinner table, guests are seated according to precedence, but a good host also takes into account functional utility—how people would be comfortable in conversation, the language conveniences of the foreign guests, and who should ideally be talking to whom, for one's own purposes.[5]

The appointment of an ambassador is subject to the receiving country accepting the nominated individual, conveyed through an *agrément*. Under a customary procedure, codified in the Vienna Convention of 1961, the sending state forwards the name and bio-data of the ambassador-designate to the receiving state. Usually within several weeks, the latter conveys approval or *agrément*, after an internal processing that usually includes the formal assent by the head of state. Rejection of a nomination is rare; it may occur if for instance the individual is perceived to have a background that renders him or her exceptionally unfit, from the perspective of the receiving state. This might happen if he is on record with views hostile to that country. Rejections are seldom made public. One US study notes that between 1910 and the late 1970s there have been three cases of failure by US envoys to obtain *agrément*.[6] Rejection usually takes the shape of prolonged delay. For instance, if approval does not materialize some months after nomination, and reminders fall on deaf ears, the sending state takes the hint that the proposed name is not acceptable, and that an alternative would be preferable—this avoids placing the rejection on record. Occasionally a rejection becomes public, often when there are strains in the bilateral relationship. This may compel each side to harden their positions, as happened between the UK and Iran in 2001, when Teheran rejected a nomination; when this became public, London insisted that it would not send forward any other name. Such a dispute is usually resolved quietly after the passage of some time.

In preparation for his assignment, the envoy-designate calls on a wide spectrum of domestic government leaders, officials and others. In these pre-departure briefings he receives a full range of instructions. Meetings with the head of government (be it a president, prime minister or chancellor) and the foreign minister are the high point of his agenda. Some countries have a formalized 'instruction' process, to convey a charter of tasks to the new envoy.[7] But even where a formal instruction system does not exist, the impromptu advice or observations provided at such meetings can be of inestimable value to the envoy.[8] The envoy also makes a round of the ministries, and meets the official and non-official agencies that are significantly engaged in the country of assignment. Most foreign ministries require that the envoy also undertake a familiarization tour in the home country, to visit different regions or provinces, and principal cities that have their own connections in the target country. Similarly, he visits business chambers, academic and scientific institutions, as well as important individual enterprises, to meet individuals who are relevant to his future work.[9] For instance, if marine product exports feature in trade with the assignment country, then visits to processing plants at home and discussions with corporates involved in that business enable the envoy to speak with conviction, if restrictions on fishery exports become an issue in the future, or if new markets are to be explored. These home tours are vital for the ambassador to keep abreast of developments.

As a final pre-departure formality, some countries organize a 'commissioning ceremony' for the ambassador-designate. In Thailand, following ancient custom, outbound envoys are 'anointed' by the King, usually in batches, and national TV news broadcasts report such events as lead stories. In Malaysia, with its rotating constitutional monarchy among nine traditional sultans, the envoy receives his papers personally from the *Yang Di-Pertuan Agong* (head of state), plus a word of personal instruction on his mission.[10] In the UK the envoy goes to Buckingham Palace to 'kiss the hand' of the sovereign, reflecting the same notion of personal representative of the monarch, though in practice he simply has tea with the Queen.[11] In some African countries an elaborate 'commissioning ceremony' is held, at which the ambassador-designate receives his credential papers from the president, with speeches by the president, the foreign minister, and by the envoy in response. These three then sign a weighty register, also an unusual addition to the ritual. The ambassador's family shares the limelight with him, together with his friends, and MFA officials.[12] In the US, credential papers are handed over by the Secretary of State at a reception attended by the envoy's family, but this may also be held at the White House for an envoy close to the President. In some countries the papers are simply forwarded by the protocol division to the embassy, to await the envoy's arrival, or are given to the envoy at the foreign ministry, to be hand-carried by him.[13]

Besides the credential papers, the envoy also receives a 'letter of commission', signed by his head of state. In a language that is formal and extravagant, he is praised for his unique abilities, and as one who merits special trust, he is charged with the task of representation in the destination country. Thereafter, if the envoy suffers from self-doubt or angst over his responsibilities, he needs only to re-read this wonderful document to obtain reassurance for his capacity to handle the mission!

By custom and logic, there cannot be two accredited ambassadors from the same country in a foreign capital, even if one of them is yet to present his papers. It means that the post must be vacated before the new envoy reaches the foreign capital. Unlike in a business enterprise, there cannot be a face-to-face handover in the foreign capital. This influences the ambassador's substantive pre-departure activity. The document that serves as the new ambassador's initial guide (at least for the first few months of assignment), is the 'handing over note' prepared by the predecessor. It covers all the accumulated ground knowledge and wisdom of the predecessor. Also included are notes on personalities and institutions that will be the local interlocutors, candid sketches of the officials posted at the embassy and in the diplomatic corps, and a narration of the unfinished tasks and suggested priorities—all that a conscientious official should transmit to his successor. When the envoy examines such a collection of notes written by some generations of predecessors, they graphically portray the evolution in that country, and the stages traversed in the bilateral relationship. In real life some handing over notes are sketchy, touching only a few major points in a relatively short compilation of a few pages. Sometimes the departing envoy even omits to write the note. The seriousness with which such an institutional memory transmission is performed is one criterion by which one may judge the degree of professionalism of any diplomatic machine.[14]

At the new post, the presentation of credentials is the ambassador-designate's first major activity. It is also a ceremonial high point of the assignment, the singular event where he is at center-stage. (Example: in Europe it may be the only occasion where he will travel, in his own right, in a limousine belonging to the head of state, flying the head's personal standard, escorted by motorcycle outriders!) National custom determines the procedure in each capital; the standard template demands only that the credential papers be handed over.[15] The sequence of events begins with the new ambassador-designate making his very first official call at the foreign ministry on the chief of protocol.[16] He is formally welcomed, and briefed on the credential procedure. He usually receives a paper giving a step-by-step ceremonial sequence,[17] sometimes with floor charts showing the placement of dignitaries, and the sequence of actions he is to undertake.[18] The chief of protocol would indicate a likely date when the ceremony may take place, and the ambassador-designate's place in the 'queue' of waiting envoys.[19] He also receives guidance on the official calls that he should make, some even prior to the credentials' presentation, and others after that event.

The next step is the handing over of the 'initialed' copies of the papers (also known as *copies d'usage*), originally intended for verification of the envoy.[20] In most capitals, the credential copies are handed over to a vice-minister or permanent secretary. That is the envoy's first high-level official encounter, and an opportunity for a brief, substantive dialogue. The old rule was that the ambassador-designate thereafter waited in a kind of limbo, unable to engage in official contacts until completion of the credential presentation. This led to situations where for several weeks, or even months, newly arrived ambassadors had to wait it out, till the head of state found the time for the credentials ceremony. In line with the progressive relaxation in diplomatic procedures, ambassadors now function more or less normally in most capitals, once the initialed copies have been handed over. But the more *protocolaire* capitals still insist that an ambassador-designate should not engage in contact with ministers or political-level personalities.[21] Where such an enforced period of low activity obtains, it is used for initial familiarization, including calls on colleagues in the diplomatic corps.

A narration of some credentials ceremonies conveys the flavor of this ritual. In London, the event begins with the bewigged Marshal of the Court, resplendent in his full uniform of gold lace, escorting the envoy in a royal horse-driven coach to Buckingham Palace, providing one more spectacle to camera-toting tourists in that vicinity. Employing a subtle, arcane distinction, a high commissioner-designate is provided with a four-horse carriage, while an ambassador-designate makes do with the two-horse version! The envoy, still bearing 'designate' status, enters the high presence of the Queen, bows as instructed on entry to the hall, and again when he stops at the prescribed distance, recites the short 'formula', to the effect that he has the honor to present the letters of recall of his predecessor and his own letters of credence (or of 'introduction', for a high commissioner). He hands over these documents to the Queen, and from that moment he is the accredited envoy. There are no speeches. In London that short ceremony is followed by the presentation of the senior embassy or high commission officials (this is customary in all countries) and finally, a private audience with the Queen. The Permanent Under-Secretary of the Foreign Office, resplendent in the British diplomatic uniform, is the only official who attends; he stands on one side, speaking only when commanded.[22] The ambassador is escorted back to his residence, and he then offers the traditional glass of champagne to the escorting British officials. An equally elaborate ritual is enacted at Vienna where the Hapsburg Palace provides a splendid setting; the Austrian flair for protocol ceremonial is given full play.

In Washington DC, given the heavy preoccupations of the US President, short speech texts are exchanged for the record, but not read out. The brief ceremony is the envoy's moment of exclusive glory in the Oval Office, an opportunity to make his pitch directly to the US President. It is preceded by a simple arrival greeting by a small honor guard.

The New Delhi ceremonial is captured in an account recorded by former ambassador M.R.A. Baig, Chief of Protocol from 1956 to 1963. He wrote:

...on the appointed day I would proceed in a fleet of the President's cars to the Embassy concerned. Here, the Ambassador and some senior officials of his staff, all in full ceremonial uniform, together with their wives would be awaiting. The officers and their wives would then enter the various cars and proceed to Rashtrapati Bhawan so as to be seated in a special enclosure in the courtyard before the ceremony commenced. Last of all, the Ambassador and I would leave. There is a long drive from the gates of Rashtrapati Bhawan to the actual place of the ceremony and, at the gates, the open car would be met and escorted in by the President's mounted Bodyguard. That part was very colourful and always greatly appreciated. Though I must have gone through the ceremony over fifty times I never failed to be thrilled by our magnificently-built men of the bodyguard, every man approximately six-foot tall, in turbans and resplendent uniforms, lance pennants fluttering in the breeze and superbly mounted.

Arriving at Rashtrapati Bhawan we would be met by the Military Secretary to the President and his household staff. Preceded by two A.D.Cs and with the Military Secretary besides him, the Ambassador would march to a saluting dais facing the Guard of Honour. On his taking up position the band would play first the National Anthem of the Ambassador's country, and then our own. The guard commander would then march up and request the Ambassador to inspect the guard. While this was being done, the members of the Embassy, and an equal number of us from the Ministry would form up. Then, led by the Ambassador and the Foreign Secretary, two by two, we would march from the courtyard and up a great flight of steps into the main building. Bodyguardsmen were at attention on each step, and trumpeters at the top of the stairs, in splendid scarlet uniforms, would sound a fanfare that would last till we entered the building.

We were now in a small ante-room leading into the Hall where the actual ceremony took place. We waited till the President had entered and taken up position. The intervening curtains would then be thrown aside and we would march in and form up in line facing the President, to whom we would bow. The Foreign Secretary then stepped forward and presented the Ambassador who would make a short speech. The President would reply suitably and then walk forward and have the members of the Embassy staff presented to him. We would then have a group photograph taken, have a cup of coffee with the President and the wives of those taking part in the ceremony, and then take leave. Several ambassadors have told me that nowhere in the world is there a more colourful and impressive credential ceremony.[23]

Over time this ceremony has undergone simplification. Gone is the full honor guard, and the national anthems. But the grand staircase in the open forecourt, leading to the Mughal Hall—the jewel of the Rashtrapati Bhavan—continues to be lined by tall lance-bearing cavalrymen of the President's Bodyguard. A trumpet fanfare sounds as the envoy walks up. In place of the single ceremony that took place on the appointed day, envoys are now processed in batches of three and four. New Delhi remains one of the rare capitals where the spouse is permitted to witness the ceremonial from a hidden balcony, much like the ladies of the royal court in times past. There are some other Asian capitals that include the spouse, but this is not typical elsewhere.

The personal meeting with the head of state is the one element that is common in all credential ceremonies, though it recedes a little in importance when the head of state holds ceremonial office and substantive executive power lies with the prime minister, or chancellor. The ambassador gets his first opportunity to put across the objectives of his mission, and to receive from this high dignitary an authentic indication of how the bilateral relationship is perceived in the receiving country, a *tour d' horizon* of important issues. The ambassador is customarily not accompanied by any embassy official,[24] while the president has with him high officials from his staff, and from the MFA.[25]

Later on, at the termination of the ambassador's assignment, there is little ceremony. The envoy makes a customary round of farewell calls, to thank the ministers and officials who facilitated his work, and to prepare the ground for the continuing relationship with his successor. He also travels to the provinces, regions, and cities to take leave of local administration officials. The number of calls he makes on high personalities depends on local custom. If the receiving country is a monarchy, the envoy can expect a meticulous departure procedure, including a farewell audience with the King or Queen. In busy capitals, presidents holding executive office are seldom available to the outbound envoy, though major countries such as Germany preserve the tradition of a final meeting with the Federal President. Kenya has an unusual custom of granting the ambassador or high commissioner a farewell call on the President, at a stand-up encounter of a few minutes' duration, held in an open corridor outside the President's personal office, with the Foreign Minister, senior officials and the media, print and TV in full attendance. Former President Daniel arap Moi sometimes used the occasion for public remarks on the state of bilateral relations and on the ambassador's performance.[26]

Some aspects of these ceremonies and courtesies are quaint, but they form the ethos of the profession. Besides providing a continuum with history, the protocol rituals also serve a practical purpose, even if this may not be immediately apparent. They provide a universally accepted framework for the operation of the diplomatic process, regardless of location and circumstance. They also underscore the envoy's status as the personal representative of the sending head of state; his immunities and privileges flow from this concept. The substantive and the symbolic constitute a single package that survives changing times.

Non-Career Appointments

Diplomatic services, as agglomerations of civil servants who spend a working lifetime preparing for head of mission appointments, naturally resent ambassadorial appointments made from outside their professional family. At the same time, as realists, diplomats have no choice but to accept that the head of government or state has the right to choose the envoy deemed best suited to represent the country abroad. There is perhaps no country where law or public regulation has as yet put this prerogative under restraint.

In countries with old, established diplomatic services, the custom has been to appoint almost all ambassadors from within the service. On a few occasions, Britain, France, Germany, and some other old school countries have appointed public figures, but these are rarities. At any point in time, a typical European country may have one or two non-career individuals serving as ambassador, if there are any at all.

Third World countries that emerged into independence in the past half century chose a different path. Most of them found it expedient to retain the option to make some appointments from outside the professional service. Generally the percentage has been around 10 to 20%, but none have a fixed formula. Who figures in these outside choices? Some are political figures, sent abroad as either a consolation prize if they missed out on a major office at home, or are sent away in political exile. Or the appointment is given as a reward to a retiring armed forces chief or a senior civil servant from the home service. Sometimes, a distinguished figure from academia or the media is rewarded. Usually, such acts of political patronage are countermanded when there is a change of regime. A common element is that most non-career appointments are made to 'comfortable' posts. This is one feature that especially arouses the ire of diplomatic services.

For instance, in India it is accepted that the Prime Minister has the prerogative to appoint some non-career ambassadors. The appointment of a *retired* career diplomat is also viewed as belonging to this category, as it deprives a career diplomat of that opportunity. India traditionally 'reserves' London and Washington DC for such appointments; serving career diplomats have been assigned there rarely. Moscow has also been a favorite for non-career appointments.[27] In contrast, one recalls only two or three political appointments to any post in sub-Saharan Africa. Heading the permanent mission in New York is quintessentially the career diplomat's job; the only political appointments made by India took place in the 1950s—

Vijayalakshmi Pandit, Prime Minister Nehru's sister, and the unforgettable, acerbic Krishna Menon. At any point in time, India has around ten non-career ambassadors, fewer than 10% of the total.

Other Asian countries similarly appoint a limited number of non-career envoys, usually to the comfortable posts. Japan, in the course of foreign ministry reforms that were triggered by public scandal in 2001 over the misuse of special funds in the foreign ministry, may have to accept a 'quota' of envoys drawn from other ministries.[28] In Africa, one might generalize that capriciousness is greater, and the protests from the professional service more muted than elsewhere. An extreme example is Uganda, where in 2003, out of 26, only one professional held an ambassadorship, all the rest were political appointees.[29] Kenya is an exception, where non-career appointments generate minimal resentment because foreign service officials have the reverse possibility of appointment as permanent secretaries in other ministries, and at any time there are two or three holding such offices. In Latin America, despite the existence of highly capable professional services, the appointment of non-career ambassadors is an endemic reality. To the public, these appear as gifts bestowed by government, with no standards applied.

The US began on a different track from the early years of independence, appointing public figures to head its legations in Europe and elsewhere. Among the founding fathers, Thomas Jefferson and Benjamin Franklin served as US envoys in Europe. This occurred at a time when the nation had no diplomatic service and the practice has continued as a special prerogative of presidents. In recent times, the percentage of non-career ambassadors has hovered around 30%, easily the highest figure among major countries (it was 36% under Kennedy and 22% under Carter). The impact is heightened by the fact that the choicest posts go to this group.

Another US custom is the appointment of non-career personalities to multilateral posts. This includes New York and Geneva, besides the permanent missions to specialized organizations like NATO at Brussels, OECD in Paris, and IAEA at Vienna. Some US Permanent Representatives to New York have been given cabinet status, not just in name but with even the right to attend cabinet meetings, as happened with Madeleine Albright when she held that job in the early 1990s, before she became Secretary of State. In contrast, almost all the other major services send their career diplomats to the top multilateral posts, barring some exceptions.

Two kinds of individuals are sent as US envoys, though in practice the distinction may not always be clear. Some are acknowledged public figures of distinction in their own walks of life, be it academia or business. Then there are appointments made from the tribe of financial contributors to the presidential election campaign, and those that have rendered personal or political service. While strictly speaking, the law forbids the latter kind of appointment, they continue and draw frequent criticism from the foreign service and public opinion.

Americans have long agonized over their system. Proponents have argued: that 'amateur diplomacy is the American method'.[30] Some have asserted that political appointments better reflect the tripartite political structure of the US and its domestic opinion.[31] The critics of the system have been no less eloquent, pointing to the weakness the system engenders. Some public incidents add grist to the mill of the critics, like the one in the 1970s when the US envoy to Thailand insisted that as the personal representative of the President he outranked visiting Vice President Hubert Humphrey,[32] or the early 1980s experience of the State Department with Ambassador Vincent de Roulet in Jamaica, when he insisted on applying his brand of personal diplomacy, in defiance of instructions.[33]

Various compromises have been suggested. One idea has been to reserve for the President some 15 to 20 appointments, those perceived as 'policy-making positions'.[34] Another idea took the shape of a draft amendment to the 1980 Foreign Service Act proposed by Senator Charles Mathias (number S. 1886), to limit political ambassadorial appointments to 15% of the total. Professionals, including eminent former envoys and the American Foreign Service Association have long lobbied hard in favor of such limits, and the deleterious effects of the spoils system, but it is unlikely that sufficient Congressional support that limits the President's authority can be mobilized.

What are the issues if we attempt an objective assessment of non-career appointments, not limited in focus to the US?

One. If diplomacy is accepted as a legitimate profession, with its own expertise, tradecraft and special skills, it stands to reason that a person inducted from outside may not do justice to the job. For instance, there are many posts where knowledge of the local language is vital to optimal performance. There is a better prospect of getting an accomplished regional specialist from within the professional service, who also possesses the other requisite skills. While exceptions can be cited of non-career individuals who have delivered outstanding performances, others have been disasters, or have performed poorly.

Two. The receiving state looks to the influence or access that the foreign ambassador enjoys with his government. If an envoy is specially trusted by the sending state, or enjoys a direct rapport with his head of government, the receiving country is gratified that it has a good friend in court. But such clout is ephemeral, and withers with a change in government. On balance, a receiving country tends to find the professional a more predictable quantity. Ambassador Malcolm Toon has written that at his farewell reception in Tel Aviv, before his successor had been named, Prime Minister Yitzak Rabin said: 'Tell Washington to send us another professional—one who can report accurately and objectively our views and who is informed on and can articulate Washington's concerns.'[35] Such public candor is rare, but it typifies the perception of receiving states that are in a close relationship.[36]

Three. Invariably the non-career envoy needs a fine Deputy Chief of Mission (DCM) to provide backup. Their relationship is often unpredictable. When it goes wrong, it compromises the functioning of the entire embassy. Empirical evidence from different services suggests that there is higher breakdown between the two with non-career ambassadors than with professionals.

Four. On appointment, a non-career envoy may become enmeshed in internal rivalries with senior officials of the home MFA, or fail to get fulsome cooperation from them. A distinguished Indian newspaper editor, sent as High Commissioner to London in the mid-1970s has written about the inadequacy of the briefings he received from the Ministry of External Affairs, New

Delhi. This can be a passing phase, rectified in time, or it may sour the entire tenure. Another problem is that such appointees may not grasp the craft of dealing with service officials, both at the MFA and in their own embassy. This can inhibit their performance.

India has favored professionals for delicate assignments in neighboring countries, be it Bangladesh, Pakistan or Sri Lanka. In Nepal it has sent a mix, contributing partly to a perception in that Himalayan kingdom of a wavering, unpredictable policy from New Delhi. An empirical study is needed to assess the performance of non-career envoys, especially in delicate assignments involving neighboring countries, but one suspects that the professionals have tended to deliver a better performance.[37]

To sum up, a diplomatic service cannot sustain morale if a large proportion of the 'best' assignments go to persons from outside the professional ranks. This is the bottom line that should be the deciding factor. Yet, a limited number of carefully selected non-partisan appointments, of outstanding public figures, can help invigorate the system and bring in fresh ideas. It is vital that the non-career envoy is helped by an able, carefully selected DCM and is proactively assisted by the foreign ministry, to help his interface with the professional system.

The Diplomatic Corps

The *Corps Diplomatique* is the collective body of foreign diplomats in a capital. The Corps was first mentioned by Sir Thomas Roe in his reports to London from Constantinople. It is a kind of brotherhood of envoys; the officials of the foreign ministry or the foreign service of the receiving country are not included.[38] The heads of UN offices and of other multilateral agencies figure on the official diplomatic list maintained by the MFA of the receiving state, but are not functional members of the Corps. Heads of Missions are the principals of the Corps, but the collective entity also includes the other diplomats from each embassy. A Doyen or Dean, the longest-serving ambassador at that particular post, heads the

Corps. But in countries that are predominantly Catholic, the Corps is headed by the Vatican Ambassador, who carries the special title, Papal Nuncio.[39]

Diplomacy guru Harold Nicolson called the Diplomatic Corps a 'professional freemasonry'. It has first of all the responsibility of safeguarding the privileges and immunities of ambassadors and their staff. It collectively represents all of them in permanent dialogue with the official agencies of the receiving country, almost invariably through the Chief of Protocol of the MFA. Similarly the Dean is the contact point for the Chief of Protocol for the transmission of information and regulations that affect the Corps. This dialogue ranges across issues like ceremonial procedures, exemption from local taxation (including traditional duty-free import privileges of the Corps), security issues and anything else connected with the smooth functioning of embassies. The Dean may be assisted by a deputy and by the deans of the regional groups, especially when the Corps is large. It occasionally holds business sessions at which collective issues are thrashed out, including matters relating to the host country. It also organizes collective social events like farewells for departing ambassadors, the presentation of traditional souvenirs to them, annual functions and the like—following custom that varies from capital to capital. Some of the ways in which the Corps affects the functioning of ambassadors are:

> One. In busy capitals, the Corps is generally less active than in smaller places, where the *esprit de corps* is also much stronger. Similarly, in receiving countries where there is a multitude of shared local problems, the latent 'trade unionism' of the Corps comes to the surface. Observation shows that the Corps tends to be more assertive in countries that are relatively weaker, or paradoxically, very solicitous towards foreigners.

> Two. The Corps is a brotherhood with shared values and other commonalities. Even in capitals that may have 15 or 20 embassies, ambassadors meet in smaller regional groups (for example the cluster of EU ambassadors, and those from Africa, Latin America, the Arabs and the Commonwealth). In very large diplomatic capitals, where there may be 100 or more embassies, the Corps

functions primarily through such regional groups. The regional deans represent their groups in discussion with the Dean. The regional and other clusters organize monthly lunch gatherings, hosted by each ambassador in rotation, where they exchange information and socialize. Sometimes these sub-groups become proactive agencies for the collective benefit of the countries they represent—it depends on individuals and the initiative they take.[40]

Three. An extraordinary degree of information exchange takes place among ambassadors, in the framework of the shared interests of the Corps and commonly understood ground rules. No one would expect an envoy to casually share information on sensitive bilateral issues, but much of the rest is often the object of mutual exchange, always respecting confidentiality. For example, a European envoy may show an Asian counterpart a cipher telegram that he has sent giving an assessment on some issue, when he expects a similar sharing of assessments by the other envoy. For any new ambassador, identifying the key envoys in a capital and establishing personal credibility with them are important goals. The same holds true of good relations with the members of one's own regional group, with the difference that all of them are valid targets for cultivation.

Four. In isolated capitals where local difficulty is encountered, the Corps can become the breeding ground for an 'us-and-them' mentality, and the ambassador has to guard against this. It can lead to pointless rounds of mutual entertainment among foreign envoys, instead of using entertainment as a device for advancing local connections.[41]

The Corps is sometimes also collectively invited to events organized by the host country, and the custom varies between countries. An annual meeting with the head of state is a standard practice; sometimes this may take the form of a reception, or a dinner. It provides an opportunity for a limited private discussion with high dignitaries, including the head of state. For example at the Chancellor's annual reception in Germany in the 1990s, some ambassadors were alerted by the Foreign Office that they were slated for a short, private discussion with the Chancellor; after the customary round of speeches, the dozen odd so selected were escorted turn by turn to the Chancellor by the Chief of Protocol for a few minutes of conversation. There are other collective activities that are organized for the Corps. In pre-1991 Czechoslovakia, the President hosted a year-end pheasant hunt at one of the old castles, Konopište, maintained as a Presidential retreat. In Japan, the Corps is invited to a peach blossom viewing, with a member of the Royal Family or the Grand Chancellor of the Court acting as host. Other places have a tradition of organizing excursions for the Corps by special train or aircraft. In the mid-1990s, Ottawa organized an elaborate special journey by military aircraft for a score of ambassadors to several places in its frozen North, visiting tiny settlements of the Inuit and some defense bases, well beyond to the Arctic Circle.[42]

The Diplomatic Corps in each capital has its own flavor and working methods. An ambassador neglects the Corps at his peril, because he cannot anticipate when he will need the support of this professional brotherhood, even if he may assign to it secondary importance, in comparison with his bilateral work. The investment of a little effort is all that it takes to derive value—sometimes of an unexpected depth and quality—from the Corps.

Privilege and Immunity

Distinguished diplomat Abba Eban has written: 'The idea of immunity, which ancient civilizations interpreted as a form of sanctity, is the first condition of a diplomatic system.'[43] The practice of protecting emissaries was well known in history, in China, India, Greece and Rome. Broadly, when a dominant empire ruled, emissaries were treated as representatives of vassals, while in situations of near-equality among states, they were treated with greater honor. For instance, the Roman civilization, unlike the Greeks, had little regard for the envoys sent to the empire's capital by other states; they were treated as representatives of supplicants. The *Arthashastra*, authored by Kautilya, declares: 'It goes without saying that the Brahman envoy shall never be harmed.'[44] The great

17th-century jurist Grotius spoke of 'the sacredness of ambassadors'. In his 1681 classic, de Wicquefort calls the violation of the person of the ambassador a 'violation of the Law of Nations.'[45]

Therein lay the key as to how envoys, episodic or resident, might be regarded. A notion of sovereign equality among all the states exchanging envoys is implicit in the concepts of diplomatic privilege and immunity that grew gradually since the first of the resident ambassadors were exchanged in medieval Italy in the 15th century. Linked with the equality concept is an acknowledgment of reciprocity, that countries are both senders and recipients of resident envoys; to treat one lot badly is to invite retaliation. This led to the development of rules of customary usage, which were codified in the Vienna Regulations of 1815. The Vienna Convention on Diplomatic Relations of 1961 further elaborated on rules and practices that had grown in the intervening years.

The inviolability of the person, the office premises, and the infrastructure of the ambassador are vital to his function. The communication facilities, including the diplomatic bag that served as the prime means of report dispatch and receipt of instructions in times past, also enjoy this protection. The privileges have survived intact in modern times, since they are a functional necessity. What attracts public notice are the instances of gross violation of privilege, rare as they are, like a shooting incident outside an embassy during a demonstration that may result in the injury or death of a citizen of the host country. Or there are personal misdemeanors by the envoy or his dependent, ranging from financial misdeeds to acts of violence against locals.[46] The maximum recourse available to the host country is to demand the lifting of diplomatic immunity of the envoy or embassy official, and when that is rejected, to demand withdrawal of the individual, i.e. to declare him *persona non grata*. It is customary to negotiate bilaterally the departure of the individual, without public announcement. An aspect of diplomatic privilege that attracts media notice is traffic offences, such as the accumulation of parking tickets by embassy vehicles. In some countries, a local practice has evolved where embassies are no longer exempt from paying traffic fines. Elsewhere, the publication of parking offence statistics in the media serves as a deterrent of sorts, at least to keep the frequency of violations within bounds.

The ambassador and his diplomatic staff are also exempt from any form of taxation in the receiving country, and from the payment of local levies. But the interpretation of what constitutes a tax varies, and many countries have shifted matters such as the exemption from payment of sales tax or VAT, to a graduated, bilateral reciprocal regime, linking exemption to similar facilities for their own diplomats in the country concerned.[47]

Privilege and immunity remains one of the pillars of the diplomatic system. It is taken for granted in times of normalcy, but functions as a safety net for the individuals and for the institution, when relations between countries deteriorate, or when a crisis erupts.

Operational Modalities: Duration, Channels and Withdrawal

How long should an ambassador serve in a foreign capital? Most foreign ministries consider 3 to 4 years to be a 'normal' term.[48] Every diplomatic service enforces the principle of rotation. However successful or singularly suited an envoy may be, no one serves for an indefinite duration in a foreign capital. But there are exceptions. The Soviet Union left Alexi Dobrynin to serve in Washington DC for 24 years. In any capital one might encounter one or two ambassadors who have been at their posts for 10 or 15 years. The chances are that they belong to one of the smaller countries. The connections they establish over such a long period of time often give prestige to that small state, especially if the envoy has also become the Dean of the Diplomatic Corps.

A US Senate committee noted in 1964 that in practice, the average time served by US ambassadors was 2 years and 10 months.[49] If we survey other services, a similar situation would emerge. A few countries like China, Egypt, Indonesia and Russia tend to retain envoys for an average of 4 years at their posts.[50] When an envoy stays on for 5 years or longer there may be a personal reason, like someone left undisturbed prior to retirement. In contrast, a multinational enterprise may find an assignment cycle of three years for a business executive heading a country operation, as convenient in a 'hard' post, but quite insufficient at a normal or comfortable station. An enterprise would want better value out of the individual, by keeping him for a minimum of four or five years. What, then, are the virtues of rotation?

Firstly, a professional diplomat is conditioned to hit the ground running, compressing his initial adjustment phase. A sharp learning curve, most of it on the job, is an essential characteristic of the profession. The value of long-stay experience has to be set off against a potential loss in momentum. As one senior African envoy remarked, 'By the fifth year [the diplomat] is tired and loses dynamism.'[51] Secondly, a prolonged stay at one post carries the risk of 'localitis', believing one's place of assignment to be the center of the world, and worse, becoming excessively solicitous for the concerns of the receiving country. Experience shows these dangers to be very real. Thirdly, for professional development, the diplomat should be exposed to different regions and work specialties. Long assignment cycles inhibit this. Fourthly—and this is crucial for the smaller diplomatic services—human resource (HR) management of service hierarchies and promotions mandates frequent turnover.

Ambassadors are customarily exchanged on the basis of reciprocity (we refer here only to the resident bilateral ambassador; permanent missions do not involve reciprocity). Sometimes there is temporary asymmetry, but unless a good reason exists, like an economy drive or personnel shortage, the closing of one embassy is followed by counter-closure. As for the great powers, small countries find it essential to maintain representation in their capitals, but the great powers do not always reciprocate. For example, the US is host to 173 foreign embassies in Washington DC, but has only 160 of its own bilateral embassies abroad; Belgium receives 162 (of course, this high number is largely on account of the EU), but has only 86 of its own abroad; Germany receives 147 embassies, but sends out only 137; Italy receives 127, but maintains only 118 of its own abroad; Canada receives 116, but sends out only 93 embassies to other countries. We may call such mismatch international 'under-representation'.[52] In contrast, the figures for France (155 to 154), UK (149 to 146), Russia (140 to 140) and Japan (123 to 119) are pretty much in equilibrium.[53]

Singapore is a city-state that consistently manages a large mismatch: against 44 foreign embassies it hosts, it has just 24 resident embassies abroad. Singapore makes up for this imbalance with another 25 'non-resident ambassadors' who live in Singapore, and visit their countries of assignment twice or thrice a year. There are other countries that are 'over-represented' abroad, that is to say, having more resident embassies abroad than foreign missions in their own capitals. India has about 110 embassies abroad, but receives only 101. Brazil sends out 92, but has 88 in Brasilia.

When ambassadors are stationed in both capitals, which is the channel of communication used by the foreign ministry (and by other agencies)? Who does the foreign ministry use to communicate with a partner country—its own ambassador or the foreign envoy?

A general rule is that each country uses its own envoy for the bulk of its *démarches*, to make soundings, or to negotiate. One's ambassador can reach out to the principals in the foreign country and report back their first-hand reaction or response. This also valorizes him, giving an opportunity to pursue other pending matters. But there are exceptions. On an issue of gravity to the host country, the foreign envoy is used to convey the message. For instance, when India carried out its nuclear tests in May 1998, most West European countries, as prime advocates of non-proliferation, summoned Indian ambassadors and conveyed strong protests through high officials, including state secretaries and even foreign ministers. This delivered a far stronger signal than could be made by the foreign ambassadors in New Delhi, though that route was used in parallel. Another instance when the foreign envoy becomes the first channel is when group briefings are organized in the receiving capital, say to cover a major development, or a reaction to an international event. In the example cited above, New Delhi conveyed its rationale for the 1998 tests via high-level briefings for foreign ambassadors, called in regional groups to the Ministry of External Affairs.

Let us consider one of the signals used in diplomacy, the temporary withdrawal of the ambassador. The explanation often given is that the envoy has been 'recalled for consultations', a classic signal of displeasure by the sending country, suggesting a bilateral problem, but falling much short of a break in relations. This device is still in use, but in an age of constant peregrination of ministers and other dignitaries, it has lost its edge as a gesture of displeasure. One danger in recalling one's envoy for consultations today is that the other partner may not take much notice, as happened with the withdrawal of the UK High Commissioner and some other EU ambassadors from Harare in 2000–1, following the confiscation of land from white farmers by the Mugabe government.

Another example: in December 2001, after a terrorist attack on the Indian Parliament, when there was hard evidence that this was the work of *mujahidin* groups based in Pakistan, sponsored by that government, India withdrew its High Commissioner from Islamabad, part of a package of response actions. Pakistan chose not to reciprocate, arguing that it wanted to keep open all avenues of contact. Three months later India demanded the withdrawal of the Pakistan High Commissioner. In June 2002, when bilateral tension had eased a bit (following several rounds of visits by Western foreign ministers and others), India indicated its willingness to consider sending a new High Commissioner, but continuing tension over new terrorist incidents originating from this neighbor's territory blocked that effort. Finally, the two countries sent back their envoys in July 2003, following a new Indian peace initiative.

The moral is that initially an indefinite withdrawal may make good sense as a gesture of displeasure, but the return of ambassadors sometimes falls victim to complex political calculations—such as the perceptions on each side of how domestic and international opinion might interpret the 'normalization' gesture. When bilateral relations are tense, it does not take much to derail new initiatives. Many countries have also realized that the envoy's withdrawal removes the professional, one's best observer and adviser on the local scene when he is most needed.[54] It is probably better to keep cool, and opt for some other expressions of displeasure.

When there is a bilateral crisis, the progressive diplomatic escalation steps, following the *ad hoc* withdrawal of the ambassador, are: definitive recall; a formal downgrading of relations to sub-ambassadorial level (i.e. embassies headed by a chargé d' affaires *en pied*); a withdrawal of embassies; or a formal break in diplomatic ties (which would still leave intact consular relations, unless these are specifically ended as well).[55] When relations are broken, the task of providing consular protection, and keeping alive some contacts becomes important. This may be entrusted to an 'interests section', consisting of relatively junior or middle-ranking diplomats of the sending country, placed under the flag of a third country. Or one may simply entrust to a third country the task of looking after routine matters like the upkeep of property, consular protection, and the like. The Swiss have specialized in offering such services, as a premier neutral country. The US maintains an interests section in Havana, long after the break in relations with Cuba, and the Cubans do likewise in Washington DC. But without a high level Cuban envoy, in the plural US foreign policy establishment there is no advocate for that bilateral relationship, and this partly contributes to the blockage.

Under autocratic regimes, a drastic change at home, through a *coup d'état* or break-up of a country, may force envoys posted abroad representing that country with harsh choices, especially for those close to the previous government. In such circumstances, some are forced into exile, and others quietly return home to face an uncertain future, as happened after the April 2003 Iraq War and the overthrow of the Saddam Hussein regime. At times, such envoys may seek shelter in the receiving state. For instance, after the 1965 exit of President Sukarno in Indonesia and the harsh clampdown on the Indonesian communist party, the country's envoy in Beijing opted to remain there, and became involved in the radio propaganda activities directed at his home country. For many years thereafter, Indonesia demanded his extradition as a precondition to the normalization of bilateral relations between the two countries.[56]

Rarely, ambassadors confront other extraordinary situations. Bangladesh emerged through the break-up of Pakistan, following the December 1971 India–Pakistan War. In the months that followed, one consequence was that all the diplomats from East Pakistan posted abroad in Pakistani embassies, including ambassadors, expressed allegiance for their new independent homeland, and gradually moved over to Dacca. In the capitals where these changeovers were carried out, Indian missions acted as facilitators, given the fact that the new government of Bangladesh had to build its foreign ministry from scratch and lacked any infrastructure.

Notwithstanding the complex circumstances, the changeover was carried out with remarkable equanimity and a minimum of bitterness.[57]

Personal Security

We live in a violent age. Ambassadors, other diplomats and their physical premises have become significant targets for terrorists and for various disaffected groups. Other official representatives of foreign states, and those working for foreign companies, especially expatriates, are also targets for acts of kidnapping and murder. Such incidents come in waves and no region is exempt. After the terrorism of 9/11, security concerns are more acute than ever before; in 2001–2 there were attacks on the US Consulate General at Karachi, church congregations at Islamabad, and the US Cultural Center at Kolkata. Over the years, the US has lost five ambassadors on duty, through acts of terrorism and assassination. Turkey is another nation that has suffered grievously on a similar count, at the hands of Kurdish separatists, and at the end of 2003 through terrorists linked with Al Qaeda. In places as far apart as Beijing, Beirut, Dar-es-Salaam, Islamabad, Nairobi, and Riyadh, to name just a few, embassies have also been targets of attacks. Embassies are also targets for violent protests and group incursions by asylum seekers.

In many capitals, armed policemen and diplomatic protection group personnel escort ambassadors representing countries facing acute threat, providing 'portal to portal' services. Static posts manned by heavily armed personnel protect the residences of ambassadors and their chanceries in many capitals. Every diplomatic mission and foreign ministry has set procedures for dealing with threats that ambassadors and their staff receive via telephone, mail and other means. Most embassies employ private security agencies as well, and in an increasing number of capitals, the sending countries deploy their own home-based armed security guards to protect ambassadors and embassies, almost always with the support of the receiving state.

Diplomatic architecture and access routes for the buildings have to take into account the new threat environment. Major powers spend vast sums on upgrading physical security in this fashion, with blast-proof doors and walls, toughening the windows, creating strong barriers at entry points and providing ambassadors and others with bullet-proof vehicles. Smaller countries find much of this beyond the limit of affordability, and believe that their best protection lies in the range of general precautions that they implement, and their relative anonymity.

Security procedures are part of diplomatic training programs in most countries, even in places that do not perceive a direct or special threat. Envoys can become enmeshed in a crisis situation by accident, as in the December 1996 seizure of the Japanese Embassy in Lima, Peru by local extremists in the course of a national day reception. Families of envoys too learn to live with these threats.

The security dimension adds to the tension of the job. The ambassador has to accept the principle that concerning his own security, he is not the decision maker. In large embassies there are security specialists, often on deputation from the home police or security forces, and they, together with the deputy chief of mission (DCM) usually take charge of the ambassador's personal security.[58] Usually, beyond a certain limit, security precautions become a burden and give diminishing returns in terms of actual safety. Enforced too vigorously, security measures inhibit envoys from wide outreach and normal activity, which too is part of the unavoidable change and adaptation in our violent times.

3

PARTNERS AND TECHNIQUES

What are the ambassador's principal tasks? How does he operate? We begin with a simple, contemporary six-word definition of the ambassador's tasks: *negotiation, outreach, promotion, feedback, management and servicing.*[1] This description differs from what is set out in the 1961 Vienna Convention on Diplomatic Relations,[2] reflecting the evolution of the past four decades. We focus here on the bilateral ambassador; the multilateral envoy is the subject of the next chapter.

The ambassador has two principal action arenas: the host or receiving country, and only to a slightly lesser extent the home or sending country. That the home base has become so important is also a change from the past. Each imposes on him different demands and obligations. Representing the sending country is nevertheless the first task, although there is sometimes tension between the two roles. While cultivating an understanding and empathy for the host country, the ambassador cannot afford to forget that his masters are at home, and he is their agent. Chapter 5 examines the envoy's home tasks.

Official Interlocutors

The ambassador of yesteryear dealt almost exclusively with official agencies; the foreign ministry was his prime interlocutor.

A British ambassador served in Paris from 1905 to 1918 and made only one public speech.³ His successor today might be hard put to name a week without one or two speaking engagements. Diplomacy has predominantly become public and multilayered. As one envoy put it, the frequent exhortation now from headquarters to every ambassador is: 'Be visible!'⁴

The 1961 Vienna Convention on Diplomatic Relations names the foreign ministry as the embassy's channel of communication with the receiving country (article 41(2)): 'All official business with the receiving State entrusted to the mission by the sending State shall be conducted with or through the Ministry for Foreign Affairs of the receiving State or such other ministry as may be agreed.' This is the classic vision of the MFA's 'gatekeeper role'.⁵

That rule is now an anachronism. The ambassador regards himself as free to deal with all the official branches of the host country, with the MFA as the entity that is *also* kept informed of all major issues, sometimes even after the event. The wise envoy treats the host foreign ministry as his natural ally, and engages it in a parallel dialogue where feasible. The MFA remains his first port of call on most important issues, but pragmatism and circumstance determine who will be the other local interlocutors.

Within the foreign ministry, the territorial department covering the envoy's country is his point of constant encounter, the singular entity where he has the greatest need for credibility, mutual confidence and 'on demand' access. It serves as the embassy's local counterpart, customarily with a full spectrum oversight of that relationship. It handles, at some stage, every bilateral issue of importance. Even when a particular action originates elsewhere in the government, the foreign ministry's territorial unit is seldom out of the information loop for long. When an action is personally initiated by a head of government, it normally handles the operational details and follow-up. When embassy–territorial unit relations function well, the ambassador's path to every official contact in the country, and to many non-official actors as well, is smooth. If suspicion or tension reigns, the relation becomes the bane of the envoy's professional life.⁶

The majority of foreign ministries now employ a 'mixed'

structure, a blend of territorial and functional units. A recent monograph of the Italian Foreign Ministry reports that among the 19 EU and G-8 MFAs, most have such structures, as against only four organized on a 'functional' basis, without territorial divisions.[7] Even in foreign ministries where functional departments dominate, or where territorial units concentrate almost exclusively on political work, these units also perform some coordination tasks in economic, cultural and other functional areas. The more usual situation is that the territorial unit acts as the coordinator in almost all non-political functional areas, embodying the integrated diplomacy concept.

Several other MFA divisions or departments are the ambassador's regular discussion partners, ranging from the other territorial units covering the regions of interest, to functional departments like policy planning, UN and conference affairs, disarmament, culture, multilateral economics, protocol, including new entities handling human rights, the environment, terrorism and drugs. The list of contacts expands as dialogue flourishes.

The ambassador needs communication channels to several hierarchy levels in the foreign ministry, starting with the permanent or civil service head (called variously the permanent secretary, or secretary general or state secretary) and the next echelon, often called directors general of political affairs and of economic affairs.[8] The frequency of high level meetings depends on the perceived relative importance of the ambassador's country, and the density of bilateral links. In a capital with a large diplomatic corps, with ensuing competition for access, the ambassador of a country seen as having medium or low importance for the receiving state might not meet the permanent foreign ministry head more than once in several months. In some capitals, the ambassador of a small nation may not see this dignitary at all, beyond an initial call on arrival. This is not a cause for despair, as long as effective working relations exist at other levels, and moreover, that in a situation of real urgency, effective communication is possible. Operational functionality is more important than appearance.[9] Further, a good deal of business is transacted at informal encounters, like at ceremonials and social events. Serendipity is the ambassador's ally at all times. He needs alertness to take advantage of fortuitous encounters. The ambassador usually leaves his deputy and other political officers to engage officials below the head of the territorial unit. Always, function is more important for the envoy than self-prestige.

The ambassador's political-level contacts commence with the foreign minister, and his deputy called variously vice-minister, minister of state or parliamentary state secretary—and in the US, the Deputy State Secretary. Given the huge growth in foreign travel by these high officials and their other obligations, routine access is no longer the ambassador's natural right. In many capitals he may wait for some months before making even his first call on them, after presenting credentials to the head of state.[10] Subsequent meetings may be rare—not counting the opportunity when the ambassador accompanies a visiting high dignitary from home who calls on the foreign minister or when that minister travels to the ambassador's country.[11] A good substitute is available via working relations with the minister's *Chef de Cabinet* or other diplomats on his staff. Further, access to the junior ministers is almost invariably easier, providing a viable alternative.

The home country has a role in building up its ambassador. It can visibly signal his advisory power, sometimes in the simplest way, such as at a meeting when the foreign minister turns to his ambassador and seeks his opinion, or appears to consult him before conveying a reaction.[12] High standing can also be indicated via the seating plan at bilateral talks, though this is less meaningful. The receiving country always values the foreign ambassador who carries clout at home.[13] Given human nature, the reverse kind of situations tend to be more frequent, where home colleagues undercut their own envoy, or show him scant professional regard!

The ambassador's access to the head of state and the head of government (if these two functions are separate) varies greatly, but everywhere the trend is towards more rigidity. The credentials ceremony apart, a typical ambassador in major capitals may now almost never meet the head for an exclusive appointment, as a matter of right, except at the time of departure if it is customary to make a brief farewell call. Yet, there is no real dearth of opportunity for brief conversation at opportune moments, which may range from airport and arrival ceremonials for dignitaries (if that is the local custom), annual greetings for the diplomatic corps, and other social events. If there are issues of substance to be raised directly at that level, even a few minutes snatched in the midst of a public engagement can be productive. But the envoy has to take care not to abuse this method, at risk of being closed out. A Canadian envoy to Germany in the 1970s has painted a different scene: 'I was fortunate in having access to Chancellor Schmidt but used it extremely rarely.'[14] For envoys representing neighboring countries, major powers and fellow-members of alliances or tight-knit regional groups, direct access to heads is still possible, sometimes on a reciprocal basis.

Outside of major capitals, access to heads of state and government is sometimes, but not always, easier. In India, for instance, Prime Minister Indira Gandhi received foreign ambassadors fairly frequently. Her successors have been increasingly harder to meet. One might expect that in small countries access should be easier, but some developing countries in Asia, Africa or the Arab world can be extremely formal, while others in the same region are quite relaxed.

The alternative is the *office* of the head of government, not just the dignitary's principal aide (who often has ministerial rank), but also the foreign affairs adviser and/or his deputies (who may be seconded from the MFA).[15] These days, with presidents and prime ministers as principal movers in foreign affairs, in direct contact with one another, ambassadors need good access to these offices. When relations are exceptionally close, the heads sometimes designate their own private communication routes, bypassing foreign ministries and ambassadors. But the ambassador is seldom left out of the information loop for long. When he is used as the channel, he invariably performs more than a post-office function. If he transmits a sealed envelope message, he usually receives from home an open copy. This provides an opportunity for informal soundings on the issues under dialogue, including initial reactions, even from the aides he meets.

Ambassadors may need to develop 'back channel' contacts to influential personalities, sometimes reaching even the heads of state or government. This can happen through circumstance, or affinity, or sustained cultivation—or even by accident. Language and region specialists and those envoys that have served earlier at the post, carrying forward their own networks, are at a distinct advantage.

This is one more argument in favor of area and country specialization, and career professionals.[16] The envoy has to seize windows of opportunity as available.[17] The ambassador's personal credibility and local reputation is an asset. His goal is effective, functional, 'on tap' access. For instance, if an important issue is under dialogue, the envoy may be called upon to convey a personal message from one head to the other. Often, time pressure mandates that the most direct route be used; for this he needs access virtually without appointment, or outside working hours.

At the other ministries and official agencies, the ambassador is personally involved in dialogue with those that rank high on the action agenda, prioritizing them and taking the help of his embassy colleagues. This includes the principal economic ministries, and those dealing with the interior, culture, education, science & technology, the environment, and/or others. The field is wide. There may be embassy contacts where the ambassador is involved minimally, and his colleagues like the science counselor or the education attaché, run the contacts. The ambassador may enter the frame only when needed, for instance to convey a political message. A good formula is to aim at wide reach, but with clear focus, avoiding over-engagement in any one segment. Contacts with the top agencies that handle government 'oversight', like the cabinet office or the national security council, and/or key political party personalities are invariably important, though not easy to develop. The US is unique, in that the National Security Adviser in the White House plays this overarching role, with a large staff that is amenable to cultivation at different levels. In many countries there is intense competition among foreign envoys for access to a limited number of influential individuals at the apex bodies.

Parliamentary institutions and political parties constitute another arena for cultivation. In authoritarian states, or in strong-fisted democracies, governments view with disfavor contacts by foreign envoys with opposition leaders. In practice, the envoys of developing states tend to be very circumspect in such contacts, since they are not animated by the same zeal for the export of democracy and human rights as their Western counterparts.

How often and on what kinds of issues would the typical

ambassador approach the MFA and other official agencies? There is no standard template, and much depends on the texture of mutual interests, the issues on the agenda, the international context, and subjective factors like the envoy's self-initiative. The relevant elements include:

One. How active are the bilateral dossiers? A new accord under exploration or discussion, or a major visit in the pipeline, or a dynamic multilateral issue would mean an activation of contacts. As the engagement among countries increases, the frequency of contact also multiplies. Invariably, important bilateral issues take precedence in the activities of the ambassador and his staff.

Two. Does the global agenda figure in the exchanges? The US is unique in working its diplomatic mechanism for the active pursuit of a host of non-bilateral or third-country issues. Typically, a US ambassador even in a remote capital, may receive two or three messages in a week instructing him to take up 'at the highest level' some issue on the agenda of the UN or elsewhere, on which the US is keen to mobilize international support.[18] No other country works the bilateral diplomatic system in an even remotely comparable fashion. EU envoys, the other fairly active element on the diplomatic scene, are unique in the joint *démarches* that they undertake—but they function at a lower frequency than the typical US ambassador.

Three. How active is the foreign policy and diplomacy of the host country? When that engagement is heavy, resident ambassadors have to mobilize themselves to track and report upon developments. The emergence of regional diplomacy as a high-growth industry has added to the *démarche*-making function of member states. Their rounds of incoming and outgoing delegations, and sectoral or specialized meetings, become kaleidoscopic. For the embassies of countries that lie outside the region too, the reporting function expands. We see this in ASEAN, as also in other regional groups such as the Contadora Group in Latin America.

Four. What is the potential for local initiative by the envoy? This partly depends on the proactive style of the individual, and his innovative instincts, plus of course the ground reality. If there is scope that the envoy is willing to exploit, he needs frequent dialogue with ministries beyond the MFA; economics is often the driver of such activism, besides the media, culture and education. The headquarters at home can exercise only limited oversight, which makes self-initiative a major driving force. In its absence, somnolence reigns.

It follows that there are a good many ambassadors who are not over-worked, and handle a very finite amount of official business. Abba Eban described this in pithy words: 'The only over-worked embassies are those of major powers with universal and competitive interests...and those in controversy or conflict with neighbors.'[19] John Kenneth Galbraith, sent as Ambassador to India by President Kennedy, makes trenchant observations that are a trifle over-stretched, calling the system of resident envoys 'a spectacular form of disguised unemployment'.[20] Galbraith has written of completing his daily work within three hours each day, which left him ample time to produce three books during the two odd years he spent in New Delhi.[21]

If ambassadors are often under-worked, it is also proof that they have a latent capacity to do more, a principal theme of this study. The foreign ministry can seldom supervise the ambassador beyond a point, or push him to take the initiative or explore new avenues in different areas. It follows that self-initiative has to be the major driving force. This reinforces one conclusion, in line with the 'agency' theory, that the individual envoy has a unique role to play, as a relationship builder. Another conclusion is that techniques borrowed from management theory, tempered with realism, are very pertinent to this profession, to motivate envoys to exploit the opportunities that generally abound. The goal should be to raise average performance levels through systemic change, monitoring, and motivation. These issues are examined later.

The problem goes beyond the actions of ambassadors. We saw that the MFA has lost its external contact gatekeeper role.[22] The MFA does not prevent other agencies from direct foreign relationships because of the huge growth in the international agenda, and technical complexity. It faces the challenge of reinventing itself as a value-provider for them, from its intrinsic position as the one organ of government without a sectoral agenda. Thanks to the ambassador system, the foreign ministry has the best institutional overview of world political dynamics, in exquisite detail. The envoy is thus a vital conduit for the foreign ministry in fulfilling that role. The MFA can use the specialized knowledge that resides with the envoy, and his counterparts at headquarters, for advancing the special agendas of the functional ministries, as well as promoting the wider national interest. Just as the MFA cannot impose its will on domestic ministries through a formalistic stand, it also must not object to the 'disintermediation' that is involved in the direct dialogue between these ministries and the envoys abroad. We examine this later.

There is another set of partners now active in international affairs—the sub-state entities: provinces, states, regions, communes, autonomous zones, or metro cities. Some maintain overseas offices to advance economic interests, be it in the shape of exports, inbound investments or tourism (e.g. German, and US states). Another example is their 'sister city' and 'sister region' relationships. A few are actors in 'growth triangles' and quadrangles with neighboring entities, like 'Euro-zones' in Europe and growth zones in ASEAN and other parts of Asia. The role played by Chinese provinces in external diplomacy is detailed in an excellent study edited by David M. Lampton.[23]

The ambassador and his team reach out to these entities, through tours outside the capital, and other local contacts. The envoy plays a catalyst role in building direct partnerships between them and counterparts in his country. For the resident envoy, it is an axiom that a country's real worth is often found outside the capital city. The ambassador normally takes care not to engage in 'political' dialogue with sub-state leaders, replicating his discussions in the capital, but in practice the latitude is wide. For example in 1999–2001, the British Ambassador in Germany carried out vital political outreach with the German Federal States of the Southern region, Bavaria and Baden-Württemberg, subtly underscoring the convergence in their standpoint, with the position of his country on EU unification. His goal was to influence the German stand, in the collegial political process of that country.[24] This may have come close to the limits of the desirable, but Federal authorities could hardly object, given the blurred internal–external boundary, and the autonomous role of regions, within the EU.

At most other places, the situation is not comparable, but a kind of disintermediation in external relations is taking place, in varying degrees, between internal regions and the central authorities of countries. Sub-state entities are especially active in the economic arena. In some countries, states directly negotiate foreign aid with donors. They also reach out to attract foreign investment from abroad. The net result is a widening of the ambassador's eco-political reach and responsibility.

Another new development is that sometimes ambassadors become entangled with internal issues in the receiving country, discarding customary discretion. The representatives of the great powers, especially the US, are the pioneers, as narrated in an unusual collection of ambassadorial stories recently published by the American Academy of Diplomacy, *First Line of Defense*.[25] One event narrated covers intervention by US Ambassador Elinor Constable in Kenya in 1986–89, when she was instructed to deliver to President Moi a letter from US Commerce Secretary Malcom Baldrige, accusing a particular minister of corruption in blocking a deal involving a US company.[26] She decided that delivering it 'would be a bad idea', and opted to show the letter to the minister concerned, to pressure him into complying with the demand of the US company.[27]

In Africa and elsewhere, other Western envoys have used the aid carrot to push for greater democracy, transparency in administration and respect for human rights. Practical experience has shown that such actions produce results up to a point, but tactical dexterity is essential. For instance, publicizing misdemeanors by the receiving country administration works in some situations, but if overdone, it becomes counter-productive. Zimbabwe in the period 2000–03 is a case in point of the limits of such coercive diplomacy. There are other instances of ham-handed, ineffective intervention.

US ambassadors sometimes play proconsular roles of an

extraordinary kind, not always in the Third World. One unusual story in the American Academy of Diplomacy study relates to the role played by Frank Carlucci, US Ambassador to Portugal in 1975, who later went on to become Secretary of Defense and National Security Adviser.[28] He reached Lisbon when that country 'was considered all but lost to communism'; his predecessor, whose proactive ideas did not conform to the policy of isolation towards that country, had been shifted out. Carlucci opposed the internal trend in Portugal with even greater fervor. He used his Washington DC network, overcame the strong resistance of Secretary of State Kissinger, and became involved with the Portuguese political process. He pushed for early elections and when the Socialists won power, worked to mobilize international financial support for this beleaguered country. There are other cases where envoys have played event-shaping roles in extraordinary situations, though these are seldom publicly documented or acknowledged.

An Indian High Commissioner to Mauritius played a political role during elections held in that island nation in 1982. The full story of this event has not been narrated. In brief, the Mauritius electorate had become disenchanted with the country's founding leader Sir Seewosagur Ramgoolam, after two decades of rule; an economic crisis compounded the situation. To cap it, the relationship with India (original home of 70% of the population) had also deteriorated. A new Indian High Commissioner, Prem Singh, played a visible role in the elections, which culminated in the temporary eclipse of Ramgoolam's Labour Party, and the emergence of Anerood Jugnauth as Prime Minister. The Mauritius press wrote extensively on the extra-diplomatic work of this Indian envoy. Such pro-activism is also part of contemporary unconventional diplomacy.

Non-State Partners

The ambassador's regular discourse with non-official entities has expanded in direct proportion to the involvement of these actors in the conduct of external relations. Rather than list them, it may be useful to describe some characteristics of these contacts, and the ambassador's role.

One. In the economic or cultural sectors, where both official agencies and private bodies are influential, the ambassador and his team have a catalytic and coordination role—to provide discreet leadership without possessing leadership authority. One way is through interactive dialogue at the embassy, chaired by the ambassador, where autonomous players representing home agencies are invited to share information on their programs and ideas. The more proactive way, which also carries some risk of failure, is to broaden such contact groups to include local agencies; of course, the potential gain is also larger with the expanded formula. This is feasible when the pace of activity is heavy, with multiple players.[29]

Two. A similar outreach device is to craft a high-level non-official advisory group, composed of influential local personalities. Who might participate? If there is a bilateral 'eminent persons' group' (a recent diplomatic innovation that is now used fairly widely, where non-officials are used as advisers, meeting annually), the members of this group, led by its co-chairman, is the natural choice.[30] For instance, in the mid-1990s the Indian Ambassador at Brussels established a local contact group of eminent persons, including three Nobel Laureates, to help identify opportunities for developing relations with the EU.[31] In New Delhi, US Ambassador Robert Blackwill (2001–03) initiated a roundtable dinner discussion group that drew the elite of the international affairs and strategic community. Of course any informal brains trust must be handled discretely, avoiding any impression of dependence on such advisers.

Three. Ethnic groups have become a strong diplomatic lever. The Jewish community in the US and other Western countries is the oft-cited model of organized mobilization of blood, religion and ethnicity connections. Others have tried to emulate this, with mixed results. In North America and the UK, overseas Indians have become a growing asset, used increasingly for diplomatic outreach and overseas connections.[32] Home country professionals and experts working in a foreign country can also be used as information sources and sounding boards.

Four. The influence of NGOs and other civil society agencies in international affairs is well recognized. Envoys are seldom comfortable with the fact that even an international NGO that is a critic and even an adversary to the home government can be a worthy outreach partner abroad. (For example: Amnesty International, which evokes mixed reactions in many developing countries, is influential at most places and therefore worth cultivating).

Five. Academics specializing in one's own country or region, think tanks, researchers and scientists are important not only for their own work, but as multipliers in a promotional outreach strategy. Through their contact networks they help to build and sustain country images. Some form of individual and collective interaction with them is always useful. Example: when Indian leaders go abroad on visits they find time to meet that country's intellectuals and specialists from different fields.[33]

The common thread is an *inclusive* work ethic. The mental barrier that the envoy must overcome is an irrational fear that he might dilute his own authority through open dialogue. If the ambassador grudgingly accepts that he has to work with non-official actors, as a matter of form, he is unlikely to derive much value. Non-state actors are sensitive, long accustomed to disdainful dismissal by official agencies. They are quick to spot patronizing behavior. In contrast, genuine proactive interest makes it easy to win their confidence, often producing innovative ideas.

Principal Functions: Negotiation, Promotion and Outreach

In the widest sense, all human communication is *negotiation*. For the envoy, presenting the home perspective to foreign partners, persuading them, and building congruence with them, belongs to the general work of negotiation. Such negotiation remains at the core of diplomacy. But when Nicolson and his generation gave negotiation the central place in diplomacy some 70 years ago, they had in view a narrower definition, of negotiation leading to 'precise agreements in ratifiable form'.[34] Negotiation so defined remains important in diplomacy, but it has receded in importance for professional diplomats. The simple reason is that states have moved from classic *political* negotiation, to a search for commonality and agreement in narrow, specialized functional areas. Now 'line' ministries and their para-diplomats handle such negotiations, often highly technical in character. Ambassadors and the MFA mainly provide the backup and facilitation. One exception is major political negotiation, which mainly takes place in neighboring countries, or in the capitals of the major powers, or for problem-solving. In all of these, the envoy retains a significant direct role.

The formal negotiation sessions at which an ambassador is an active participant may be rather few in a typical career.[35] When specialist delegations arrive from home, say to revise an old agreement on civil aviation traffic rights or finalize a new treaty giving protection to foreign investments, the ambassador is unlikely to join the delegation, leaving this task to the commercial or economic counselor. He briefs the team on arrival, receives feedback on the progress of negotiations, advises them if blockages develop, and pushes things forward, as needed. He may have a more active role in the inter-negotiation phase, to convey messages on behalf of the home team, and unblock local obstacles. He has a more central role in developing ideas for future agreements; some of which can take several years to move from concept to reality.

'*Promotion*' is one word from the 1961 Vienna Convention definition that has gained in relevance. It encompasses the classic function of 'protection', expressing it more proactively. Furthermore, promotion extends to every work area: politics, economics, culture, education, science & technology, information and media, and even consular affairs. In each, the embassy is tasked to advance home country interests, utilizing local partners as allies. Everywhere, the cultivation of individuals provides opportunity for action, often moving from person-to-person relations to the higher stage of institutional contacts, which is even better. In the promotional mode, the envoy essentially works on his personal initiative rather than a set of instructions.

'*Outreach*' is linked with promotion, and encompasses relation-building actions by the ambassador and his team, aimed at both traditional and the non-obvious local partners. In its operation, this word includes, in the broadest sense, the classic diplomatic activity of explanation, persuasion, and negotiation. It involves the sustained pursuit of targets, to win them over for support and collaboration. It operates through the envoy's contact network. Outreach and promotion are intertwined. Let us examine the working of promotion and outreach in the key areas.

Political work. This retains primacy in diplomacy even in an age when at most locations, the ambassador devotes more time to other activities, especially those of an economic native. The political understanding between countries forms the base upon which other sectoral activities are built and elaborated. What exactly is the envoy's political work?

a) First of all is the task of communication, presenting the views of the home country on issues that are important, or directly concerning the two nations, or affecting third-country, regional or global issues. The home foreign ministry invariably wants the ambassador to transmit its views, immediately, and 'at the highest level possible'. It is left to the ambassador to decide on the level to which he will actually make his *démarche*, the timing and other details. This choice is relevant to the reaction he will obtain; he must consider the frequency at which he has used a particular channel, the interlocutor's responsiveness, and above all the efficacy.[36] After the *démarche*, he reports the reaction, usually via a cipher message. If he is wise he will concentrate on the interlocutor's reaction, rather than hold forth excessively on his own performance.[37] As noted earlier, it is the envoys of the great powers that most often visit the MFA with representations on third-country and global issues. In contrast, ambassadors of the middle and lesser powers stick to bilateral themes and subjects where their country has a strong stake.[38]

b) The ambassador may raise political issues at his own initiative, to probe intentions, and to convey assessments home that will warn, alert or advise, in anticipation of some event, or analyzing an ongoing situation. It is left to the envoy's imagination to pursue such topics, on the basis of local events, or information that he and his team may have gathered. Beyond his first contact channel, the foreign ministry, he has a wealth of other avenues—official, in the media, academia and elsewhere. The envoy will generally not raise a new bilateral issue on his own initiative, without clearance from home, but he might float a trial balloon, or make a tentative sounding that fits in with home policy. In such cases he makes it clear that he is speaking on his own authority, not on instruction. The essential point is that he has a zone of autonomy. An example: when a Western envoy in an African capital found that his intervention on a domestic issue was not productive, he used the Internet to locate and reach out to some international NGOs, to persuade them to raise the issue. They did so, arguing that if not rectified, this situation would affect their sizable aid programs. Narrating the story, the envoy doubted if his action would have received official sanction, had he sought it![39]

c) In the US, lobbying through hired professional specialists is an activity that challenges traditional canons. Many countries now use lobbyists for political work, and for media outreach, in Washington DC, often to generate access for the ambassador in the Congress. The custom has not spread to other capitals, except at Brussels, for work related to the EU.

d) In the ambassador's contacts with high personalities, traditional routes are supplemented with back-channel contacts. Besides the principals, often a good intermediary or senior adviser may do nearly as well, as long as this delivers result. Even in Beijing and Moscow, non-official contacts are creatively used to reach out to key individuals.

e) Contacts with opposition groups can pose a dilemma for the envoy. One study notes: 'If a diplomat is to...maintain the confidence of the government to which he is accredited...[it] could be forfeited by attempts on his part to establish relations to individuals opposed to the existing regime, or disaffected groups within society.'[40] Action has to be tailored to circumstance. For instance, astute embassies cultivate the foreign affairs advisers to leading contenders in US presidential elections, long before Election Day. But all democracies are not equally transparent, while quasi-democracies and authoritarian regimes impose different standards. Some Western ambassadors openly court opposition figures in authoritarian states, and have contributed to change. Example: the easing of internal restrictions on the opposition leader Aung San Suu Kyi by the Myanmar military junta in mid-2002 and the start of a dialogue with her, though it culminated in a fresh spell of incarceration for this brave leader. Non-Western democracies are less interventionist; their envoys are more circumspect in dealings with opposition political parties.[41]

The above listing gives a flavor of the political actions undertaken by the ambassador. In all of these, the constant is a continual accretion of the home country's zone of influence, through connections with individuals, institutions and systems. The levers of power and decision-making in nations, small and big, are invariably complex. This can be visualized as 'programmed, layered outreach...[the envoy] must especially cultivate, or try to cultivate, those who do not like us, be they think-tanks that are in adversarial positions or others'.[42] The ambassador's guiding star is to accept the legacy of contacts that he inherits, representing the work of his predecessors, and build on it, in effect creating concentric circles of influence, who are actual and potential allies for relation-building. Invariably, there are interconnections; a cultural contact may prove vital for advancing political or economic interests. This too is a facet of integrated diplomacy.

Modern communication speeds up the political work of advocacy. A case that occurred in 2000 was recounted widely at the time in American diplomatic circles.[43] The US Permanent Mission in New York sent an internal email to the US Embassy in Mauritius, asking them to obtain support from that country for an issue that the US was pursuing. The Ambassador asked the DCM to forward the request electronically to the Mauritius Foreign Ministry. In turn the Director of the UN Division at the Mauritius Foreign Ministry who received this by email, sent it via the Ministry's computer network, to the Permanent Secretary for instructions. The latter conveyed approval and an email came back to the Embassy the same day, with all the notations. The US Embassy forwarded it to the Permanent Mission in New York and the entire action chain was completed in 24 hours. Could the work have been done without the Embassy? It may seem that the Embassy's role was passive, confined to relaying the New York request. But in fact it depended on a personal rapport of mutual trust already established. The situation could just as easily have demanded a personal *démarche*. Thus, improved communication does not supplant the personal relationship, but becomes a multiplier when used aptly.

Economics. Beyond political work, economic diplomacy is almost invariably the ambassador's second priority, with sharply etched requirements, often making the largest demand on his time.[44] It covers economic promotion for trade, investments, aid and technical cooperation, image building, tourism promotion, plus special activities that circumstance dictates. It may include: accompanying a visiting industrial delegation from home at a meeting organized at a chamber of commerce, where the embassy may have set up appointments or even organized the entire program; joining a meeting at a ministry on financing projects in third countries, in which civil construction enterprises of the home country want to participate; meeting officials of regional entities, or a group of local businessmen, to discuss a 'promotion week', or a cultural event that has a nexus with economic objectives; the list is endless. The chief executive of India's powerful industry apex body, the Confederation of Indian Industry (CII) graphically told the author: The ambassador's task is 'meeting corporates, Indian and foreign; building networks and relationships which support trade and investment.'[45] The principles underlying all these activities are:

> One. The envoy is his country's first salesman. If exports are the target of the day, he might focus on new products that his country is promoting, as a net addition to the export basket, or assist home exporters to pursue a new niche market. He might advise the Commercial Counselor on the marketing plan, leaving the

elaboration of tactics to his colleague. He thus *concentrates on new initiatives*, and oversees master plans.

Two. Ambassadors and their teams particularly support home companies involved in big projects—in much the same way that mega-projects figure on the agenda of dialogue during visits of high dignitaries. The ambassador *supervises ongoing activities*, looking particularly to the moral compass (see below).

Three. His local access is especially relevant for economic and media promotion. Whether meeting the chief executive of a company or the editorial board of a leading journal, the ambassador utilizes the briefs prepared by his team (e.g. the commercial or information counselors), creating the initial openings that are exploited by embassy colleagues. Dialogue with the journal may involve a proposal for a special economic supplement, or a business conference with the journal as a sponsor. With the corporation, it may involve new investments, or a proposal to source some item from the home country. In each situation the ambassador is the point man and door opener, winning initial support for the project. Thus he *becomes a multiplier* for the entire team.

Four. Between the ambassador and his deputy, resides the full overarching real-time panoramic picture of the bilateral relationship, from the concepts and objectives to the operational detail, plus new activities in the pipeline. Working with the rest of the team and the territorial department at home, they use this holistic view to locate the interconnections and *potential for leverage* and possible trade-offs. Of course this applies to all the activity areas, but often economics act as the persuader.

An example taken from a journal describing the activities of the Canadian Ambassador to the US from 1994 to 2000 is illustrative:

Swinging a weatherbeaten leather briefcase, Raymond Chrétien strides into the office of Connecticut Governor John Rowland with a smile for everyone. 'Glad to meet you at last!' he booms. Canada's Ambassador takes a seat and briskly urges the Governor to lead a trade mission to Canada. 'I've talked to colleagues of yours who have done the same and never regretted it'. 'Good idea,' says Rowland, 44, a rising Republican star. 'We'll work on that.' ...Chrétien strides out—a salesman who has landed a new client.[46]

Of course, every envoy does not have the clout, or the purposeful direction, of a Canadian ambassador, the closest neighbor to the world's economic powerhouse. But the principle of promotion and outreach is the same—a striving to expand the action envelope, to make connections and deliver value.

The ambassador can easily overplay his hand as an economic salesman. The baleful saga of the Texas-based Enron Corporation that unraveled in early 2002, as a massive case of corporate fraud, political corruption and auditor complicity, remains to be fully exposed to public view. It has produced echoes in India (and elsewhere), since Enron had invested heavily in a major greenfield power project, Dhabol, near Mumbai, and several US envoys and others had lobbied very actively during its controversy-laden history. A leading Indian economic journal, in an editorial in February 2002, criticized the role played by the US Ambassador and went on to make a wider point:

Driving change in the envoy's role and function are the economic interests of his government and those of domestic business. The ambassador might achieve political objectives, but his focus is elsewhere. He helps to swing major business deals for companies as he lobbies developing country governments on far-reaching economic policy changes. His priority now is the business arena and his favorite podium a business conference room from where he publicly warns governments that appear to be dragging their feet on critical economic issues.[47]

This begs the question, how far should an ambassador go to lobby in favor of a particular business enterprise? What is the limit of 'public interest' in such advocacy?

Export abroad of a product, service, project, or the mobilization of investment and technology for the home country, clearly serves home country interests. The ambassador might face a hard decision on the extent and manner of his intervention to support a particular business activity. Good judgment dictates the limit to single-beneficiary assistance, but times are changing. Example: two decades back, a Western embassy in Latin America was approached by a home-based company that felt it was being closed out of a local purchase tender on technical grounds, through suspected manipulation by a competitor from another country. While the commercial secretary recommended intervention, his ambassador turned this down on the ground that he did not know if there was some other bidder from home. In fact there was no other bidder from home, the ambassador was simply being over-cautions.[48] Most diplomatic services have moved beyond mindsets of super-caution, but the issue remains, how far should one go? A pragmatic answer: it depends on the circumstances. A large flagship project, important in itself and as a precursor to other contracts, is likely to garner stronger diplomatic advocacy. Business promotion now engages even presidents and prime ministers in personal advocacy, especially in countries where the state is the deciding authority. On journeys to China or Russia by foreign dignitaries, the media often compiles a scorecard of the deals signed and their value.

Most envoys would consider it legitimate help to an individual exporter, or home enterprise, as long as the action is transparent, and the headquarters are informed, even after the event. It helps if larger public interest is clearly served by the business deal. Another rule-of-thumb is that as long as there is no kind of personal stake for the envoy, or even the perception of a personal angle, he can afford to be proactive. But at the slightest whiff of subjective motivation, it is in his interest to draw back and leave the active advocacy to other actors, preferably home-based.[49]

In terms of national styles, Western envoys are active in business promotion, especially the Americans, the British and the French, as are the Japanese while Germans still show a degree of reserve. The Russians have a long tradition of intertwining political and economic advocacy, while the Chinese are cautious, still evolving their methods.

Public diplomacy and country image. In the remaining workfields, it is culture, media and public diplomacy—including national image-building—that represent the ambassador's third sector of concentrated attention, straddling as they do across all diplomatic activity. An experienced Canadian Ambassador who served in the US for 7 years has written: 'The new diplomacy, as I call it, is to a large extent public diplomacy and requires different skills, techniques and attitudes ... Traditional diplomacy, I came to understand, was a recipe for ineffectiveness ... Almost everything I regarded as a qualification was, in fact, closer to being a hindrance to carrying out my tasks effectively.'[50]

A US task force, representing the Council on Foreign Relations and the Center for Studies in International Security, reported to Secretary of State Colin Powell in January 2001: 'The professional culture remains predisposed against public outreach and engagement.'[51] Such strong indictment is surprising when we consider that American diplomacy has pursued public diplomacy in all its dimensions, more assiduously than others. The report urged that the US should treat such outreach as 'a core function in diplomacy and statecraft'. Since the events of 9/11, there has been an outpouring of other US studies on public diplomacy, some of them treating it as a panacea for all failings.[52]

This concept of public diplomacy carries varied nuances. Some British scholars tend to view it as mere propaganda.[53] In contrast, the German Paschke Report states:

... in Europe public diplomacy is viewed as the number one priority over the whole spectrum of issues. I intentionally avoid using the German term 'Öffentlichkeitsarbeit' (public relations) with rather different connotations. The English words 'lobbying' and 'networking' give a better indication of what public diplomacy really is: reaching out to people in the host country, actively communicating through ongoing dialogue with all sections of the informed public in order to generate interest in and understanding for both our European and bilateral concepts.[54]

Evan H. Potter draws a distinction between public diplomacy, which aims to 'influence publics or elite opinion of another country', and public relations, which uses 'similar activities and techniques directed at own citizens'.[55] Potter adds that the aim of public relations by the foreign ministry is to help its own citizens 'to help them interpret the outside world from a nationalist perspective and to raise awareness of their country's role and that of its diplomatic service'; at the same time, many of the Department's activities identified as public diplomacy are directed at domestic audiences. For our purpose, 'public diplomacy' is used to cover both the activities directed abroad and at home.

Public diplomacy involves an active engagement with varied non-state agencies, the shedding of traditional reserve, and the operation of networks of influence, many of them in non-conventional arenas. Considerable new learning is involved, because both at home and abroad, the role these constituencies play in international affairs expands in unexpected ways. There is no standard template. Training programs for diplomats are still playing catch-up in this specialty. Hard-won field experience is the best available guide.

Public outreach should not be treated as an add-on activity for the ambassador, but as an essential, operational dimension, integral to most actions. It also serves to convey signals, direct and indirect, to official and non-state partners. The more vital the bilateral relationship, as in a neighboring country, the greater is the role of public diplomacy. In situations of antagonism, the media is used to communicate with one's own people, and to develop support abroad, both among adversaries and the international community. Nor can the envoy overlook his domestic public, as we see later.

Public diplomacy obliges the ambassador to embrace the media closely. The envoy often becomes a media performer, as for instance a permanent representative to the UN, or an ambassador in a major capital. In the age of 24-hour global networks, and their national counterparts in many countries, no location is immune from news worthiness, and a well-honed media ability is vital for the envoy everywhere. If he becomes a familiar face on local chat shows and is in demand for interviews, he wins visibility for his national brand.

Image building is closely tied with public diplomacy, but has a wider focus, though some may argue that they are both concerned with the country's image. Events in the political or economic field influence the image one's country enjoys abroad. Business decisions on investments abroad and foreign trade are influenced by political events, terrorism and other kinds of crisis, as well as by the attractiveness of the country as a location. Tourism, depending on decisions by individuals and families on where to holiday, is even more sensitive to image and perceptions. Images of foreign countries are actually collections of stereotypes embedded in our minds over time, in part by history and ethnic memory. TV and news media add to the volatility of images.

The international reputation of countries is a composite of many elements. Some images are deeply ingrained, such as those learnt by school children (example: the simplistic, distorted picture of Africa in most countries), or form part of collective memory (as in the case of neighbors with a history of mutual antagonism). Sociologists posit that cultures need 'the other' to act as a counterpoint, to embellish one's self-worth. Be as it may, in the practical business of diplomacy, all countries are concerned over how they are perceived by others, since this affects concrete inter-state activities such as the inflow of tourists, visits by businessmen and foreign investments, and the credibility of a country as a worthy partner in all types of foreign dealings. Many of the global South believe that the world media, dominated by the West, does injustice in the images that it broadcasts, but in reality all countries have some grievance over their external image.

In the world of integrated diplomacy, image lies at the core, directly affecting outcomes in many fields. For example, in 1993–94, attacks on Turkish migrants in Germany by ultra-rightists were publicized in the international media as an 'anti-foreigner' sentiment; a globally renowned German company found US partners canceling business visits, apprehending problems over personal security. That exaggerated reaction brought home to Germans the fragility of image, even for a major European power. In recent times, the UK, Spain and Germany have undertaken coordinated actions, in pubic–private partnership, to improve 'country branding'.[56]

It is an illusion that images can be easily ameliorated. But on the downside, images are susceptible to rapid degradation. This conditions the actions of envoys—and their governments—but does not reduce the importance of incremental actions that envoys undertake to improve the images, and actively combat adverse developments. In special situations, image-building events are organized in foreign countries through the embassy—'festivals' of culture are one example. It is even more effective to pursue the image dimension in all diplomatic activity, and continually work for improvement.

Feedback

The principal recipient of the ambassador's reportage—analysis and policy recommendations—is the home government, particularly the MFA. The ambassador also communicates local developments and gives some form of advice to non-state partners at home, such as chambers of commerce, academic institutions seeking foreign partnerships and others, depending on their interests in the target country. Raymond L. Garthoff, who served as US Ambassador to Bulgaria in 1977–79 identified a central limitation of diplomatic reportage.

There was of course a substantial gap between what we would like to know and report (for example friction between Bulgaria and its neighbors, or within the Politburo, or on Bulgarian or Soviet activities in foreign affairs) and what we were able to learn and therefore did report (mostly on internal policy and economic development, of little interest to the State Department).[57]

Such limitation in reporting on closed societies—the sheer opacity of the political system and problems of access to credible local interlocutors—often leads to an informal alliance among embassies, not leaving out the foreign journalists. Their information exchanges attempt to decipher the real local situation. Over the years, such networks have functioned informally at locations like Beijing and Moscow, animated by a special *esprit de corps* among all of them.

Our age of 24-hour global news networks raises a basic question. When presidents and foreign ministers rely on CNN, BBC and their ilk for breaking developments, which are consistently faster than the most resource-rich intelligence agencies, do the ambassador's reports have any value? Would not a subscription to *The Economist*, and to *Le Monde*, furnish all the international analysis that one might wish? True, these are valuable, instant information sources. Their lean, fluid style is the envy of many an envoy. But there are profound differences as well between these and what an envoy can produce.

One. Journals do not present the needed analysis, centered on the perspective and interests of the home country; nor are they focused on prognosis and recommendations. Facts are freely available; the diplomatic system needs pointers on what may happen a month and a year later. One interlocutor remarked: 'Current information is not needed. What is required is good judgment and assessments based on this.'[58] Two. The media cannot deliver news which is not reportable under customary guidelines. Thus, they cannot reveal an inside story that rests on speculation or insufficient data. Diplomats cover this, with the needed caveats, often providing early warnings. Three. The ambassador's comments take into account the media reports. He anticipates the queries that must flow from all that reaches headquarters from diverse sources. Ideally, his reportage is more rounded and complete. In sum, forward-looking prognostication oriented to policy or tactical recommendations is the envoy's special goal, which no media source can replicate.

Virtually all the reports that originate from the embassy bear the ambassador's imprint, as well as his approval, explicit or tacit. He may write a covering note that accompanies a 'dispatch' prepared by junior colleagues, say an exhaustive survey on a single theme. Or he may write a preface to the annual report, or simply furnish guidance on a draft prepared by the political or information counselor. The dispatches that he sends over his signature, even when others have prepared initial drafts, are crafted to command particular attention.[59]

The one reporting instrument that uniquely belongs to the ambassador is the cipher telegram, or more precisely, the cipher message. In all but the very largest of embassies, he is the principal originator of these messages.[60] The message may report on an official conversation, or convey information that has reached the ambassador through an indirect source, or convey his analysis of a local or international development, or respond to a query from headquarters. The power of these messages lies in their urgent and parallel distribution at home to senior personalities, within and outside the MFA, including to the heads of state and government and their principal advisers. Given the contemporary inflation in information, MFAs are flooded with cipher messages that rely on the easy use of encrypting technology. Custom-designed 'intranets' and 'virtual private networks' that are increasingly the norm, as exclusive communication networks for sophisticated diplomatic services, have also devalued the medium. Despite this, a single cipher message can command attention, mollify or anger policy makers, or in some manner shape policy.

Cipher messages are classified in levels of security and distribution; heavy usage leads to inflation. In practice, few of the messages that bear the highest classification truly warrant it, if they are judged by their content. This classification becomes an attention-seeking device, exploited by envoys. One US practice is the 'NODIS' appellation, signifying that the message is to go only to the named recipients. Such messages paradoxically attract the widest attention and readership, despite or rather because of the label![61] Other countries use the appellation 'personal' to mark messages that are to have limited distribution at home. Used well, 'cipher diplomacy' is an art form that envoys should master, contributing to their personal credibility and reputation. The timing and style, and of course the content, are all notable features of the best exemplars.

The ambassador also uses the less urgent reporting formats, like the special dispatch and analytical notes, increasingly sent via the intranet communication channels rather than the traditional diplomatic bag—though the latter device remains in use in most systems. These convey policy recommendations, suggest initiatives, or simply furnish assessments that carry his personal imprint. On the eve of major events, like visits by high dignitaries, a session of negotiations, or even an encounter between leaders that may take place on the margins of a multilateral event, the ambassador forwards a briefing paper that sets out the overall context of the relationship at that point in time, and his recommendations on the issues to be tackled. He typically forwards this directly to the principals, or to their personal staff, with copies to the territorial division as well. The final 'brief' for the event will come from the MFA system (with the territorial division as the initiator of the paper), but the ambassador's views are both read directly and factored into the final briefing book. This is his advisory role as played to the hilt. And if he has strong personal credibility, he will prevail.

This feedback role has now expanded in other ways, giving the envoy more direct access into high-level briefings, as well as the process that leads to decision and policy. Flexible new reporting instruments have emerged. We consider these later.

The public has no early access to the ambassador's political reportage, unless a report is leaked, which occurs rarely. This makes it impossible for a scholar or journalist to assess independently the quality and value of reportage in real time. A full-exposure reality check comes only when classified reports, like other government documents, are released under public access formulas that operate in democracies, such as UK's '30-year' rules. Historians then have a field day, with an abundance of raw material for historical analysis. Many developing countries have such procedures on the books, but fail to implement them, fearing a disclosure of their inadequacies. For instance, India allows the release of official papers after 30 years, but this is not implemented on the grounds of a continuing need for secrecy. The few scholars that gain conditional access find that what resides in the National Archives in New Delhi are sanitized documents, with the trail of drafts and internal noting (showing the action process), frequently eliminated.[62] The simple point is lost, that public access to historical diplomatic documents is essential to good governance in foreign affairs.

Management

There are three management dimensions that involve the ambassador: first, day-to-day tactical management of the overarching relationship in the assignment country; second, fulfilling the performance objectives set by the foreign ministry; and third, overseeing the internal functioning of the embassy, including its human resources.

Take the first task. The ambassador's role in bilateral relationship management was a theme at the end of Chapter 1. He has always been viewed as the man in the field, running the embassy as an outpost of the sending country, offering expert counsel on that country. Viewing him additionally as a 'co-manager' of that relationship expands the focus, and involves his acceptance as a member of the headquarters management team, with a *right* to be involved on the elaboration of strategy and tactic, along the entire decisions chain. Modern communications permit and facilitate such consultation. But are MFAs willing to conceptually accommodate the ambassador in this role?

Historically, the envoy has been seen at the receiving end of the communications link, tasked to implement the instructions given from headquarters, and provide feedback and advice, principally on a one-shot basis. Just a little thought shows that current real-time communication systems work both ways, and using the envoy in a wider fashion makes optimum use of his capacity. That is precisely the altered picture that is leading to some rethinking in European foreign ministries. We consider this further in the final chapter.

The second management task makes the ambassador directly answerable to headquarters for his performance. Many countries are experimenting with different systems. These developments, and the third task, relating to the internal management of the embassy are examined in subsequent chapters.

Servicing

The embassy's service role brings it in wide contact with the public, both its own nationals and those belonging to the country of assignment. Three of these segments are consular work, commercial activities, and public diplomacy. The first of these, and sometimes the second as well, often receive low priority in the embassy, while the third—public diplomacy—is a new sector, currently much subject to hype, as we saw earlier. Each should engage the ambassador in a particular way.

Consular work comprises, first, the facilities for local citizens to travel to one's home country (e.g. the issue of visas; permission to visit restricted areas, if any; accreditation for journalists and scholars who often need special authorization; the issue of student and work visas, and assistance to foreign nationals facing special problems). Second, there is the protection and services offered to one's own citizens—such as the assistance to those under detention or judicial process or needing special help from the local authorities; the issue or revalidation of passports; replacement of lost passports; registration of one's own citizens in the foreign country; and help in emergencies. This work is handled by the embassy's specialist consular staff, which is often under heavy pressure of visitors (such as visa seekers and 'illegal' migrants from home). Much of the work is of a repetitive, routine character.

Why should this engage the ambassador? He needs to keep it under personal oversight, if only on the periphery, to provide leadership and ensure efficiency. Performed well, it becomes a multiplier. Examples: in 1998–99 in London, Indian High Commissioner Lalit Mansingh astutely converted a large consular section, the inefficiency of which was legendary, from a local problem into a tactical asset. Using personal clout, he implemented a computerized visa application processing system that delivered a visa across the counter in less than ten minutes.[63] The result was a major reduction in overcrowding for the several hundred daily applicants. It won him a letter of appreciation from the British Home Secretary who called it the most efficient foreign visa service in the UK, plus a large amount of goodwill from the public, especially ethnic Indians. There are other consular posts—Indian and others—that cry for similar initiative. The US consulates in India have similarly applied information technology to offer 'online' visa processing and firm interview appointments for applicants, due to public pressure and in order to gain goodwill.

A new consular issue with heavy political overtones is the tide of 'economic migrants' from the Third World to the rich nations, either illegal entrants or those exploiting liberal political asylum provisions. The flow is mainly from Africa, Asia and Latin America to the West, often transiting through a long chain of third countries.[64] Illegal migrants also go from the transition countries of southern Europe and Central Asia to west Europe. Japan, Australia and some South-East Asian countries are also destinations for some. The socio-economic conditions in the supplying countries producing the exodus are known. Often overlooked is the demand in rich countries for 'dirty' work, which domestic labor is unwilling to handle; plus their demographics—shrinking, aging populations—compound the issue. This will surely figure prominently in the future.

Looking ahead, it is likely that routine consular work in embassies will diminish. Visa application processing will surely be handled remotely in 'back-offices', for cost-efficiency, while visa delivery may be outsourced to specialist enterprises. The use of biometrics in passports, such as digitalized fingerprinting techniques, will also simplify work. On the other hand, consular issues will be complicated with problems of movement of people, taking political overtones. At the same time, the growth in tourism and business will keep consular sections occupied with personal emergency tasks—leaving this an active arena within the embassy.

Routine commercial work seldom engages the ambassador, be it queries from home exporters looking to new markets, or local businessmen seeking counterpart information. Like some of the routine consular work, this should shift out of the embassy to dedicated back-offices utilizing the Internet, leaving the embassy team to concentrate on promotion and problem solving. We have already considered the ambassador's involvement in trade and investment mobilization. Business disputes may involve the ambassador when either an issue is complex and involves important enterprises, or if a business problem casts a large shadow on the economic relationship. A proactive stance by the embassy at the initial stage of a problem can sometimes push business parties to actively negotiate a solution, but if the 'good offices' stage has passed, and disputing parties are entrenched in set positions, it is often best to leave the issue to the arbitration or legal process.

In the Internet age, the well designed webpage and portal are the most efficient medium for public outreach, giving basic information on the home country. Economic diplomacy is advanced via the commercial and market notes that the embassy posts there, plus the home contacts and hyperlinks. E-commerce is best handled from centralized home locations, and the embassy has a secondary role here. But the alert ambassador who is aware of technology can convey home timely information on new methods, such as 'virtual trade shows' and other marketing devices. The ambassador needs to keep an eye on the good operation of Internet-based public diplomacy outreach. Prompt responses to queries from local students, potential tourists and others serve as building blocks towards good image creation, for the mission and for the country, and therefore merit his personal attention.

Overall, the service function demands the ambassador's policy direction. Treating with sensitivity and a problem-solving attitude the general public that approaches the embassy is a method of 'customer satisfaction', and good basic diplomacy.

4

THE MULTILATERAL AMBASSADOR

Multilateral diplomacy has been defined as 'diplomacy via conferences attended by three or more states'.[1] Besides the constantly expanding activities or global and regional gatherings of states, it includes work at the international inter-governmental organizations that total several hundred, though only 30-odd have full-time diplomatic missions accredited to them. These organizations have become independent actors on the international stage, to a degree that few could have anticipated when the League of Nations and the International Labor Organization, the first such entities, were created in 1919 in the aftermath of World War I.[2]

Multilateral diplomacy has been described as 'diplomacy of process' where the actual evolution of negotiation determines to some extent the kind of agreement that emerges at the end.[3] This is easily visible in the European Union and in other regional organizations. Multiple players and the constant shift in the contours of debate require an adaptation in tactics within a consistent strategy, from the perspective of member-states, i.e. agile diplomacy.

Out of a total of about 8300 full-time ambassadors stationed in different foreign countries (Chapter 1), the full-time multilateral envoys, usually called 'permanent representatives' (PRs) to the international organization concerned, number around 600, some 8% of the total. The work they perform is sufficiently differentiated from that of the bilateral envoy to treat them separately in this chapter.

Besides the full-time multilateral envoys, there are a large number of bilateral ambassadors who bear a concurrent designation as permanent representatives to an international organization that has its headquarters in the capital where this envoy is stationed. For instance in Paris, a large Western country may have three ambassadors: one accredited to France, and two more as permanent representatives to UNESCO and OECD. Smaller European countries that are members of both those international bodies might deploy a single ambassador wearing all three hats, with perhaps one or two specialists on his or her staff to concentrate on the multilateral agencies. In Nairobi, home to the environment agency UNEP and the smaller UN agency dealing with human settlements, HABITAT, most countries' bilateral envoy to Kenya doubles up as the PR to the two UN agencies. In this chapter we primarily deal with the full-time PR, but some of the analysis applies to the part-time PR as well. The two major organizations that do not have permanent representatives are the World Bank and IMF, where the major powers have a system of 'executive directors' placed within the organization, who look after the interests of the country; some regions also have their executive directors. They work differently from permanent representatives and are not designated as ambassadors.

Multilateral and Bilateral Work

One question needs to be answered right away: is multilateral work a specialized branch of diplomacy? Or do the activities at global conferences, regional meetings and the international organizations, essentially involve the same knowledge, craft and skills as bilateral diplomacy, differing only in focus? The reply will not be unanimous.[4] The very best multilateral diplomacy practitioners tend to insist that theirs is a specialized skill, while the majority of bilateralists are inclined to disagree. There is another way of addressing the issue: should multilateral diplomacy be treated as a speciality within a diplomatic service?

Large services have some officials who mainly work on

multilateral diplomacy. These are individuals who have spent two or more assignments at their permanent mission in New York and Geneva, interspersing this with the odd stint at the foreign ministry also in the multilateral affairs department. This group would surely assert that theirs is a distinct speciality. Although there is no disagreement that within multilateral work, particular fields like disarmament and security affairs, global environment issues, and multilateral trade regimes—to name a few—are established areas of special competence. The issue is whether multilateral diplomacy as a whole also qualifies for this appellation. In most diplomatic services, the majority of practitioners undergo a blended career, spending the bulk of their time abroad at bilateral assignments, leavened with some multilateral experience, international and regional. These bilateralists would probably concede that there are differences in the two kinds of work, but not to the degree that we must speak of the multilateral as a special branch of the genre.

This distinction involves more than semantics. First, if we accept the contention of the multilateral aficionados, then the 'specialized' branch justifies that a significant number within the service will spend the bulk of their careers in New York and Geneva, interspersed with a stint or two at Brussels, Rome, Vienna, or Nairobi, and maybe just the odd term at a typical bilateral post. These poles of multilateral work are among the most comfortable of all diplomatic assignments. For most diplomatic services, this raises a practical problem: if a cluster of officials serves abroad only at such charmed locations, the bilateral foot-soldiers are left to work in the trenches, the many places of physical hardship, insecurity and multiple discomfort. Family welfare, opportunities for children's education, a favorable employment environment for spouses—these are practical concerns for diplomats, at all levels. Precisely for these reasons, even large Western services find it impractical to operate sub-categories of multilateral specialists. The problem is worse for developing countries, with less personnel and sharper expectations of an 'equitable' rotation in assignments abroad.

Second, which envoy is likely to be more effective in multilateral work—the one who has spent an entire career in it, or the one who has cut his teeth in the hurly-burly of bilateral diplomacy, and comes to multilateral work with that solid experience base? True, it helps a new ambassador heading a permanent mission at New York or Geneva if he had served there earlier in a junior or mid-level capacity. He will be familiar with UN rules and operational procedures. But in a normal career, every career ambassador gathers the experience of conference and regional diplomacy (e.g. through work in bilateral embassies that are concurrently permanent missions to international agencies, and as a delegate to meetings of international and regional bodies). Thus the typical 'bilateral' diplomat accumulates a fair breadth of multilateral experience by the time he is appointed an envoy at a multilateral post.

Third, are there conceptual differences in the two kinds of work, if we look to the six tasks of diplomacy, i.e. outreach, promotion, negotiation, feedback, management and servicing? As we see below, the principal difference is that 'negotiation' is the centerpiece of conference activity, but it is performed via the same instruments of advocacy, persuasion and communication that are also the *leitmotif* of bilateral diplomacy. True, there are some differences as well—the work of 'promotion' has a limited place. The 'management' task is also different, covering the multilateral diplomacy process, and the delivery of the end result at conferences (of course besides the efficient operation of the permanent mission). Further, 'servicing' responsibilities are restricted, mainly confined to the realm of public diplomacy. Taken together, this differentiation is insufficient to qualify the multilateral as conceptually divergent.

In practical terms, if we examine the typical career profile of the permanent representatives in New York, the holy shrine of multilateral diplomacy, we find that while many envoys may have had one or two previous assignments at New York or Geneva, they have handled a vast amount of bilateral work, including often a couple of ambassadorships at bilateral posts. There are even a fair number who come to a full-time multilateral assignment for the first time. This shows that there is no career specialization in this arena. The one possible exception is China, which has retained a much higher degree of area and functional specialization than other services. Chinese diplomats spend the bulk of their career in one 'speciality', or region, but this too is now changing.[5]

To sum up, diplomatic services generally resist the temptation to treat multilateral work as a career speciality, while taking care to produce some experts in the functional areas, such as disarmament, environment issues and international economic affairs.

Form and Substance

We noted in Chapter 1 that the bulk of multilateral envoys tend to be professionals. The US is unique in its tradition of mainly sending eminent public personalities to New York, interspersed with an occasional professional. Michael Dobbs, biographer to Madeleine Albright, records criticism by former UN Secretary General Butros-Ghali,: 'She [Albright] was a beginner at diplomacy, an amateur. She would never give you an answer...from the smallest problem to the greatest, she would always say: "I have to consult Washington." But over time she became more spontaneous and exuberant.'[6] One cannot fault Ambassador Albright for her prudence at the start of her diplomatic career, after a lifetime in academia and being on the fringes of the political process. The biography also makes it clear that as a permanent representative who held an exceptional position in the Reagan administration (i.e. cabinet status), she tended to have limited time for the other PRs and for diplomatic niceties. With such a high-profile non-career envoy, the US gained something in domestic public projection, and that was clearly important. But it hardly serves as a model for other countries. Europe and Japan almost invariably appoint professionals to head multilateral missions. Canada has blended professional and political appointments. Major developing countries almost always send professionals to both these places.

The archetype of the multilateral envoy is the ambassador and permanent representative to the UN at New York and at Geneva. He or she begins a typical new assignment with little fanfare. The only ceremony is the handing over of the 'letter of introduction' from the envoy's foreign minister to the UN Secretary General, or to the head of the concerned agency; the event is duly photographed for record but has limited news value. Dark suits are the usual dress code in that kind of working environment, *sans* other ceremony.[7]

At the termination of his assignment there is no ceremony at all, other than a business-like farewell call, or a working lunch to bid *au revoir*, besides the larger reception that the envoy, or the regional group to which he belongs, may host in the envoy's honor.

Much more than the bilateral envoy, the multilateralist depends on the connections with fellow permanent representatives and the diplomats in the other permanent missions. They are his constant negotiation partners, sources of intelligence and allies in shared labor—and sometimes adversaries as well. Consequently, he needs to rapidly locate or construct connections with them, through courtesy calls, working lunches, the regular meetings of regional and sub-regional groups, and the multitude of caucuses in topical issues and *ad hoc* groups that may exist. Even more than his bilateral counterpart, he must hit the ground running. He is bound by none of the protocol limitations that apply to the bilateral ambassador. Nor is he distracted by too many interests outside the multilateral group of official representatives, though activist NGOs now figure on his contact agenda, as a new dimension of public diplomacy. Other partners are business and industry associations, and different kinds of specialists that are called in for expert advice. Non-state agents are also vastly more assertive today in multilateral diplomacy, especially the NGOs that flaunt their claim as authentic representatives of civil society—often camouflaging their status as special interest promoters, however well motivated.

The ambassador also needs friendships with the key officials of the secretariat who exercise a powerful influence in the UN and other multilateral agencies. The UN Secretary General, the heads of the agencies, their *chefs de cabinet* and personal advisers, plus the other senior officials, are all autonomous agents with whom the multilateral ambassador deals at all times. The nationals from one's own country serving within international organizations are of two kinds: the international civil servants who have spent a lifetime in that career, and those from the home country seconded on assignment, sometimes from the diplomatic service. They are natural allies, if handled with discretion.

The multilateral ambassador heads a mission that is less heterogeneous than the large embassy. He has no commercial, cultural or consular staff, but may have instead specialists in multilateral economic diplomacy, from the economic ministries at home, and experts in other fields. Legal specialists play a role too, especially in the large missions. He also uses media experts, plus advisers on issues that are prominent on the functional agenda, though it is more likely that such specialists will come from home on temporary duty, for conferences or for sessions of the UN General Assembly. The bulk of his team is made up of regular diplomats. Unlike the bilateral embassy, his mission will also have a floating population of experts and even political advisers, which can double the strength of the permanent mission in the busy season (e.g. during the annual September to December session of the General Assembly). Handling them becomes a task in itself, calling for delicate internal diplomacy.[8] Permanent missions at New York have evolved their own creative methods to deal with the non-official delegates, and their extra-curricular activities. A similar phenomenon occurs at Geneva, though on a smaller scale.

A significant contrast with bilateral work is that in most foreign services, multilateral work attracts the cream of the crop. The typical permanent mission at New York has a finer collection of talent than might be found in the embassy of that country in a major capital. We may call this a byproduct of the 'glamour of the atmospherics attached to multilateral diplomacy'.[9] Multilateral diplomacy's self-image, of immersion in acute global issues—political, economic, social and human—and coping with these through finely crafted resolutions and declarations, all produce a sense of power. There is substance as well as deception in this image. The same UN at New York, where vital issues of security and peace are effectively addressed at the Security Council sessions, is also the locus of much wasted effort, such as in the General Assembly and many of its committees. We should accept that diplomats from Third World countries are attracted to multilateral work, in part, because life in the Big Apple is easy, and the foreign allowance paid to officials are among the best that the service may offer. Further, in many services, multilateral work provides a fast track to career advancement.

Notwithstanding the above, multilateral ambassadors from most countries are consummate professionals, often regarded by their peers as among the best that country has to offer. Even countries that appoint many non-career ambassadors generally send seasoned professionals to the two prime multilateral posts, New York and Geneva. The contrasting US method is special, but its political appointees perform very well, partly through the clout they carry in Washington DC (including direct access to the US President), and partly because they are well-selected public figures with enormous experience of their own.

The multilateral ambassador of a developing or emerging nation, differs in one way with his developed country counterpart. The latter has at the home foreign ministry a fairly sizable backup unit (the UN and multilateral affairs directorate or division), which follows the principal issues under debate in various committees and conferences, providing him detailed instructions or 'briefs' on the stand to be taken. The home officials—at the foreign ministry and at the functional agencies concerned—even track in real time the final document drafting process, giving continual advice to the mission. In contrast, in the MFAs of developing states, the oversight over the activities of the permanent mission is far less thorough. The briefs sent to the PR concentrate on issues where the country has a sizable stake, and on matters of global importance. For the rest, matters are left to the good judgment of the PR, to take positions that are broadly consistent with national policy. Consequently, these envoys enjoy considerable latitude in their conference statements, even on the votes they cast, as long as they respect the policy framework. Of course, the ambassador sends copies of statements, *post facto*, to the home MFA, and may even show them a draft when he prefers to clarify some doubt. But the envoy's domain for autonomous action on low diplomacy issues is fairly large. It follows that whenever support has to be mobilized, it becomes vital to cultivate such ambassadors and their staff. This is one concrete instance where, despite modern communication systems, the envoy does not operate on a tight leash.

Besides conference and committee work, the multilateral ambassador has an increasing public diplomacy role. For the US permanent representative, this means a continually high domestic and international media profile, virtually as a spokesman parallel to the

State Department, using the pulpit of the UN to speak out on global issues. He may also testify before congressional committees, helping to mobilize domestic public opinion as needed. A few other countries, particularly the UK, deploy the PR in New York in similar fashion, albeit at a lesser frequency. Global TV networks are also plugged into this process, given the practice of live broadcasts of important meetings of the UN Security Council whose images are carried around the world, transforming envoys into instant media performers. This also produces some competition among the PRs of middle and small powers for international media visibility.

In comparison with his bilateral counterpart, the PR has two sets of media targets: the global media and his own domestic constituencies. When major issues are under debate, be it at the Security Council or an international conference, the permanent representative virtually becomes a national spokesperson, even more than home counterparts. For instance, in 1994–95 the Indian Ambassador to Geneva, Arundhati Ghosh, became a public figure in the Indian media, during the extended lead-up to the Comprehensive Test Ban Treaty (CTBT), which India eventually refused to sign. In developing states, such media attention at home for envoys is rare.

Diplomacy theorists have not as yet advanced any notion that the multilateral ambassador is dispensable or irrelevant. Leaving aside this non-question, we should note that the increased technical issues under global debate challenges the professional diplomat in his role as a synthesizer and integrator, and sometimes as an internal mediator as well, dealing with different specialists on his own delegation. As with the bilateral ambassador, he is responsible for finding connections between different subjects, and offering ideas to the home administration on possible trade-offs and linkages.

Methods and Goals

Permanent missions are of two kinds, those accredited to the UN (at New York and Geneva), and those accredited to specialized agencies, be it UNESCO in Paris, IAEA in Vienna or NATO in Brussels. The latter kind of permanent missions work on a relatively narrow range of issues, relevant to that organization's mandate. One consequence of globalization has been a breakdown in clear boundaries between subjects and the emergence of complex interconnections. For instance, the International Labor Organization (ILO) now deals with the social aspects of global trade, in parallel with WTO; some European countries, especially France, would like it to become a stronger enforcer of labor standards, to counter the low labor input cost in developing countries, i.e. as a trade protectionist measure. Consequently, experts on WTO affairs have to keep an eye on the way these issues are debated in ILO, and vice versa for labor specialists. The PR has to handle the blend of technical and political issues. In his interface with home-based experts, he needs a sufficient understanding of technicalities to place these in the context of national political objectives.

The UN headquarters at New York and Geneva deal with just about every subject, political, economic, cultural, social and humanitarian. Some of the less obvious issues recently tackled have included the deployment of boy-soldiers in Africa, and the Indian caste system as an expression of 'racism'. The PR heading these missions especially needs broad-based knowledge and acute political understanding.

Let us examine the way the six diplomatic tasks are performed.

The multilateral ambassador handles *outreach* within a narrow work zone: safeguarding his country's interests in the organization where he functions. Unlike the bilateral envoy, his interlocutors are finite, principally the states represented through the other permanent missions, observer missions and the non-state agencies active there (such as those with 'consultative' status, some wielding influence), and the officials of that organization. He needs to cultivate them intensively. For instance, envoys that have worked in New York speak eloquently about the quality of trust built with fellow-PRs and key officials as a basic success factor.

At first sight, *promotion* is unlikely to be important for the multilateral ambassador. But special situations arise for imaginative initiatives, at conferences and at multilateral organizations— windows of opportunity that the astute manage to grasp. Two examples: at the Belgrade Non-Aligned Summit in 1987, the Indian team led by Prime Minister Rajiv Gandhi advanced a novel idea, the creation of a group of 15 prominent developing countries from Africa, Asia and Latin America, calling itself G-15, for consultation on global economic issues, indirectly a counterpoise to the G-7 group of leading industrialized powers. The boldness lay in the fact that there was no mandate or decision in support, from either the Non-Aligned Movement or the G-77 group of more than a hundred developing countries.[10] It is another matter that this effort at advancing the interests of the South has produced limited impact, and the biennial G-15 summits have been desultory. The more successful example is the creation of the ASEM Summit group in 1994, an Asia–EU annual meeting of principal countries, an initiative steered by 'Team Singapore'. Several Singapore ambassadors played a key role in convincing major EU capitals on the utility of the concept, a task facilitated by Europe's keenness for a platform that could match the APEC initiative, where Europe has felt left out.[11]

We witness the full expression of the classic *negotiation* function, which Harold Nicolson had described as the profession's centerpiece in multilateral diplomacy.[12] Multilateral negotiation is the *raison d'être* of the PR. Compared with bilateral negotiation, the multilateral variant is more dynamic, where the negotiator operates at several levels, seeking consensus or support in fluid situations. Leaving out the speeches, opening statements and plenary or committee activities, the decisive conference work that determines outcome occurs in small working groups—some of it preceding the conference—as well as in drafting committees and contact sessions. The ambassador and his team mobilize support within their own sub-regional and regional caucuses, or among a nucleus of states that may cut across regions, and on the strength of that, seek wider consensus with other groups. Some countries play a disproportionately large role; these are the smart operators at New York or Geneva. Their permanent representatives and delegates frequently find inclusion in the small groups where substantive work is conducted. While the elective offices of conferences, the committee chairmanships, the positions of *rapporteur* and the like follow the geographic rotation principle, the best envoys get the lion's share.

The multilateral environment has increased in complexity—in its participants, themes, and extraordinary time pressures, even compared with the early years of the UN. One factor is the presence of 192 member-states at the UN, and a comparably expanded number at the other multilateral institutions (such as the global trade regulator WTO that has 134 members and continues to grow). This diversity translates into varied cultural mores and styles of work that the multilateral envoy has to master. The same is true of the non-state negotiation partners that enter the calculation. Thus, cross-cultural management skills have become essential.

The *feedback* produced by the multilateral envoy resembles that in bilateral reportage, with one significant addition. This concerns the elective offices, including membership of committees and other offices to which that country aspires. The envoy is called upon to give his honest assessment of the prospects for success, and once a decision is taken to pursue an elective position, to run the campaign using all the tools of diplomacy, both multilateral and bilateral. Countries invest vast efforts in some of these campaigns, such as the membership of the UN Security Council. For instance, Singapore withheld offering itself for one of the elected seats for many years, despite its role as an active diplomacy player, until it completed an intensive preparation, at home and internationally, not just to be certain of winning the election, but also to determine in advance the role that it should play during its two-year term. Sometimes the election becomes important, in the domestic public eye, only in the event of a negative outcome, as happened in late 2000 when the US failed to win what used to be the almost automatic re-election to the UN's Economic and Social Council, ECOSOC; this was blamed on insensitivity with which issues of concern to other states had been handled in Washington DC, besides the long-running problem of non-payment of UN budget contributions, because of Congressional intransigence.[13] India's 1996 Security Council election defeat is an enduring negative example.[14] In some elections, like appointments to the International Court of Justice at The Hague, national purpose blends with the private ambition of the nominated candidate, and the envoy has his work cut out in resisting the pressure exerted by individuals and conveying objective assessments.[15]

The PR's *management* role (besides running the mission), involves safeguarding and advancing the country's interests at that particular forum, be it at the WHO and the annual sessions of the World Health Assembly, or in relation to international trade access, or anti-dumping threats, at the WTO. In any political or security crisis, the PR in New York becomes one of the key voices for the country, projecting country interests and perspectives to the world community, via the Security Council and to a lesser extent at the General Assembly. The performance of each country's ambassador in New York, on international crisis involving national interests is sharply etched in public memory. The 24-hour news networks bring the drama of live debate and impromptu interviews into every home. Thus Americans instantly recall the one-liners of Madeleine Albright during the Bosnia events of the early 1990s; few Indians can forget the performance of its PR, Samar Sen, during the Bangladesh War of 1971.

The multilateral envoy's *servicing* function is relatively minor, since his mission performs no commercial or consular work. Responsiveness to the public and the general duties of public diplomacy are the only exception, as already noted. In terms of communication with the public, an effective website that is constantly updated is essential to putting across the home country perspective.

Work Procedures

Is a legal background essential for multilateral work, as was past custom in many classic diplomatic services in Europe?[16] If we look at the educational backgrounds of contemporary envoys and their work demands, this is not the case, though legal training hones some of the needed skills. The PR has legal specialists available for consultation, especially at the legal department in the foreign ministry at home. He needs mastery over conference procedures and regulations, and the aptitude to use these creatively in the heat of a debate, in the shape of 'points of order', amendment devices giving tactical precedence, and other procedural devices that help to mobilize support during tight voting situations.

In an interview, a middle power envoy offered a remarkably

incisive analysis of the work of the contemporary multilateral ambassador.[17]

One. Unlike in bilateral diplomacy, multilateral work is still focused on the classic tasks, 'liaison, negotiation, representation, and conflict-resolution; the skills involved are communication, advocacy and persuasion.'

Two. It is extremely labor-intensive; a great deal of effort has to be expended in building personal relations with counterparts, especially those representing smaller nations. Situations arise when a particular foreign colleague has to decide if you can be trusted, in an atmosphere that is very frequently fluid and clouded with suspicion. This is where the time taken to build personal credibility and an investment in relationships, pays off.

Three. There are situations where the ambassador has precise instructions from home and little latitude for local initiative, or adaptation. But the more prevalent situation is one where the PR has a choice of action. Sometimes the PR has to create that elbow-room, and interpret instructions with flexibility, because without that it becomes impossible to negotiate multilaterally.

Four. In any committee or conference, there is an 'inner group' that runs affairs, involved in all the key decisions. The first challenge for a newcomer is to identify the power brokers, and then to work to join that group. This is much harder than it sounds, because it involves understanding the different players, and their motivation. One has to determine, for instance, when a delegate blocking a particular move is acting on instructions from home that give no possibility of that delegate giving up that stand. Or there may be occasions when that same kind of blockage comes from an individual's personal agenda, or even factors of ego and self-projection. Good multilateral work involves being able to decide when it is good to back off a bit, or even let pass an adverse development, for reasons of longer strategy; or to determine if that development deserves to be challenged.

Five. Chairing a committee means being alert to the mood in the chamber, and to gauge incipient unease of one or more delegations, especially those that are influential, before an issue boils over. The counter-action may involve sending out a 'runner', to convey a message of reassurance, or an indication that the troubling aspect will be handled. Again, personal credibility is often the key. In particular, delegates need a communication style from the chair that is clear to those that may not be completely familiar with the languages used at the conference, even at the risk of repetition. Often, a reassurance has to be conveyed that delegations will not be taken by surprise. The aim is to eliminate as much as possible, any potential misunderstandings over language and intention, which in practice often ties up multilateral negotiation in protracted debate.

Six. The multilateral ambassador should ideally be adept in at least two principal languages, besides English. Within the mission and the diplomatic service there should be an adequate 'bank of languages', to support multilateral diplomacy. Outreach is always easier when practiced in the language of the interlocutor.

Another description of the skills is: unassertive or 'discreet leadership'; to find a consensus out of a multitude of contradictory positions of other delegations; and finding compromise and creating bridges among opposed camps, while remaining steadfast on one's basic goal. Moreover, timing becomes extremely important, as also the 'ability to spot openings in an impasse as soon as these appear ...envoys should have the ability to react promptly, propose initiatives and improvise within the broad margins of their instructions.'[18] Multilateral work is also more democratic than bilateral—diplomatic ranks count for little in a committee or a drafting caucus.

A former permanent representative offered a related comment. 'There may be occasions when substantive issues can be incorporated or deleted from documents (e.g. resolutions) through amendments to an original, carefully negotiated text. In these situations, a good knowledge of the rules of procedure is essential. The PR or his deputy should anticipate roadblocks and ensure that a few friendly delegations are briefed appropriately either to move the amendment or lend support to it from the floor.'[19]

There are other points. Drafting skills is an obvious asset, especially the ability to think on one's feet, to find an apt phrase or word that seemingly bridges differences on a contentious point, while at the same time preserving the essence of one's position. Action unfolds rapidly at times; there are other delegations trying the same, to their own advantage. Much of the vital finalization of documents takes place in small clusters of delegates, usually under time pressure and often at late hours; informality prevails, and distinctions between senior ambassadors and low-rank diplomats from other permanent missions are blurred, in the cut and thrust of putting together a consensus text. Much of the work is done in English, and an envoy lacking mastery in it is at a disadvantage. Often, Indians are often among the more adept draftsmen, together with those from the English-speaking countries. But language savvy can also become a disadvantage if other delegates, be they Asians or Africans, find these envoys domineering on account of their natural language advantage. Over-competitiveness at drafting is also a liability.

As the chief executive of the mission, the permanent representative has to be selective in the choice of areas for personal involvement. The delegation of responsibility to the mission team is essential, especially to the deputy PR, who is invariably an experienced official, often given the personal rank of ambassador. In a large mission, that rank may also be given to one or two others, or they may be designated as permanent representatives for particular work functions (such as PR for disarmament affairs in Geneva). Typically, the US mission at New York has up to four senior diplomats with ambassadorial rank, who tend to be professionals and are a big help to the PR who is often a political appointee.

As the captain of a talented team, the PR needs to continually track the pulse of multiple debates. Daily meetings of the mission team, chaired by the PR, identify the tasks and tactics. He guides the team on issues of substance as well as detail, and this hinges on total professional familiarity with the multilateral process of that particular agency of conference. Rules of procedure, and the customary practices of committees and plenary sessions, as well as a knowledge of the other players, are all part of the PRs calculus.

Regional Diplomacy

Regional diplomacy is a special variant of multilateral work involving virtually permanent dialogue with neighbors. The European Union is the world's most advanced model of this genre, in its intensive 'unification' process, and the expansion to 25 members in 2004. The EU's political engineering has no parallel in the world. No wonder, member-states regard their permanent mission in Brussels as their most important diplomatic mission.

The work of the PR at Brussels merits a study by itself; he has a task that is literally almost unmanageable.[20] There is simply so much happening in the complex web of inter-government, inter-region and European Commission initiated activity. It is impossible for a single mission to track everything. They perforce prioritize and apply a selective focus on the key issues before the EU Commission and the Council of Ministers and their subsidiary bodies, also keeping a weather eye on the third of the triumvirate, the European Parliament. Beyond that, it is left to each national agency or unit engaged in the EU process, to work out its own way, reporting back to the central coordinators on EU affairs in the home capital, where warranted. There is a guiding national policy, but no single, total operational control.

The EU ambassador acts like a conductor of an orchestra, though even this analogy is inadequate. One of his tasks is to interface with the European Commission, via a continual round of meetings with the Commissioners and their senior staff. The second major function is the servicing of the meetings of the EU Council of Ministers that is virtually in continuous session, at the level of the principals who are the foreign ministers, and the permanent secretaries, the political directors of foreign ministries, and all the territorial and functional department heads, who too meet regularly in their own separate networks, often once a month. His permanent dialogue with member-states is via the Committee of Permanent Representatives (COREPER), subdivided into COREPER I, which deals with domestic business at the level of the deputy PRs (the so-called 'first pillar' activities), and COREPER II, which the PRs directly handle, covering EU external affairs, including the Common

Foreign and Security Policy (CFSP) and the work of the Political and Security Committee (PSC) which is a product of the Nice Treaty of 2000.

The daily 'prayer meeting' at the embassy may be attended by over 100 officials, some on the ambassador's permanent staff and many more visiting Brussels for one or another meeting or negotiation round. The ambassador typically spends 30 minutes or less with them, listening to terse reports on new developments on the main activities of the day, issuing brief guidelines on instructions that are to be obtained from home, and his own advice pertinent to the discussion themes. The majority of the participants are there to listen and get an overview of the full process under way. The ambassador then departs, and it is left to his deputy to conduct the rest of the internal coordination session, always in a very business-like fashion.

The EU permanent representative does not involve himself directly in the work of the European Parliament that meets in Strasbourg, but he is occasionally invited to appear at committee meetings and the like. He does have a role with the other EU institutions, such as the EU Court of Justice. It adds up to a very full plate.

Bilateral ambassadors in individual EU capitals are tasked with conveying to the home administration developments on major issues such as the unification process, the attitude towards on-going negotiations with new applicants, or the position of the collective entity on some external developments. In turn, the same ambassadors transmit to dialogue partners in the receiving state the home country's perspective on these issues. The PR in Brussels is a vital cog in this two-way information collection and lobbying mechanism, sometimes able to convey a first warning of an incipient change, or to probe for chinks in opposing positions, via his networking contacts. One can easily visualize the furious exchange of communications and the concurrent dialogue on multiple issues that this dynamic produces. As a recent study of the EU observes, bilateral diplomacy is not redundant, it has produced a new kind of 'multiple bilateralism'.[21]

The other major regional organization where the PR system is replicated, though at lower intensity, is the Organization of American States (OAS), with its headquarters in Washington DC. Given the focus of OAS on hemisphere security and military–political cooperation, these issues shape the work content of this second set of ambassadors from OAS member-countries stationed in the US capital.

As for other regional bodies, ASEAN has a large headquarters in Jakarta, and the South Asian group SAARC has a much smaller one in Kathmandu, Nepal. SADC of Southern Africa is headquartered in Malawi, and so on. None of them have a system of PRs, full-time or part-time, accredited to the collective entity. It is left to the home administration to directly interface with the secretariat, perhaps on the premise that the quality of engagement with these regional bodies makes it counter-productive to deploy the envoy as an intermediary.[22] The OAU based in Addis Ababa (the acronym used to stand for the 'Organization of African Unity'; it now denotes 'Organization of the African Union') has full-time PRs from a number of member countries, while others appoint a single ambassador to both Ethiopia and to the OAU.

One feature of regional diplomacy is the support network it produces for bilateral ambassadors in different capitals, for local networking and outreach. The regional group becomes their common platform, for mutual consultation, to make and receive joint *démarches* in the receiving country, joint tours inside the country, and other group activities. Integrated networks such as those comprising the EU ambassadors, perform many shared or joint activities. These include: periodic, structured meetings at different levels, involving ambassadors, DCMs, political and commercial officials, etc.; writing joint reports that go to all member-state MFAs; collective *démarches* on CFSP and other issues;[23] temporary local exchange of diplomats among embassies; and pooled logistic facilities. The list does not end here. At the other end of the spectrum, a group such as SAARC has so far produced a limited mandate for joint activities, reflecting the stunted regionalization process. SAARC envoys only meet at monthly lunch meetings; even that limited interaction does not occur at places where only two or three of the seven member-states are represented.

The Home Base

The foreign ministry and other official entities at home that the PR represents have, firstly, their expectations of what the PR should deliver to them; secondly, he in turn has a sizable requirement for support from all of them. Let us examine the first issue.

Governments abhor being taken by surprise with international developments that their envoy, bilateral or multilateral, should have anticipated. At a conference or an international organization, this means that the negotiation process should be predictable, producing no surprises of the unwelcome kind. When an adverse development is anticipated, headquarters needs early warning on the contours of an expected outcome to prepare and cope with the aftermath. Naturally, the importance of good anticipation becomes acute when vital interests are at stake. The ambassador, say at the UN in New York, is seldom the only player on any international issue, but in the midst of sharp multilateral debate he is the one present in a dynamic arena, charged with representing national interests. With diplomacy more public than ever before, if anything is perceived as affecting national prestige, the envoy comes under tight scrutiny.

Accuracy in forecasting is difficult with multiple players. It becomes complicated when the same individual is immersed in the lobbying process, say in the course of a lead-up to a major vote where the home country has a large stake, and has to gauge the possible outcome. Objectivity is often the first victim in such situations. The extent to which the ambassador can de-link the estimation of an initiative's results from his own lobbying efforts, becomes a measure of his professionalism.

The foreign ministry's expectations from the multilateral envoy are no different from what it demands of the bilateral counterpart— the safeguarding and advancement of national interests across the full gamut of activities undertaken. Beyond the obvious, this covers several specifics. First, the envoy has to provide early warnings of any adverse development that impinges on national interests. Second, he should be wary of the political dimension of technical issues, or those that seemingly relate only to narrow functional areas, especially when the lead ministry or agency may not be in close coordination with the foreign ministry at home. Or there may be an unanticipated political dimension that emerges in the course of a conference. He thus helps in the coordinator role of the MFA. Third, he looks for opportunities to make connections between disparate issues, say a request from a country for support in an election, and one's own need for support from that same country on some unconnected technical issue handled by another ministry. Such trade-off identification for leverage is very similar to what the bilateral ambassador attempts. Fourth, he looks for openings in secretariats and in subsidiary bodies where officials from one's own country can be placed, on short or full-term assignments (the latter may run from three to five years). Such placements are subject to 'quotas' that are calculated on the basis of the budget contribution of each country, usually applied with some flexibility; some countries are 'over-represented' and face difficulties in getting new placements. For instance, India and some other South Asian countries, home to talented people adept in the English language and at cross-cultural skills, find it hard to get openings. Fifth, headquarters may require the envoy, especially at New York, to pursue bilateral dialogue with countries not represented in the home capital, or in some special context, if the issue does not warrant sending a special emissary. Small countries with a limited network of embassies routinely use their permanent representatives for bilateral contact.

What does the envoy need from headquarters? The first requirement is clear, realistic and actionable instructions; he is sorely handicapped without these. Conferences are volatile by nature. Delegations, individually or in clusters, act in ways that cannot always be predicted. The interaction among multiple players can throw up completely new situations. The PR who handles the day-to-day management of a conference requires tactical flexibility within the master plan; this gives him latitude to work and identify compromises that serve the essential objectives. A scholar sums this up as 'the authority to recast priorities, propose initiatives and improvise within the broad margins of the instructions.'[24]

Many of the instructions sent by the foreign ministry to the multilateral envoy are based on the envoy's recommendations. This enhances his responsibility in guiding headquarters, on strategy as well as detailed tactics. Lack of conference instruction flexibility can be disastrous. During an earlier set of interviews, an Indian official who had participated in several international economic conclaves had spoken of the difficulty with rigid briefs. When pressures against a delegation holding such a brief became intolerable, usually in the final stages of a conference, the delegation was often forced to give way completely, bereft of a fall-back position. This kept the delegation out of reckoning, and usually left it worse off, compared with the deal it could have crafted, had it remained an active, flexible negotiator.[25] At the November 2002 Doha Ministerial Conference of WTO there was an echo of this problem when the press reported that India's holdout on the final day, awaiting approval from home, paradoxically allowed France to squeeze into the consensus its slanted interpretation of the compromise on agricultural subsidies.

In the case of PRs to specialized agencies, the performance of their role depends upon a close understanding with the functional ministry at home having the lead role in that agency. The foreign ministry can assist on important issues, or coordinate political angles. But the MFA cannot substitute for the PRs personal equations with that lead agency, such as the agriculture ministry on FAO affairs. This is essential domestic diplomacy.

A Downside?

Is there a downside to multilateral diplomacy? What limitations does the multilateral ambassador face?

In the aftermath of 9/11, the global revulsion against terrorism produced a rare solidarity within the international community, and a strong commitment to multilateralism. Some expected this to produce a wider multilateral action to resolve complex issues on the world agenda, especially development and poverty elimination. But the two major international conferences held in 2002, at Monterey, Mexico, in March on the international financing of development, and at Johannesburg, South Africa in September on sustainable development, produced little result. The expectations of an international compact to address the growing chasm between the world's rich and poor, and to mitigate the harsh impact of globalization, did not materialize. The Iraq war of April 2003 launched by the US–UK coalition, circumvented the UN and was seen as a demonstration of US unilateralism and its diminished faith in the multilateral system. Surely, both these interpretations are simplistic. The system of global consultative diplomacy represented by the UN system and other international institutions is a reality, and no country can afford to walk away from it. The problem is that the multilateral process is 'routinized'; it evokes neither innovative methods nor any real commitment. Its institutions have become huge bureaucracies that have taken a life of their own, in ways their founders never anticipated.

Unsurprisingly, interest among the rich in multilateral dialogue is low. In countries like Australia and the US, the high tide of engagement to multilateralism has receded. True, the European Union retains some interest, as do Japan and much of the developing world. But we see that the once important UN Conference on Disarmament at Geneva, the forum where major nuclear arms control documents like the Non-Proliferation Treat (NPT) and the Comprehensive Test Ban Treaty (CTBT) were negotiated, is in its doldrums, with almost nothing substantive on the agenda for its weekly meetings. This leaves the delegates, including some 20-odd full-time ambassadors who are stationed in Geneva exclusively to deal with this subject, with nothing more than make-believe work.

Developing countries confront another deception. Many of them have viewed multilateral diplomacy as the most vital area of the work of their foreign ministries. The *crème de la crème* of their diplomats are assigned as permanent representatives, especially in New York. The same applies to the other diplomats appointed to these missions. There is often an over-concentration of talent.

Dealing with fundamental issues of peace and development, and other global issues that seem vital to states and their peoples, it is easy for the professional diplomat to get caught up in a heady atmosphere of multilateralism. The complex confrontation of ideals and interests that occurs continually at conferences of all kinds, from the political to the technical, produces absorbing drama. But much of this output is simply verbiage that is forgotten even before the ink is dry on the printed paper. Take, for instance, the end products of a typical UN General Assembly session—the resolutions passed and the speeches delivered are forgotten instantly, ignored even in the sponsoring countries. They have but archival value for researchers. They seldom relate to the solutions of real issues.

The UN system as an employer is a talent magnet for the developing world, including the ambassadors assigned to New York as PRs. The manner this works in practice is legitimate. The UN needs senior staff, special representatives and heads of task forces for many problems around the world, and the best of the PRs, especially those on the eve of retirement from diplomatic services, offer a ready pool of quality. Many countries send their senior-most envoys to New York, often on final assignments, which makes it inevitable that they seek UN jobs. Some Western envoys also find these jobs attractive.

When almost all the retiring permanent representatives from particular countries end up with UN jobs, it conveys an impression of a 'revolving door'.[26] It leads to the question whether an envoy in the final year or two of his term, harboring expectations of a UN assignment on retirement, will always retain an objectivity in his dealings with the secretariat. Just as old-fashioned civil services insist on a 'cooling off period', before those who have spent a lifetime in public service take up private sector jobs with those who were their interlocutors, a similar time gap would be logical.

The situation is a product of the high, tax-free emoluments that the UN pays at all levels; the same scales apply at most international organizations. These earnings are many multiples of what equivalent officials in most countries can earn. The counter-argument is that high UN salaries are essential to attracting top talent; remuneration must be comparable to the earnings in the top tier of advanced countries. This is perhaps true, but the kind of problems narrated above is an unintended consequence. Perhaps each member-state should lay down its own rules to prevent such envoys from using their assignments as a launch pad for personal gain. It is a sensitive theme, but it is essential to shed light and to provoke a debate that is missing today.

To sum up, the multilateral envoy is a practitioner of professional skills, typically chosen from the ranks of the most experienced diplomats of each country. The relatively few non-career appointees survive only if they are quick learners, blending into their jobs their public affairs skills. Multilateral diplomacy is the arena where the classic skills of negotiation are practiced, almost to the relative exclusion of the other elements of the diplomatic craft. And yet, few diplomatic services regard this branch of diplomacy to be an area of exclusive specialization. This is a powerful argument that conforms the integrated nature of diplomacy, where specialization lies in the craft skills of the *métier*, not the action arena where these skills are practiced.

5

THE DOMESTIC DIMENSION

A scholar notes: 'Diplomacy has lost its insulation from domestic politics.'[1] More than ever, an ambassador has to keep one eye focused on his home front, both as his vital support base and the beneficiary of all that he attempts in the country of assignment. Diplomacy in a foreign land has always been predicated on the confidence the envoy enjoyed at home, but the domestic part of the job has become more prominent, complex and demanding. The main reasons are the new players in external affairs, consisting of official agencies, non-state elements and the publics. The ambassador has become answerable to them all, in varying degrees.

Working conditions were radically different in the past. Until a couple of decades back, domestic politics were seldom an active factor in diplomacy—defined in the narrow sense of implementation of foreign policy—even when foreign policy drew the attention of home constituencies. It was routinely assumed that envoys abroad enjoyed the support of all their political leaders, unless there was some partisan action or lapse by the envoy compromising this confidence. The career ambassador did not have to make a special 'diplomatic' effort on the home front, as long as he performed within the parameters of his assignment and brief.

What, then, is the origin of this change? In a word, it is a byproduct of globalization. The democratization of information and the blurring of the external–domestic boundary mean that home constituencies are keenly interested in, and affected by, say, the debate on climate change and the Kyoto Treaty that impacts on their own lives. Audiences in poor countries keenly follow the manner in which national interests have been advanced in global trade negotiations when a major meeting is held under the WTO banner. Equally, live coverage of key discussions at the UN Security Council attracts tens of millions around the world. Similarly, the bilateral ambassador finds his or her conduct in crisis under close scrutiny, even when he is not at the direct locus of the event. The instant TV interview, plus the live or immediate playback of telephone conversations in the midst of a crisis are standard media practices in every country. The ambassador at key assignments becomes an actor on the domestic stage. The volatility of international affairs sometimes thrusts in the limelight the envoy stationed in a distant backwater. Politicians also take their cue from this interest of domestic publics, and even drive this change. For the envoy, building ties to politicians, the media and other opinion leaders is a good career option. Young diplomats learn from their mentors.

Credibility is the envoy's capital stock, both in the receiving country and at home. Credibility at home is the hardest to earn, and the one element that facilitates his work best of all. An envoy going abroad with a reputation for sound judgment carries a reservoir of working capital, to which he can add through subsequent actions. For a new ambassador launched on a first assignment, or entrusted with a particularly challenging job, credibility is earned gradually; it depends both on personal efforts as well as opportunity.

A serving ambassador illustrated this graphically in an interview.[2] At his overseas post he saw an important opportunity, which he felt merited a visit by the foreign minister, to reciprocate several ministerial-level visits from that country. The ambassador's strong recommendation was viewed with disdain in the home capital—a situation that even experienced envoys encounter from time to time.[3] Other priorities and competing demands on the foreign minister's time led to a negative response, accompanied by the minister's caustic comment informally conveyed to him, that the ambassador should restrain his enthusiasm. Undaunted, the envoy persisted, in a less assertive fashion. Eventually the proposal was accepted, and some months later, the foreign minister reached there. At their first private moment, he asked the ambassador: 'Why have you brought me here?' Taken aback, the ambassador gave his best justification. As the visit progressed it became evident that the envoy's assessment had been sound and that an overdue visit had been worthwhile, judging by the results. The ambassador later received a grudging acknowledgement for his sound advice! The envoy walks a thin line in pushing his proposals, often risking criticism that he is over-enthusiastic, or out of touch with reality. This incident also illustrates the foreign ministry's challenge in managing competing priorities.

The Home Context

Is the ambassador today more subject to domestic political influences than before? The short answer is yes, true for most parts of the world. One Western envoy told the author: 'The ambassador is 95% free from political constraints.'[4] But such an insulation is not universal. Another Western diplomat affirmed that the diplomatic service could no longer assume that it was aloof from the domestic processes.[5] One problem is that envoys abroad sometimes face politically motivated criticism from the home media.[6] Those from developing countries may concede readily that they are very much subject to political influences in their work, although usually not to the point where it involves their professional judgment. Let us examine the factors that have led to the present situation of the mounting importance of the home front, to the point where the ambassador finds himself 'facing both ways'.[7]

First, this situation results from the entry of multiple players, official and non-official, into the external policy process. The foreign ministry remains the envoy's mooring point, but he deals with all the other constituents as well. The list expands continually. They generally deal with the ambassador directly. A few foreign ministries fight a losing battle, insisting that they remain the routing channel for instructions to ambassadors. Until the early 1990s, the German Foreign Office insisted that all such instructions pass through its portals. This led to the situation where, for example, the Ministry of Economic Cooperation would fax advice on aid issues directly to the ambassador concerned, as an 'advance copy' of the papers sent through the *Auswärtiges Amt*. The common practice is for ministries to deal directly with the envoy abroad (e.g. conveying instructions on ongoing negotiations or seeking information), endorsing copies of important messages to the foreign ministry at home. When in doubt, the cautious ambassador checks with the foreign ministry, that it is aware of the actions being undertaken.

In the other direction, the envoy today reports directly to other ministries as often as he does to the foreign ministry, but it would be rare for him not to keep the concerned department in the foreign ministry (often the 'parent' territorial unit), informed via copies of such messages. The breadth and quality of the ambassador's dialogue with 'line' ministries, taken collectively, forms a component of the foreign ministry's relationship with these agencies. Conceptually, the envoy represents the government in its entirety, but it happens all too often that he, and the diplomatic machinery that he symbolizes—perceived as the instruments of the foreign ministry—are consequently under-utilized by the other government agencies. Experience and observation show that this happens in many countries. Therefore, the envoy's effective dialogue with functional ministries also assists the MFA in these relationships.

For the ambassador, direct contact with the non-state partners at home is no less vital; many are his permanent interlocutors. Examples of such contact are: institutionalized cooperation among business chambers; periodic exchanges of think tanks, scientific institutions and educational institutions; dialogue between voluntary bodies engaged in development work. The breadth of their operational activities abroad frequently needs the embassy's follow-up on the ground. The proactive envoy sees himself as a facilitator, who gives initial introductions and then withdraws to a discreet distance, but continues to observe, assisting when needed. Keeping the territorial department at the MFA informed serves two purposes: the home base gets real time inputs on the evolution of relations, and this provides a platform for the embassy to get help when problems arise.[8]

Once in a while an ambassador risks a sharp rejoinder from the

MFA for direct communication with a home agency that the MFA perceives as a rival on its domestic turf. The envoy has to be cautious in advancing a new proposal to another agency that has not been cleared with the MFA, the more so if he doubts its acceptability to the MFA. Exceptional cases of 'independent' action by rogue ambassadors are discussed later. At all times, the envoy needs special care in communications with the country's external intelligence agency, since it is often in contestation with the MFA.[9]

Second, the public at home is increasingly attentive to foreign affairs, realizing that it is closely affected by external developments. In many countries, the domestic political consensus on foreign policy that was typical of the past no longer exists, or is qualified. The old adage that domestic politics ceased at the country's borders seldom works now. In democracies, sharp divergences on foreign policy are routine, whether covering policy or tactics. Consequently, even career ambassadors can be pulled into political debate, becoming identified with partisan positions, sometimes unfairly. This may be less a problem in the US where ambassadors—career and noncareer—hold office at the pleasure of the administration in power, and even the professional envoy is routinely expected to be engaged in the domestic political process, testifying before congressional panels, and drumming up support for the administration through media interviews and speeches to interest groups.[10] In most other countries such explicit involvement does not occur; it would be unusual for an ambassador to appear before a parliamentary panel in India, Germany or the UK, except in an inquiry covering activities under his jurisdiction. But carefully tailored speeches and interviews by envoys that support domestic policies, indirectly pitched to the home audience, are part of the external policy process. The permanent representative in New York must always consider how his speech will play at home. An envoy may be asked to reinforce a public message at home, if he is at a location that is politically sensitive. This may take the shape of mobilizing public opinion, via platforms like business seminars, gatherings of intellectuals, and other activities not in themselves of a political nature. Or the envoy may be encouraged to give media interviews in home journals and TV. These activities do not necessarily transgress into the political arena, but come close to a conservative limit of the permissible for a professional diplomat. The non-career ambassador has fewer inhibitions.

What has caused this loss of domestic consensus on foreign policy in many countries? In part it is the blurring of dividing lines between the home and the foreign fronts. In an age of interdependence and globalization, decisions taken far away, some even by private firms, impact on states. Examples: Decisions by foreign firms on the credit rating of countries, whether Japan or Brazil, impacts on the inflow of portfolio investments into that capital market and stock exchanges, and affects economic growth. In the same way, actions by activist foreign NGOs, taking up the cause of child labor or ill-treatment of animals, lead to boycotts against products from countries seen to contravene such ethical standards; this affects jobs and business activity. In many developing countries the domestic electorate is hypersensitive to allegations of 'the foreign hand', and this too becomes fertile ground for exploitation by politicians; it becomes easy to argue in over-simplistic terms about how actions by rich states, or by the World Bank or WTO acting as their 'agents', threaten a country's agriculture, industry or even the entire economy. The envoy representing the developing South has to understand such domestic mindsets, and both offer realistic assessments to the policy formulators at home, and cope with Western agencies to blunt the adverse impact of their actions. This involves a dialogue with influential home agencies, and networking to induce greater understanding.

The demands on career civil service ambassadors to provide domestic political support are not limited to democracies. Under autocratic regimes, or where governments are less accountable to the people, envoys face stronger demands from home. The overt and hidden pressure to act in support of political masters at home is harder to resist. In general, when foreign policy is subject to domestic divergence and political debate, the implementation of that policy also becomes an object of attention and frequent controversy.

Third, the ambassador's professional conduct comes under close political scrutiny. Sometimes he also becomes a scapegoat for lapses that lie beyond his control. This applies particularly to envoys stationed in neighboring countries and in the capitals of major powers.[11] Those at more distant locations, both in geography and in terms of the sending country's interests are lower on political radar screens at home, unless a crisis intervenes. It makes good sense for the envoy to develop domestic connections with influential media editors, business associations, industry leaders, think tank intellectuals, academics and even political personalities. These friends serve as insurance in times of need.

Fourth, ambassadors based in countries with a sizable ethnic diaspora are prone to unusual political pressures. Take an Indian example, which surely applies to some other countries.[12] Thanks to large migrant communities in the UK and the US, the major Indian political parties have developed support bases there, even branch units. Ethnic leaders in these countries have their New Delhi connections, and demand special status in their relations with the Indian ambassador and his consuls general. Under particular circumstances, the most prominent among them has sometimes functioned as a parallel envoy. Their local clout is used to convey messages or get political access for visiting Indian personalities to high leaders in these countries.[13] It is interesting that the ethnic Indian communities in the old migration countries (South Africa, Guyana, Fiji, Mauritius, East Africa and the Caribbean) have limited interest in Indian politics, despite exceptionally strong cultural roots.[14]

Diaspora concerns may also lead envoys into misguided actions, as became public in April 2003 when an Indian high commissioner in Mauritius was withdrawn, partly because of unauthorized involvement in local politics.[15] Yet, ethnic communities are useful assets, operating through levels and methods that are beyond the domain of the ambassador—for instance, as financial contributors to political parties, supporters of their parliamentarians and congressmen or as party activists. The essential ingredient in the situation described above is the presence of a large and economically powerful ethnic community, often of the first or second migration generation, which retains an orientation towards their country of origin, and a tendency by home political elements to exploit such communities.

Israel has rich experience in using the Jewish diaspora as an instrument of foreign policy. China has also used the access that its overseas community offers in diverse countries, and has organized structures at home for sustaining these links, such as the Chinese Commission for Overseas Chinese, reporting to the State Council. Italy and Spain, sources of major European migration to the Americas, have used their overseas communities for local connections, but domestic feedback into their own systems has weakened over time.

For the envoy, overseas communities are potentially difficult partners. When there is a change of government at home, a new set of local ethnic allies emerge, and the earlier ones sometimes treat the envoy in an adversarial fashion.[16] At the best of times, they force the ambassador and his team into a political choice that has nothing to do with the situation in the country of assignment, but hinges on the home connections of these individuals. All this offers rich material for an objective study.

Fifth, modern communications and time zones location have a strange impact. Some envoys report that when they are stationed at places that lie ahead of the home time zone, the Internet enables them to scan the major home newspapers of the day and anticipate the urgent queries that they may receive on foreign media coverage or foreign reactions on issues. Conversely, those at disadvantageous time zones can count on losing sleep with late-night phone calls, when headquarters is provoked by a news story at home that they have not seen. Overall, the electronic global village and 24/7 news channels shorten reaction times and demand ever quicker responses from envoys stationed abroad.

All these elements require the envoy to keep a wary eye on the home front, and to employ networking and outreach *vis-à-vis* the home interlocutors. Some experienced envoys testify that domestic diplomacy becomes almost as important as diplomacy at the place of assignment, a significant departure from the classic era.

Performance Management

The foreign ministry is the envoy's direct master. As noted earlier, within it, the territorial bureau is where he is most accountable, and this serves as his operational base. Much of his effectiveness, including relations with most official agencies at home, even some non-state players, depends on the quality of this link. One interviewed diplomat aptly called the territorial unit the embassy's 'parent division', portraying this intimate relationship.[17]

How does the foreign ministry–ambassador interface operate? In brief, it directs, supervises and evaluates his performance; it receives and absorbs all the feedback; and it provides him support and logistic assistance. Let us consider a key aspect that currently dominates this multi-faceted relationship—performance management.

Before the ambassador takes up an assignment abroad, the foreign ministry—acting on behalf of the entire government—provides his or her overall instructions on the task to be performed. These 'briefings' include several elements, but generally have a diffused shape. The new envoy meets the foreign minister, and other ministers, and a more intensive dialogue is held with the other senior officials. As noted earlier, it was customary for ambassadors-designate to meet the executive head of government—the president or the prime minister—for a personal pre-departure briefing, or to receive a formal communication setting out a work directive (e.g. in Turkey). But sheer numbers and work pressures have led to change; the personal meeting is possible only for the ambassadors going out to major assignments. Where available, these are invaluable, especially when actionable advice is proffered to the envoy. It can provide inspiration that guides the envoy through the length of an assignment.[18]

The French have pioneered a system of 'ambassador's instructions'. Every envoy going out on a new assignment receives from the Secretary General of the *Quai d'Orsay* a customized document setting out the tasks he is expected to accomplish at that particular post. It is the end product of a process of collective analysis, in which other ministries and departments having significant interests in that country also contribute. Within six months of taking up the post, the ambassador presents to the Secretary General his 'plan of action' for executing the instructions, plus a demand for additional resources, as needed. Thereafter, during the course of the envoy's term, the implementation is tracked through annual programs, work-plans for individuals and timelines. The method is Cartesian, and elegant. It has the merit of tying resources to objectives. Strangely, no other diplomatic system has used the same method, though some EU countries have recently adapted the French system for their own use.[19] For instance, outbound German envoys now hold a final session with the Foreign Office State Secretary, where a document serving as his Foreign Office guideline is given. But it does not as yet involve other ministries.[20] In other countries it is tacitly assumed that the ambassador knows what his task is, but this is not spelt out. Some argue that those who have risen to an ambassadorship after many years of junior apprenticeship do not need written directives on the basics of their work. And yet, if we apply a corporate analogy, it is unthinkable that a new country manager would be sent out by a multinational enterprise without a precise plan of the tasks he is expected to accomplish.[21]

An annual 'action plan' that binds the ambassador to precise objectives is another method applied increasingly. With variations, Australia, India, New Zealand, Singapore, UK, US, and others use this system. Typically, the annual plan is drafted by the embassy; after approval by the MFA territorial unit, it is sometimes integrated into the master plan for the region prepared by the latter, and then into the complete program of the entire ministry or department. This is the US method, which has evolved over two decades, currently called the Mission Program Plan; it focuses on the resources that are deployed by the embassy in pursuit of its assigned key priorities.[22] In the UK, the elaboration of an annual program is left to the ambassador, as long as the 'milestones' set by the Foreign Office, that are part of 'public performance targets' for each ministerial department are met.[23] New Zealand applies a rolling two-year plan, with objectives for the second year set out in an indicative fashion. Australia and Singapore have refined this concept further with periodic performance report formats that are simple and powerful.[24]

In India, the Annual Plans currently have a *pro forma* character, but were taken seriously in Prime Minister Rajiv Gandhi's administration (1984–89).

Some question whether diplomatic objectives can be quantified. They argue that even in the economic sector (where goals can be set for exports, foreign investment, aid and the like), an ambassador and his team cannot be held responsible, since results depend on other actors. True, ambassadors do not control the enterprises that generate exports and investments, and a mechanical linkage between promotional actions and actual results is unrealistic. Yet it is not hard for astute observers to judge the extent to which the ambassador and his team have performed, as contributors to these goals. Some countries pay a performance bonus to envoys (and to foreign ministry officials) on the basis of the achievement of set targets, or the fulfillment of objectives set out in individual contracts.

Ideally, resources should be tied to the annual plan. This is not common, but the practice is expanding. An ambassador should have the delegated authority to use the funds budgeted for his mission—of course, subject to both standing rules and the customary *post facto* audit processes. Singapore, and some others, let ambassadors switch funds within major accounting lines or heads, say, between local travel and expanded representational entertainment, or even the renovation of office premises or the replacement of official vehicles, as long as assigned mission targets are met. Paradoxically, Singapore initially found that some ambassadors did not want the delegation of authority, fearing the responsibility that went with it, but subsequently the system has worked well.[25] Other countries disallow that same degree of flexibility, but most have expanded the delegated financial powers of envoys.

Those unfamiliar with the workings of embassies might be astonished at the extent of micro-management from headquarters. Sometimes, an embassy may devote half its correspondence to requests for spending approvals, with the ambassador pitching in with personal appeals at high levels to break administrative logjams. The larger delegation of financial authority carries a responsibility to deliver results. Also implicit are strong systemic controls, plus rigorous auditing to ensure that ambassadors and embassies stick to the straight and narrow path of probity and good judgment!

The oldest management oversight method used by headquarters is the 'foreign service inspection' system, handled in the larger services by a dedicated team of Inspectors at headquarters. Large services ensure that the inspections take place at regular intervals of 3 to 5 years, to assess the performance of the ambassador and the entire embassy team.[26] China is a rare developing country that has a strong inspection system. Hard performance appraisals are not easy to accomplish during on-site inspections that may last barely a week (given the number of missions each team must visit). Therefore much hinges on the preparatory work, including the scrutiny of all the outgoing correspondence of the mission several months prior to the team visit, interviews with the user ministries and departments, and the accumulation of preliminary data through informal sources. Ambassadors are customarily given a chance to comment on recommendations before decision-makers take action.

The application of management methods adds to the ambassador's responsibility and accountability. It also breathes new vision into the system. The French, innovation leaders, recently obtained ISO 9000 certification for the economic services provided by their embassies. Thailand has similarly obtained ISO certification for its consular services. In 2000, Australia carried out a vast benchmarking exercise, comparing their diplomatic process against about eight other countries with a questionnaire that ran to some 200 pages. Others have engaged management consultants to optimize their services.[27]

How effective is MFA supervision? Corporate management techniques have developed slowly in most systems, as in other public service branches, and there is much leeway for improvement. The point not fully grasped is that the object of good supervision is to improve overall performance rather than judge individuals. Developing countries, at the slight risk of over-generalization, have not done enough. Even the management methods they apply often follow the form, but fall short of substance. Sound performance management is an attribute of good foreign policy governance.

Foreign Ministry Interface

The capacity of the foreign ministry to guide and assist the envoy in his outreach and promotion tasks depends, *inter alia*, on its manpower strength. One way to assess a diplomatic service is through the ratio between its personnel at headquarters and those at missions abroad. Empirical analysis shows that a good ratio is: for every 1 person at headquarters, there should be around 1.2 to 1.8 home-based officials stationed abroad.[28] Some well-managed foreign ministries have virtually the same numbers at the two locations, i.e. China, Singapore, and the UK, three radically different systems. Unbalanced numbers point to problems. If the proportion of officials abroad is greatly in excess of the home figure, say a ratio of 1 to 2.5 or more, it indicates gross insufficiency at headquarters; i.e. not enough officials to absorb what the field produces, or even guide them in their tasks.[29]

Of course, numbers do not tell the entire story. There are other factors, like the chemistry between individuals, and the ambassador's ability to deal with ministry officials at varying levels. A senior ambassador often outranks the head of this territorial unit; in many systems, he may often be of the same seniority as the permanent secretary or close to that.[30] Some envoys get carried away with their status, developing a notion that they should exclusively deal with the foreign ministry at its highest level, i.e. the permanent secretary or even the foreign minister. Non-career envoys are especially prone to this kind of mental blockage,[31] but there are career ambassadors who too are prone to an excess of ego. Most envoys realize before long the cost of status preoccupation, i.e. the neglect of those very individuals who handle every proposal and initiative that come from themselves, including advice on policy, regardless of whom these messages are addressed to. Ambassadors that understand the system treat with due respect all the home officials they deal with, from the youngest desk officials upwards. Nor do they take umbrage over professional disagreements over their recommendations.[32]

We noted earlier that the foreign ministry is the envoy's permanent interlocutor, even when his messages are directed at other government agencies, or to non-officials. The MFA has to guide the embassy on changing priorities and the issues important to others at home. It has to engage the envoy with comments, queries and the assessments as these coalesce. The depth and quality of such two-way dialogue is one of the distinguishing characteristics of a good diplomatic system. In developing countries, and in some advanced states as well, this is one issue on which complaints of inadequacy are at the loudest from ambassadors posted abroad. There is never any justification for poor responsiveness from headquarters, besides a lack of personnel to process the reportage. True, the foreign ministry is often overwhelmed, given its obligations, to the political leadership, to parliament and to the wide range of domestic constituencies. But this does not minimize its responsibility in two-way dialogue.

Communication technology now determines the structure of this dialogue, and through it, the level of headquarters–mission integration. Foreign ministries utilizing contemporary systems (intranets and 'virtual private networks') have real-time, secure links with their embassies. Obviously, when used well, technology intensifies the dialogue; reaction time radically improves.[33] Further, the experience of diplomatic systems that have lived through a changeover to these systems is a *qualitative* communication change—hierarchies become flatter, and a culture to engage in dialogue, and to consult becomes the standard mode.

Small states like Botswana now link envoys abroad with the foreign ministry through the Internet. In contrast, India has hesitated in switching to the new system because of a worry over communications security, despite a domestic software industry that achieved an output of some $16 billion in 2003, around 60% exported. Some other developing countries face a similar indecision in applying this technology. A consequence is that these diplomatic systems are unable to take the essential step in achieving a close integration of the entire system, thereby failing to utilize the ambassador and his team as components of the headquarters team.

Traditionally, the missions abroad and the headquarters were seen as two distinct entities, each cast in its own work ethos and function. The revolution in communications and information technology has realigned this paradigm. The September 2000 German Paschke Report declares:

> ...is there much validity in the old argument that our headquarters staff, by reason of their familiarity with the whole spectrum of foreign policy automatically have the superior expertise? In the Berlin E2 Directorate there is usually only one and often only 'half' a desk officer with an intimate knowledge of an EU partner's affairs. At the embassies, by contrast, there are always several officers at different levels concerned with all aspects of our relationship with the host country on a day-to-day basis. That clearly has organizational implications. The various documents needed in Berlin (briefings for the minister, draft speeches, reports, information for visiting politicians, dossier contributions) should normally be prepared by embassies *and be recognizable as embassy products*. Any comments added or diverging opinion expressed by the responsible division in Berlin should likewise be recognizable as such...*Berlin should conduct the ongoing dialogue with embassies as if embassy staff were in fact members of the country division on the ground* [emphasis added].[34]

In mid-2001, the German Foreign Office acted on the above concept and the recommendation implicit in it.[35] Some other Western diplomatic powers tacitly acknowledge the same situation of the *de facto* empowerment of the ambassador, but explicit recognition by most MFAs has yet to emerge. One interviewed ambassador felt that while an able, resourceful ambassador may establish such a relationship with his ministry, the territorial departments would probably continue to regard their missions abroad as units to be used intensively, but also kept at a distance.[36]

The astute envoy profits from this (as recounted by several during interviews) by tracking a decision, or a set of instructions that may be under consideration at home for him, interacting informally with officials along the entire action chain. Used well, this ideally produces a new flexibility, where he can intervene in the process at different stages, and thus becomes continually available for consultation. A few foreign ministries are formalizing this through a tighter integration of the embassy and its supervising territorial unit. This is a far cry from the classic notion of the ambassador tendering his recommendation as a one-shot affair, and then awaiting instructions from a remote, sphinx-like foreign ministry.

Official Partners

The ambassador needs fluid and open links with all the other ministries and departments that are relevant to his work in the assignment country. In developing these, he must shed institutional inhibitions, of the kind that may affect his foreign service colleagues at home. For instance, a rivalry between the MFA and the economic ministries is traditional in many countries, often involving the ministries of economics, finance, trade and industry.[37]

Good personal equations with these 'line' ministries produce insights into their interests in the country of assignment, and enable the ambassador to perform his own limited role as a foreign affairs coordinator and promoter of that institution's agenda. When these ministries are comfortable with him, all the activity in those functional areas goes smoothly. The onus falls on the envoy to build the initial contacts, utilizing consultation visits and other opportunities to sustain these, ensuring that in the eyes of the line agencies, he is regarded as an ally.

The envoy indirectly contributes to the MFA's cooperative relations with all these home official agencies that are active in the target country. The efficient execution of his role helps the MFA as their value-provider. This happens in several ways. First, he should be accepted by these agencies as their man in the target country, not just the MFA representative. This entails effort, and does not happen automatically. Second, he must initiate proactive actions to advance their interests, and demonstrate personal commitment—not wait for instructions. This task is too vital to be delegated to embassy colleagues, unsupervised.[38] Third, the envoy should resist temptation and steer clear of disputes over jurisdiction or turf between ministries.

The institution of the ambassador is only a cog in the foreign ministry–official agency relationship. But it is also one of the foreign ministry's assets in retaining centrality in the system of external governance.

Political Masters

The direct involvement of the executive head government into foreign affairs means that the envoy sometimes finds himself serving two masters, the president or prime minister (and his staff), and the foreign minister leading the MFA. True, the hierarchical lines of authority are clear, but this does not mitigate practical problems. Situations of nuanced divergence occur despite the fact that normally the foreign ministry works in close harmony with the office of the executive head and that office usually supervises the MFA more closely than any other branch of the government.[39]

Personal initiatives by the head of the government routinely bypass the foreign ministry; information on these may reach the ministry after a delay. Sometimes the direct correspondence between the executive head and his foreign counterpart does not involve the foreign ministry at all. There are documented instances when this happens in almost all countries.[40] The increasing frequency with which leaders use the telephone for personal contact is partly the result of the spread of the institution of summitry, multilateral and bilateral, which produces a degree of personal intimacy between them. For instance, on the eve of the Gulf War, between August and December 1990, the presidents of the US and Turkey exchanged over 40 telephone calls.[41] In most countries, the foreign ministry and the ambassadors seldom receive timely information on the telephone conversations between leaders, much less have regular access to the transcripts of the dialogue that takes place, even when such transcripts are maintained.[42]

A practical consequence is that the astute ambassador needs to build a channel to the office of the executive head at home. As noted earlier, it used to be customary for the envoy-designate to call on the head of government, to receive personal instructions. Envoys at major posts still meet national leaders when they come for consultations; this gives the leader a better feel for the situation abroad than any formal report. Increasingly, the expansion in government work truncates this procedure. Former US Ambassador to Iran William H. Schulman, who witnessed the collapse of the Shah's regime in 1979, has written that President Carter refused to meet him, having established a 'very limited quota' of American envoys with whom he would meet.[43] In many countries, the office of the president or prime minister has diplomatic service officials serving on deputation from the MFA, acting as foreign affairs advisers.

They help the envoy in such domestic diplomacy, through the professional brotherhood. It is useful for the envoy assigned to a country of potential importance to have a channel for direct access, to be used as needed.

An ambassador from outside the career track is often better placed in such contacts—his appointment implies a special choice by the political establishment. On the flip side, domestic political developments can make that envoy's proximity to home leaders a liability, especially if it is personalized. An envoy perceived as especially close to a former government, can find that his value in the receiving capital drops sharply, even in advance of his recall by the successor regime. The professional envoy treads the median path by avoiding an excessive identification with political leaders, and by insulating himself via good institutional contacts, especially at the home MFA.[44]

The proximity between ambassadors and home politicians has a downside—the use of political contacts by diplomatic service officials for career advancement, especially for gaining attractive assignments, as well as other benefits such as extensions and post-retirement appointments. Officials with political orientations, even ambitions, have existed in every civil service, but the trend has accentuated, no doubt fed by proximity. Proof is seldom visible, but on occasion, allegations surface in the public that are not denied—for instance, press stories in India about jockeying for ambassadorships to Washington DC and other major posts involving political lobbying by aspirants, as well as the entry of former envoys into the political arena. In Western countries there is a similar phenomenon, even if it remains subterranean most of the time.[45]

Non-State Agencies and Public Diplomacy

Because of the expanded range of issues in relations between states, private organizations figure among the ambassador's domestic constituents, some of them very rewarding partners. Dealing with them demands an un-bureaucratic, informal working style, often with an initial effort at overcoming their past grievances. A banker friend put it well over 20 years back when visiting Prague, on the author's second ambassadorial assignment. He remarked that approaching an Indian embassy as for business promotion was very disconcerting, because he had no way of knowing in advance if he would encounter warm cooperation or total indifference. 'Why can't you chaps be more consistent?' he remonstrated. The short answer was that like many diplomatic services, we were in a stage of transition, from one set of mindsets and values to another—from indifference or reserve towards non-officials (even in economic diplomacy), to an active mode of unsolicited assistance. But honesty also demands the admission that one does not know if in India, as in other countries in the same boat, a successful transition has been made.

Be it in culture, media affairs, education, S&T, or economic diplomacy, it is the non-official actors who are often the source of dynamism. Their connections are broader and deeper than anything that official agencies can replicate, given the pluralization process that has taken place in international affairs. The ambassador and his team need a close interface with them in their self-interest—to keep track of all that is happening, and to fulfill their mandate as the country's best observers of the bilateral relationship, with a real-time mastery of significant developments.[46]

The ambassador has to invest effort into creating and sustaining these home contacts. The initial pre-assignment round of meetings, and the familiarization tour across his own country, identifies the constituents that have a stake in the assignment country. In the foreign capital, visitors from home add to his knowledge and contacts. Each subsequent visit home, when the ambassador goes to regions outside the capital, builds on this network. Nothing compels the non-official agency to keep the ambassador informed of its activities, other than perceived self-interest, or friendship with the envoy or an expectation that the embassy team will reciprocate with something of value.[47] If the envoy takes the ultra-conservative view that he has no role in advising non-official agencies, he will find his contact network shrinking. Conversely, a proactive envoy realizes that his 'private' visitors are among his best general information sources on a wide spectrum of activities. Example: Germany annually invites foreign journalists from many countries;

with characteristic thoroughness, the forms that the journalists fill out on their preferred activities have a column asking if the journalist's embassy is to be informed. Many decline, unless they find through experience that the home embassy will give them something worth their while.[48]

We saw that NGOs and other civil society organizations are non-state agencies that diplomats must cultivate. But as one experienced ambassador observed, to do this they have to 'overcome the allergy in dealing with NGOs'.[49] There are also countries such as France that believe that the influence of NGOs should not be exaggerated.[50] Any objective assessment confirms that these new actors are integral to the international community. It is another matter that in France they are less influential than in other European states or in North America. A dialogue with NGOs should involve the ambassador, of course assisted by embassy colleagues. High-level attention is what they crave; patient listening is vital in these dealings.[51]

In developing countries, domestic NGOs dealing with humanitarian, developmental or public policy issues are not normally among the constituencies that are in dialogue with their envoy based abroad (they are much more likely to be in contact with Western embassies in the home capital, which are often a source of funds). But even without this dialogue, the envoy representing a developing country needs to be aware of the issues that are in the global debate among such groups, since such NGOs operate internationally with great efficiency, networked via the fax machine of yesterday, and today's Internet. This envoy may encounter in the developed country echoes of issues at home.[52] The situation is reversed for developed nation envoys stationed in developing countries where they may come across their own NGOs that have strong connections in these countries. Western envoys cannot afford to neglect such NGOs, given their political and parliamentary influence. Some international NGOs receive funding from Western official development aid budgets.

Business chambers, research institutes, think tanks and academic institutions, as well as professional organizations in the home country are invariably active in their own international networks. The diplomatic system needs practical and non-bureaucratic ways of plugging into these contacts and using them in external outreach. Often, it is the individual initiative by the envoy that produces result. Consequently, the emulation of good examples produces an advantage for the whole system.

Latitude and Innovation

Writing a couple of decades back, former Indian ambassador to Jakarta, Badr-ud-Din Tyabji, disclosed that in 1955, when he presented his ideas to the Indonesians for using the Afro-Asian Conference for building strong economic links, he found the Indonesians more receptive than his own foreign ministry in New Delhi.[53] As things turned out, nothing came of the effort, but his statement indirectly reveals the extent to which an envoy of that time could undertake an initiative on his own, without prior approval. Of course, the envoy needed good judgment, as he was accountable for the results.

The latitude available for local initiative by an ambassador varies from one national system to another. In the past, slow communication produced a penumbra of incertitude, giving scope for local actions on an *ad referendum* basis, where the envoy could honestly say that he was acting on his own, and that the home government's approval was awaited. Today, such excuses do not hold, but it is still possible to float trial balloons, and make soundings of a deniable kind, using local initiative as justification. This may happen at the early stage of a negotiation when the agenda is being developed, or to break an impasse on a complex issue, or to sound the receiving state on a completely new proposal.

Some individuals are prone to greater autonomy, and pay the price when a local initiative is rejected at home. As a general rule, an ambassador should not pursue anything of importance without home approval. Yet, on the ground, the situation is not so stifling. At tactical levels, and as long as he acts within overall policy, the envoy retains a fair degree of initiative, especially if in his judgment there is a narrow window of opportunity to be seized, and the *post facto* approval method is justifiable. The other kind of situation where local initiative can be used, is to convey an instant reaction to some new proposal by the receiving country, where the envoy does not want the other side to be in the slightest doubt over his country's reaction; in such a situation, the standard formula of 'I shall convey this to my government' may not suffice.

Constraints on local initiatives do not mean that innovation is taboo. At operational levels, ample opportunity exists for the envoy to apply new ideas and working methods. By its very nature, as a craft that deals with human and societal interactions, diplomacy continually throws up the opportunity for new ways of handling issues, and applying innovative methods. Further, since diplomacy acts as a link between different disciplines, tactics in implementing policy tend to vary and change over time and circumstance. Noted scholar Jan Melissen writes:

Confronted with change at many levels, and at a breathtaking pace, diplomacy must be inherently adaptive and elastic...If it is agreed then, that diplomacy is the management and facilitation of change in international relations, by means of adaptation and innovation in the modes of diplomatic practice, it becomes clear that the title of this volume is in fact a tautology. Diplomacy could not be about anything other than innovation.[54]

As the field representative dealing with dynamic events, enjoying the relative autonomy of a field commander or a ship's captain, the ambassador has more opportunities to apply new methods than his counterpart at headquarters. For the diplomatic machine as a whole, the receptivity to innovation and to new ideas is one element that differentiates and identifies a good system from the banal.[55]

6

♦

LEADERSHIP IN THE EMBASSY

The ambassador depends on his entire embassy team, traditionally composed of three categories: diplomatic officers, home-based non-diplomatic support personnel, and locally recruited staff. Like the chief executive of a corporate enterprise, the envoy must lead them, through personal example. Solo brilliance is never sufficient.

More than the most 'closed' or isolated company subsidiary situated abroad, the embassy is an insular, inward-oriented community, with a distinct ethos—a home outpost implanted in a foreign land.[1] With some adaptation to the local context, the embassy operates on the norms, procedures and style of the home administration. If the local environment is restrictive, or presents a security hazard or political difficulty, the embassy team's unity becomes all that much stronger. Diplomatic services find that adversity of any sort produces togetherness, plus a mood of shared purpose. The converse has also been observed. At the most comfortable assignments, the problems of discord within the mission, as also a paradoxical sense of loneliness among individual officials and their spouses, are uncommonly high. It is a feature of the profession that living conditions at posts abroad vary greatly. There are just too many places characterized by acute discomfort, insecurity and physical hazard—on a global checkerboard of continual flux.

The Ship's Captain

The analogy with a ship's captain is appropriate to the ambassador on several counts. Both depend on team effort, in which each working individual has an assigned role, and none is unimportant to the complete enterprise, from the lowest functionary or service provider to the high-ranked executives.[2] Like the ship, the embassy is guided to a shared purpose. Like the captain, the ambassador assumes a personal responsibility for all that occurs in the execution of the venture—the buck always stops with him/her. In both situations there is a sense of living in a self-contained community, a bit distanced from the actual environment, and remote from the home base. Modern communication gives instant contact with the headquarters, but does not eliminate the physical separation. The envoy can seek instructions or advice from home, yet no words can describe the complete situation that each leader on the spot faces. There are responsibilities that cannot be delegated. The loneliness of command is a palpable reality.

Like any manager, the ambassador has to apply limited resources to multiple tasks, prioritizing the goals, set by himself and/or by the system. Beyond specific political, economic or other objectives, he has to keep in mind the overall interests and credibility of the country he represents. He must ensure that all actions undertaken by the embassy team produce some advantage, however incremental, for his country and its reputation in the receiving state. It makes a great deal of sense for the envoy to view the country image as akin to corporate brand equity that shapes everything connected to the totality of that enterprise.

The ambassador is responsible for the welfare of all his staff. He particularly needs to be sensitive to the junior home-based non-diplomatic service personnel, on whom prolonged separation from the extended family in the home country bears heavily. They enjoy neither the perks of representational level officials, nor have the opportunity of returning home as frequently. When there is a family bereavement or some other personal problem, distance and separation magnify distress. Far more than in comparable situations at home, the ambassador acts *in loco parentis* to all of the staff, and has to be accessible to listen to problems and assist as best as he can.[3] The wife of former British Ambassador to France and the US, Lady Henderson, wrote in 1976: 'An embassy is like a family, in some ways a rather old-fashioned family. But you will find that if and when you need help, as in a family, you will always find someone that will help you.'[4] The implicit notion is that the ambassador (and his or her spouse), are not alone in helping out embassy colleagues. But the envoy and the spouse—the latter a key asset in soft management—provide the leadership.

It is the experience of most diplomatic services that a career of constant flux, especially a rotation between posts abroad offering vastly different living conditions, plus a protracted absence from home, produce severe family dislocation in addition to personal stress. The pressures of a competitive career, and the urge to stand out and win a fast-track, early ambassadorship, also impacts on personal and family life. Children continually move from school to school, even in their final years of study, which multiplies pressure. The prolonged separation from friends and family at home magnifies dysfunction for the individual, the spouse and for children. Among ambassadors and other diplomats, the rate of breakdown of marriages is higher than in comparable social groups of that country. So too is psychological trauma, though the author is not aware of any hard study confirming the anecdotal, episodic evidence.

The ambassador faces a special loneliness of his own. He has many acquaintances, contacts and profession-based friendships, but is seldom able to establish real personal friendships at the country of assignment. He must guard against excessive contact with or reliance on any local individual, both for the professional hazard this presents to his work, and for the image it might convey of dependence on anyone. One essayist advises: 'cultivate friends but not intimates.'[5] The envoy quickly learns that on overseas assignments he lives in a glass bowl, and must not only do the right thing, but should also be perceived as doing so. All too often his own national or ethnic community living in the country of assignment is his strongest critic, looking over the ambassador with a magnifying glass, and alert to the slightest perceived gesture of favor to someone else. The envoy has to exercise a special balance in his relations with this sensitive community.[6] Within the diplomatic corps, the ambassador finds kinship and partly a sense of shared purpose, but unless he chances upon someone with whom he had served earlier, often in another corner of the globe, the opportunity for deep bonds is slender.[7]

Within the embassy, the envoy has people on whom he depends and supervises, but he cannot open up to them or involve them in all his concerns. Even with his deputy, who may bear the title of 'deputy chief of mission' (DCM), he has to maintain a degree of caution, since that particular relationship needs to be handled with special care (see below). These factors together with the isolation of command responsibility lead to the psychological pressures that the ambassador handles.

There is one bit of discretionary power that both the ship's captain and the ambassador share. In crisis, they can take disciplinary action on their own initiative. The appeal by subordinates challenging their action lies far, even while they both remain eventually accountable to a higher authority. Much of such power is latent, not usable in normal situations. Finally, both have the legal authority to conduct marriages for the duration of the command that they hold![8]

The Embassy Team

The size of the embassy varies greatly. There are micro-embassies where there may be just one diplomatic official apart from the ambassador, plus one or two home-based staff.[9] The UK now even has a few one-man missions, where all the support staff is local—and over 30 consular posts where the entire staff is locally engaged. At the other extreme, there are the large embassies of the great powers that may have a hundred or more officials on the diplomatic list and an even larger phalanx of non-diplomatic personnel. Consequently, the ambassador's responsibility for internal coordination varies greatly.

The ambassador needs an optimal performance from the collection of individuals that he has to accept as a given. He has less flexibility than a home official in changing the team, because diplomatic services typically provide a relatively fixed tenure that services, an ambassador does not have even the theoretical option of sending back an official belonging to another agency. Sometimes, if there is a difference of views between the ambassador and such non-MFA personnel, the former may not even win the support of his own senior colleagues at home, if the headquarters decides that not rocking the boat with that agency is of greater value than the local contretemps.[15] The ambassador needs man management skills in handling a large team, plus a clear focus on his real priorities, in effect tolerating the minor divergences as and when they arise.

The ambassador's right hand is the deputy chief of mission (DCM).[16] John Kenneth Galbraith, narrating his experience at heading the US Embassy in New Delhi under the Kennedy administration in 1960–63 wrote:

The most important man in the embassy, not excluding the Ambassador, is often the Deputy Chief of Mission...He deputizes for the Ambassador, provides professional continuity, handles subordinate offices, and with suitable tact, tells his superior what he should do.[17]

The above description applies with particular force to non-career envoys, who need the best DCM that a foreign ministry can provide. A career ambassador is less dependant on his DCM, but profits greatly if this senior colleague can relieve him of a portion of his routine supervision tasks, leaving him free to concentrate on those activities of outreach, promotion and public diplomacy where the ambassador delivers the best value. In large missions, the DCM is sometimes one who has earlier served as an ambassador at one or more small embassies; he or she almost invariably has the rank to hold such office.[18] The DCM needs such an edge in seniority to be able to deal confidently with the heads of other departments, some belonging to other agencies. Occasionally, the appellation 'deputy ambassador' is used for the DCM, but this has no sanction in either tradition nor in the ranks prescribed by the Vienna Convention.

One of the hazards in the profession is the breakdown in working relations between the envoy and his DCM. This is a generic problem that all diplomatic services confront, but it is seldom viewed as a systemic issue, rather than a problem of individuals. It can result from a combination of factors: professional divergence over policy uniformly applies to all. Only an ambassador with exceptional clout might be allowed to hand-select a deputy, or someone to work as his 'chef de cabinet'.[10] In the normal course, given each diplomat's personal requirements (children's schooling, spouse's employment and the like), it takes time to implement personnel changes.

The presence of representatives of different ministries and agencies within the embassy complicates team management. Invariably, officials from other agencies come to the embassy on temporary attachment; they view themselves as ultimately answerable to their parent institutions and not to the ambassador. In practice, it means that they correspond independently with, and follow instructions from, their home offices. Such instructions may not fully conform to the objectives and tactics determined by the foreign ministry for that country. Differences in work culture and other factors also sometimes lead to personal differences, threatening the harmonious functioning of the embassy team. In extreme instances it may lead to a breakdown in discipline. Countries use different methods to deal with the issue.

We noted the US practice, originating in the days of President Harry Truman, for each president to issue a personal order affirming the ambassador's overriding authority as the head of the 'country team'. But as one observer has noted, the ambassador 'has the authority but sometimes not the tools to manage conflict within the mission'.[11] The 2001 joint report of a task force headed by Frank Carlucci declares: 'Ambassadors deployed overseas lack the authority necessary to coordinate and oversee the resources and personnel deployed to their missions by other agencies.'[12] An article in the September 2003 issue of *The Foreign Service Journal* quotes a recent book that describes how the regional commanders of the military 'have become more powerful and influential than ambassadors, often assuming their role'.[13] Clearly despite presidential directives and latent power, coordination remains a serious issue.

David Newsome, one of the *éminence grise* of US diplomacy, has pointed out: 'Good ambassadors achieve that control not through letters, but by overcoming bureaucratic obstacles, establishing confidence among their staff, and leading.'[14] In other diplomatic and tactics; competitive ambition, personality clashes; or even indiscipline. Whenever the service seniority difference between the ambassador and the deputy is small; the risk increases. Sometimes the situation reaches such an impasse that the deputy is removed prematurely—but seldom the ambassador! While cases of extreme breakdown are few in any diplomatic system, the more frequent situation involves tension, and poor cooperation. This inevitably percolates to other levels, eroding the embassy's effectiveness. Diplomatic services treat such problems within the family, but sometimes they become public. The author is not aware of any study of the phenomenon, nor of ground rules devised by any service, to better delineate the DCM's responsibilities *vis-à-vis* the ambassador. Canada uniquely runs a week-long training course at its Foreign Service Institute that is mandatory for all those assigned as DCMs. This deserves emulation.

Other relationships within the embassy are less complicated. The counselors and first secretaries in the embassy are usually heads or deputy heads of departments or sections, forming a part of the ambassador's brains trust. In large embassies, the work divisions tend to be rigid, which limits the application of 'multi-functionality', a vital characteristic of the profession, and of integrated diplomacy. In small missions, diplomats have no choice but to adapt, tackling different tasks as they arise, without being stuck in one sector. Even in a large or medium-sized mission, the ambassador can apply a 'task force' method that mobilizes all embassy officials to handle special jobs. The sectors typically amenable are: media outreach, economic diplomacy, and political networking.[19] Some may consider this unconventional, but in the self-contained world of the embassy, given its limited personnel, temporary redeployment is a practical device to cope with special needs and hone integrated skills.

The ambassador uses simple devices for management control, particularly in the large embassy. First, he needs an oversight of all inward and outbound communications. Without undermining the autonomy of department heads to handle their own correspondence, 'float' copies of messages sent out should be scanned by the ambassador (or by his DCM or *chef de cabinet*, in very large missions). Similarly he must see all inbound messages received by the embassy, by cipher, fax or email (though with the vast growth in communications flow, oversight over intranet-based e-messages is difficult). However this is enforced, the ambassador needs to be aware of the totality of embassy communications. Second, he should make it his business to meet a maximum of visitors from home, whether they are politicians, officials, media persons, businessmen, scientists, academics or whatever. They are a vital information source; the envoy and his team also often brief them on the local scene. Such an interactive dialogue reinforces the envoy's outreach and networking. Third, the ambassador needs daily or frequent internal coordination meetings with all the diplomats under his charge (and less frequent meetings with all other personnel as well), for an effective two-way dialogue. These are the tools of leadership and command.

Young diplomats assigned to the embassy, whether as 'officer-trainees' on first assignment, or at their first substantive job after confirmation in the diplomatic service, are the ambassador's special responsibility. He should mentor them, ensuring that they gain a broad experience. Typically, they can be periodically rotated to different work areas. The ambassador invites them to representational events at the residence expressly to inculcate social skills and improve their confidence in dealing with different sets of interlocutors. If the ambassador has no time for his young charges, these impressionable people suffer alienation, especially in the large mission. Most career professionals vividly recall their own experiences as young officials. As heads of missions they have a strong obligation to the career development of the next generation placed in their trust.

It is essential for the ambassador to view himself as the chief executive of the enterprise, in relation to *all* the personnel who are under his charge and not as a foreign ministry official or a senior member of the diplomatic service. A sense of inclusiveness is essential to win the loyalty of the personnel from other agencies, and to deploy them as needed, sometimes even giving them responsibilities that lie beyond the formal work boundaries. If the envoy tolerates or participates in an 'us-and-them' differentiation between the foreign ministry personnel and the remainder, it becomes impossible to exercise effective leadership. In real life, such situations arise all too often, eroding the delivery capacity of the entire team.

Intelligence, Defense and Other Specialists

The specialists in the embassy belong to different agencies outside the foreign ministry—be it the defense ministry, the intelligence establishment, or line ministries. Working with them poses a special challenge when they are embedded within the embassy family.

The public might wonder at the rationale for placing intelligence officials within embassies. This is an old tradition, linked to the notion of diplomacy as 'war by other means', justified in the fact that an 'undeclared' diplomat-intelligence official is immune from action by the receiving state; the worst that he faces if caught is expulsion, through the *persona non grata* route.[20] In practice, intelligence agencies of the receiving state manage to identify these officials; calculations of reciprocity ensure cautious treatment. When tension escalates among countries, or if an agent is caught red-handed at espionage, a round of mutual expulsions takes place; as during the Cold War between the US and the former Soviet Union, or as occurs periodically between India and Pakistan. Sometimes embassy-based espionage incidents emerge between friendly states, and those caught are expelled, without fanfare. Thus, use of embassies for intelligence collection is a normal activity, much more widespread than at first sight.

Most sizable diplomatic systems play host to these covert intelligence officials. They function within the embassy under special internal procedures, and are answerable only in a limited way to the ambassador. The end-product that intelligence systems deliver, i.e. information and predictions relating to international affairs, is similar to what diplomatic systems generate. The primary difference lies in the operational methods that intelligence officials utilize, especially the use of clandestine agents as sources. This justifies the secrecy with which they function, the need to safeguard their techniques, and their exclusive allegiance to their parent organizations. Foreign ministries and diplomatic services do not customarily broadcast the problems created in the functioning of embassies. It is only in special circumstances, like crisis, that these surface in public.

The degree of transparency between the ambassador and intelligence officials depends on the national template, and the nature of autonomy that the intelligence service enjoys at home. Ambassadors are invariably given special instructions on the relationship—hands-off or limited supervision—that they should maintain with their intelligence officials. A typical procedure may be that intelligence officials do not disclose the 'operational' aspects of their work to the ambassador, but are expected to share with him the hard information obtained. They are sometimes required to also show the principal reports that they send to their parent organization. The rationale is that the ambassador may use the important information that has been garnered, adding pieces to the larger mosaic. He should also have an opportunity to comment on the intelligence operative's analysis. Typically, the ambassador is enjoined not to share such information with others within the embassy, not even his deputy.

Some intelligence systems show almost nothing to the envoy, as was the case with the KGB operatives in the erstwhile Soviet embassies.[21] In the US system, while reports sent 'officially' to the CIA, have to be shown to the ambassador, this does not apply to the 'official–informal' communications. Additionally, data sent via 'backchannel' routes is by definition kept clandestine.[22] In real life, the procedure may not work smoothly. Ambassadors sometimes depend on their personal friendships at the home intelligence organizations to obtain cooperation from these officials. Intelligence services are loath to give to ambassadors—and to foreign ministries—complete access to reports. They much prefer to demonstrate to political masters at home their special capabilities. Competition between the MFA and these agencies is a normal state of affairs.

One generic reality is that there may not be much of original value in the intelligence reports! Situations are fairly common where these agents collate information from embassy colleagues, and pass it off to their headquarters as data gathered by themselves.[23] There are worse instances of misdirected or contradictory actions, all of which are preventable through a unified discipline system within the mission. Former Indian Foreign Secretary J.N. Dixit has written graphically about the huge miscalculation made by India in Sri Lanka in 1987, when an 'Indian Peace-Keeping Force' was sent to combat the separatist movement LTTE, based on erroneous calculations of Indian intelligence agencies that ran counter to the advice of both the Indian envoy in Colombo and the Ministry of External Affairs in New Delhi.[24]

The overthrow of the Shah in Iran in 1979 is a well-documented event where the assessment of the envoy on the spot was ignored, and the Carter administration chose to rely on other sources for what turned out to be a gross misjudgment of the ground scene. The common thread in each spectacular intelligence setback abroad is the failure to question assumptions, and the reliance on a single line of analysis. Contributory factors include the unwillingness of intelligence officials to disclose to their own ambassadors their special bits of information, and much worse, to share the analysis they present to their parent agencies. On the other hand, the practical experience of envoys serving at sensitive posts is that where the envoy has a strong personal equation with the head of the intelligence agency, he will receive fulsome cooperation from his intelligence operative, and the entire system will function smoothly.[25] The two professions have much to gain from real cooperation.

Armed service attachés are conceptually different from intelligence officials, in that they are 'declared', handling open and not covert duties, even though there are similarities, in the sense that they collect sensitive information, typically focused on the armed forces of the receiving country, their equipment and state of preparedness, as well as local activities of third country adversaries.[26] An ambassador seldom faces difficulty in dealing with the service attachés; their discipline and hierarchy-orientation generally makes them a positive factor in the internal life of the embassy.[27] One frequent professional weakness of this fine uniformed cadre is a tendency for rivalry with the intelligence officials within the embassy. Also, as with the other officials from outside the diplomatic service, the issue of substantive control over their work remains.[28]

Some of the difficulties in getting the embassy team to operate in a unified manner also apply to the representatives of other departments, although in practice only the large diplomatic services face excessive heterogeneity. An Angola or Bangladesh may have officials from the tourism board, or a commodity export promotion bureau at a major diplomatic capital such as London or Paris, but these specialists have clear-cut work areas of their own, which seldom produce internal contradictions.

The more frequent situation is the presence of a separate set of officials from the foreign trade or commerce ministry, in the case of 'non-integrated' diplomatic services. While countries such as China, Germany, Singapore and the US handle well internal coordination issues created by the separation of commercial and political work, for some other countries of the South, a division of tasks leads to a disconnection between economic and political diplomacy, especially in the way the ambassador is engaged in promotional activity. A single cadre of officials is better placed to handle the full range of economic and political duties than two separate entities.

The core issue is simple. How does an ambassador generate a team spirit out of diversity? Can these officials be persuaded to give more than temporary loyalty to the ambassador? The attributes of leadership are similar in any activity. The leader has to lead from the front, offering personal example, a sense of fairness and personal commitment to an objective that the others are induced to share. For an embassy, the advancement of national interest is a cause that is large enough to mobilize the team, regardless of their origin or permanent affiliation. But team sprit has to be built and sustained through leadership. There is no simple magic formula. In training programs for ambassadors, where these exist, the management of heterogeneity should be an important component, now more important than ever before. This is a theme for the next chapter.

Consuls—Career and Honorary

The consulates general and the consulates operate directly under the supervision of the ambassador.[29] They form a network of subsidiary offices that widen the embassy's reach, providing it the means to engage local authorities at the levels of provinces and cities. Designed for consular and commercial tasks, they extend the outreach and promotion network in other sectors, including the political. Best of all, they give access to the heartland of a large country. Ambassadors find a qualitative difference in the relations established at local levels, often marked by less reserve than in the capital.[30] While local ties can be pursued even without a consulate, an effective local post becomes a powerful intermediary. But the physical separation creates problems of coordination. A system of periodic meetings between the ambassador (accompanied by embassy department heads) and the consuls general is an essential management mechanism.[31] A recent innovation is trade and 'representative' offices in cities outside the capital, sometimes run by local recruits, that are also useful in enlarging the embassy's reach in large countries.[32]

The honorary consul is an unpaid individual who voluntarily undertakes a limited, part-time local role on behalf of a foreign government. Permission is needed from the receiving country, both for establishing the honorary consulate, and for nominating an individual to the post. He or she may receive reimbursement from the appointing country for services (like visa issue or trade promotion assistance). He is usually a national of the receiving country, or a home country citizen long-term resident there. If the honorary consul is well connected and genuinely disposed to helping the country whose flag he flies, he is an invaluable asset for the ambassador. He gets doors opened in business, media and local political sectors.[33] Small countries like Malta, Mauritius and Sri Lanka use the system very effectively, for a presence in places where full representation is not affordable.[34]

Honorary consuls and consuls general are also appointed in foreign capitals by states that cannot afford full-time diplomatic representation, but want their flag to be flown. It is rare for the appointing state to conduct official diplomatic business through these honoraries, but they provide limited consular and commercial services, and are especially helpful when delegations visit the capital.

The downside of the honorary system is that it attracts social climbers and others who seek the glamour of 'joining the consular corps', and enjoying the token immunities that the host country may extend as a courtesy, like exemption from minor parking or traffic violations. Some ego massage is fine, and the ambassador has to take care to keep the honorary consul in good humor. But situations arise where honorary consuls forget to help the country they are supposed to represent. In extreme cases, active local lobbying is conducted by some to obtain appointments, with wily agents emerging to 'market' such opportunists.[35] The ambassador needs great care in recommending a nomination to such posts, since the home authorities have no means or inclination to carry out their own scrutiny. As the man on the spot, he has also to make the system work, and derive full value from it.[36]

Country Team

Apart from the embassy team, there are almost always some nationals from one's own country to be found in foreign capitals—representatives of public sector enterprises and private business, industry or export promotion bodies, journalists from home, as well as professionals such as bankers or engineers working with organizations in the host country. Many of them are well disposed to the advancement of home country interests, in ways that are transparent and do not run counter to the interests of the receiving state. They can be treated as members of the ambassador's 'country team'. Such a definition is wider than the one used in the US, where the term originates, limited to representatives of official and quasi-official agencies.[37] But as we have seen, diplomacy today operates on a more inclusive basis than before. A widely defined country team empowers the envoy's compatriots sharing the vision of the home country, and becomes an act of public–private partnership.

Envoys customarily cultivate good relations with all the categories of the persons mentioned above, so there is nothing new in the fact of such contacts. The novel element is to install a mechanism for a regular two-way dialogue with these potential assets. For instance, the ambassador may find at a particular location in Africa a handful of experts from home working in the host country, some on programs run by the home official agency for technical cooperation, and others working on UN, or other multilateral assignments. Inviting them to periodic discussion meetings not only enables the envoy to communicate information on developments at home (which is traditional), but also to receive their ideas on new opportunities in the political, economic or other sectors. Expanding participation to include those who are not under the ambassador's authority widens the process. The interaction among different experts and professionals produces synergy, and gives the envoy and his team unique insights into the local scene.

In corporate terminology, such groups might be called 'advisory boards'. One general principle in open networking is to ensure that activities are not in contradiction to the interests of the receiving country. Obviously, the extent and manner in which such concepts are put into operation at any location depends on local circumstances. The environment usually provides ample opportunity for adaptation and innovation along the lines sketched above.[38]

Mission Size and Management

The size of diplomatic missions varies greatly. The smallest may have just one official from the sending country—besides a few local staff. The largest may have a total that approaches a thousand. Cuba and Singapore, two very different countries, have in common a reputation for lean missions, and the optimal use of manpower. Most Cuban embassies have just two or three officials from home, with a good number of husband-and-wife teams. Singapore deploys minimal home personnel, and leaves around 50% of its authorized posts abroad vacant. Like some other countries, it makes extensive use of local staff, taking advantage of the fact that at many places, quality support personnel are available, of course for non-sensitive work. They also invest in local staff by sending them on training programs.

Countries view their interests in a particular foreign state in radically different ways. For instance, in 2002, the UK had two home-based officials at its Uzbekistan embassy; France had 17, and Germany 27![39] A comparative study of foreign ministries shows that the average number of personnel in Japanese embassies is 42 (17 from home and 25 local); Germany, 43 (35 and 8); UK, 47 (11 and 36); US, 119 (58 and 61).[40] Thus the ambassador's mission management task depends on the ethos of that diplomatic system.

When J.K. Galbraith arrived in New Delhi as ambassador in 1961, his embassy had 300 home-based officials and 726 Indian employees. He found that many in the diplomatic community were grossly under-worked. With caustic wit, he has described some of the rituals, such as the exchange of ambassadorial courtesy calls among members of the diplomatic corps and the endless rounds of entertainment, calling these 'a valuable alternative to unemployment'.[41]

Globally, the trend is for smaller diplomatic missions, driven by cuts in national budgets, and a downsizing of government machinery. It is also a byproduct of technology application. Some routine service functions (especially consular work and responses to routine commercial inquires) are being transferred to cheaper 'back-office' locations at home, as noted earlier. A leaner embassy magnifies the management challenge, but also produces tighter focus on the core objectives of diplomacy, forcing stronger prioritization. Australia, New Zealand and the smaller European states are among the pioneers of these new methods. My experience has been that even a small reduction in personnel helps the embassy to focus on its tasks, and reduces the latitude for frivolous internal disputation.

Another development is a more extensive use of local staff, and an investment in training them to improve their skills. Australia, Canada, the UK and the US are trend leaders, driven in part by the fact that such personnel often cost 20% or less than home-based personnel, and provide continuity as well. Devoting attention to their welfare and morale pays handsomely for the envoy.

The Spouse and Families

Diplomatic history is replete with instances where the ambassador's wife played a vital, and usually unrecognized, role as a team member with the husband, both in the past when living abroad was an adventure, often accompanied by hazard, and in contemporary times. It has always been tacitly understood that the spouse has a direct responsibility for oversight of morale among spouses and children within the 'extended family' of home-based embassy officials. A contemporary ambassador in Washington DC has noted, echoing others, that in capitals marked by an acute competition for 'access' to high officials and politicians, the personal contacts established by the ambassador's wife can be the real determinant in ensuring that their dinners and receptions attract the top priority targets needed for cultivation and outreach.[42] But the diplomatic spouse of today often has an independent career and interests. How do these changes impact on the envoy?

First, 'the notion of "serving one's country" in the capacity of being a helpmate is becoming outdated', writes Dr Annabel Hendry of the British Diplomatic Spouses' Association.[43] With two-career couples increasingly the norm, it can no longer be assumed by diplomatic services that the female spouse will be automatically available to act as an unpaid second half of the ambassadorial team, a vital adjunct in his representational entertainment, as also a substantive companion for contact-building and outreach activities. Second, the 'ambassadress', a quaint British term for the female spouse, was the focus of an entertaining study, *Daughters of Britannia*.[44] It notes that in 1998, 13% of the spouses of diplomats in the UK service were male. One consequence has been that various associations of diplomatic 'wives' have changed names to gender-neutral 'spouse' associations. Another change is that a certain proportion of diplomatic male spouses have gradually slipped into homemaker roles. This has produced a term, used half in humor, *Monsieur l'Ambassadrice*.[45] Third, it is now harder than ever to get the ambassador's spouse to automatically take on responsibility—unpaid—for running the residence as a representational duty, overseeing official entertainment, and receiving official house-guests. The British Diplomatic Spouses' Association runs two-day courses that focus on catering skills, to assist spouses to take on responsibility for the large scale entertainment that is the ambassador's obligation, on national days, and special events such as major incoming visits. We witness a trend for major events being held in hotels and conference facilities, but the official residence remains the venue of choice. One solution is for the spouse to be paid for the home management function. In the UK this is implemented via an application made by the spouse to take on the job of 'housekeeper' of the residence, and payment is made on local employee terms. Another method, used by Canada and some others, is to pay a spouse allowance to those that accompany the diplomat abroad—unlike the housekeeper allowance, this is not limited to the ambassadorial spouse. Fourth, until recent times it was anathema for the spouse to take up employment locally. Even those professionally qualified, like doctors and teachers, were forbidden to take up paying jobs. Part-time work in an honorary capacity was often permitted, with advance permission. This is changing. Some countries now apply no restrictions. For instance, in 2001 India permitted local employment for the spouses of heads of missions, having some years earlier liberalized the rules for other embassy officials.

A few countries allow the ambassador's spouse to be employed in the same mission, if he/she is qualified. When the People's Republic of China sent out senior party cadres and generals as its first envoys after 1949, the wives of ambassadors were not allowed to work. In the early 1950s, some of them threatened to divorce their husbands, and Premier Zhou Enlai was forced to send his wife to mollify them, and change the rules, which enabled many of them to work in a senior capacity within the embassy.[46] Cuba has a large number of husband-and-wife teams posted together. But these are rarities. In most countries, if the spouse is part of a tandem couple and both are of ambassador rank, almost automatically the best they can expect is an assignment in neighboring countries, which hardly means proximity on a vast continent like Africa or South America. When even this is not possible, the two ambassadors serve out their careers at vast geographical distances.[47]

The Residence and Entertainment

'Above all do not fail to give good dinners, and pay attention to women', counseled Napoleon to his Ambassador in London in 1802.[48] This crusty advice is of timeless value. Any ambassador seeking influence and access in the country of his assignment understands the value of social interaction and good manners as essential professional skills.

The official residence is a symbol of the home country, a kind of mirror to the personality of the ambassador, and his spouse.[49] Its *raison d'être* is representational entertainment. A fair bit of diplomatic work is conducted in social settings, especially that part that we have identified as outreach and promotion—networking and dialogue at receptions and meals which the envoy hosts, or where he is a guest. His government provides ample public space for entertainment at the residence, in the shape of reception and dining rooms, and all the ancillary facilities. It is customary to set apart at least one bedroom suite for official guests. Some countries provide a full guest wing for high-level dignitaries and their immediate staff. For instance, every Nepalese ambassador's residence must have accommodation for members of the country's royal family for their visits to that capital. The British custom is that unless a visiting minister from home is accommodated by the hosts in a special guesthouse, he normally stays at the envoy's residence, in preference to a hotel—though this is no longer rigidly applied. Members of the British royal family often stay at the envoy's residence, unless they are offered official hospitality. Other countries leave it to individual choice whether the ambassador puts up high-ranking official guests. At places of security hazard, or to deal with emergencies, such accommodation at the residence becomes useful.[50]

Maintaining and operating the envoy's residence is expensive, especially the large historic properties that big countries own in major capitals. The costs include: regular upkeep of the property to high standards; professional gardening services, and cleaning and maintenance of the public rooms (i.e. usually excluding the personal apartment of the envoy); plus staff to provide household and entertainment services, sometimes supervised by a housekeeper; and a resident cook—or even a set of cooks; Japanese envoys in major capitals often have two master chefs supplied by *Gaimusho*, one each for Japanese and French cuisine. The French, the British and other major powers likewise provide full-time chefs for their principal ambassadors. The envoy also needs reliable access to temporary service personnel for large events. Developing countries do not send full-time chefs or other personal staff, and in consequence, compromise arrangements are made, often to the dissatisfaction of the envoys concerned, and leading to the inadequate use of the residence for entertainment.[51] The custom among the embassies of 'socialist' countries in the past, representing the Soviet Union and East Europe, was to provide ample public rooms within the chancery complex or in a special entertainment villa that formed part of the embassy estate, to be used by the ambassador and his senior colleagues. Such shared diplomatic entertainment centers are still used by China and a few others, as a poor substitute for social entertainment at the envoy's home.

The goal is always to offer high-class hospitality, without being too ostentatious. This is usually financed via the 'representation grant', a special sum of money paid to the envoy, to cover the cost of official entertainment. The size of the grant depends on the norms laid down in that country's diplomatic system, such as the location, and the envoy's seniority. In most cases it is sufficient for the country's objectives, though the quantum varies considerably between rich and poor countries. The grant is usually supplemented with special funds for major events, like a high-level incoming visit, or the launch of a major exhibition. Other diplomats in the mission have their own representation grants or allowances, but some countries provide a single amount to the head of mission, leaving to him the distribution—sometimes leading to malpractice or unfairness.

Diplomatic entertainment has multiple objectives. One is to create a setting that generates access to influential persons. It enables the host to persuade and influence his guests. It also provides a forum for a visiting delegation or others from home to converse with useful people, and to promote their business. For instance, it may enable a visiting parliamentarian to meet a cross-section of people that he wants to influence. It can also enable a visiting businessman to project a credible image of the standing of his enterprise to a potential local partner, or flatter his local contacts with access to the ambassador's residence. The structure and atmosphere of the event is adapted to facilitate that objective, be it a working lunch for intimate dialogue, or a glittering reception featuring a music performance, or a fashion show, to act as a social magnet for broad outreach. Presenting an authentic ambience of the host country, its cuisine and its culture, burnishes the country image. Social visibility is also an image goal.

Often it is the small function that provides the best setting for the ambassador's representational activity, facilitating relaxed conversation. This is often favored in lieu of big events. But in practice, the ambassador offers a mix of events, tailored to the circumstances. The craft of good hospitality is acquired by observation and practice, and goes beyond the rules of table seating-plans, or the selection of wines that go with particular dishes. The ambassador has a special obligation to expose and train young colleagues to this art and technique.

Despite the vast sums spent on the residence, an increasing number of ambassadors take an easy way out and entertain outside the residence. Hotel reception rooms and restaurants may offer convenience, but are poor alternatives, not just for traditionalists. Major diplomatic players regard official entertainment outside the residence as an inadequate substitute to the special ambience that the envoy's home provides. The exceptions are a reception during a conference, or the permanent representative's working lunch at New York or Geneva. Since the function of 'representation' lies at the root of the envoy's work, the residence is the mandated, ideal setting.

That hardy perennial, the ambassador's large reception, particularly in celebration of national days, is undergoing a slow evolution. Many envoys treat it as an inescapable obligation that allows them to return hospitality to a large number, especially diplomatic colleagues, in a single gesture. A few question the utility of a mass event where the host and his spouse meet properly with almost no one at all, busy as they are in the receiving line, where the principals that show up come out of obligation, and some of the crowd that actually attends consists of individuals that hardly anyone in the embassy knows. Countries such as Australia have abandoned the big national day diplomatic bash, and are shifting to smaller events in other cities in rotation, using these to build connections with regional officials and others.[52]

In many diplomatic systems, the foreign ministry's oversight of the quality and effectiveness of the ambassador's representational entertainment is inadequate—some argue that it amounts to micromanagement; someone entrusted with representing the country's interests should not be subject to petty regulation. In fact, the issue involves not just the efficient utilization of public funds, but also the manner in which a core task is performed. It is imperative for the diplomatic system to establish uniform norms, encouraging envoys to perform the representational role effectively. In major diplomatic services, such an accountability is implemented through a detailed monthly statement of the ambassador's representational activity sent to headquarters for scrutiny, the same way that the ambassador scrutinizes the representational expenditure of all embassy officials. The enforcement of oversight is a measure of professionalism. This is one area that inspectors examine closely, when embassy inspections are carried out.

Sometimes public criticism surfaces on the representational entertainment by envoys, usually based on the disclosure by aggrieved individuals within the system. Ostentation and excessive costs draw comment, as does the opposite kind of situation where ambassadors are accused of under-spending the funds for the intended purposes, and living off their entertainment budgets.[53]

In the face of the high costs of these symbols of diplomacy, a contrarian's view is beginning to emerge, that expensive official accommodation for the envoy is *dépassé*, unnecessary in contemporary times. If representational entertainment moves from homes to hotels, some of the rationale for lavish ambassadorial residences disappears. But for reasons of prestige, major countries are unlikely to abandon glitzy residences for envoys. After all, the physical assets already exist in most world capitals, the prime properties that governments own in foreign capitals. The inertia of practice and entrenched interests would surely block any shift from this traditional model. Economy and function are a factor, but in a complex, globalized world, the lure of symbols is ever strong.

Other changes have emerged to cope with high costs; one is 'corporatized' entertainment, with business enterprises meeting a part of national day reception expenditure, or completely funding a special event, say for business promotion, where the ambassador acts only as the nominal host.[54] We should expect to see this applied more widely, as an aspect of public–private partnership that is a dominant trend of our times. If such practices become more widespread, they would provide a fresh lease of life for the existing pattern of high-profile residences and conspicuous entertainment.

7

◆

HUMAN RESOURCES

A professional diplomat's career prior to his first ambassadorial assignment is an apprenticeship, a time for learning, harvesting experience, honing skills, and expanding one's personal horizon. In most diplomatic services, the career progression to an ambassadorship is a realistic goal for each official of normal competence.[1] But in the US, new entrants to the Foreign Service are warned that they must not expect to become ambassadors; out of an average annual intake of about 300, perhaps 5% make this rank. The non-career ambassador is in a different situation, having spent a lifetime in a different field, coming to diplomacy ideally as a person of eminence in his or her field, to learn the rudiments of a new profession.

Training and Conferences

Let us first look at the training of non-career ambassadors. In countries that appoint non-career ambassadors rarely, no special programs exist. In the US, non-career ambassadors attend a week-long course at the Foreign Service Institute, located within the National Foreign Affairs Training Center, on an attractive 75-acre campus in Arlington. Though not limited to non-career envoys, the course is specially designed for them. It covers basic familiarization, and an introduction to embassy and State Department procedures, rudiments of protocol, and the like. Some critics assert that it is not a serious exercise that teaches the skills of effective ambassadorship. But in the majority of African and Asian countries that make extensive use of non-professional talent, no training is given at all. At best, their customary initial briefing at the foreign ministry may be stretched to cover the basics of protocol, and the administrative regulations that the head of mission is expected to uphold. Such a lack of grounding handicaps non-career envoys at the outset, contributing to problems over levels or modes of communication to the foreign ministry, and the handling of embassy human resources.

Canada requires all ambassadors, whether on first appointment or at a final pre-retirement assignment—including its few non-professionals—to attend an intensive two-week training program, devoted to all aspects of running the embassy, including management methods, new technology and techniques relevant to their work.[2] Probably the most intensive training for ambassadors is run by China, a two-month program held thrice a year, compulsory for all. Besides conventional training, it includes high-level briefings by senior leaders and ministers, plus site visits and travel to the provinces, showcasing new developments in the country. Informal interaction within the group also leads to experience sharing. Everywhere, the training for envoys is more essential than ever, and it is a wonder that more countries do not follow this practice. The traditional excuse, that officials cannot be spared, is simply irrational.

What should be the content of an ideal training program for ambassadors? Their typical 20 years or more of service experience is their craft base. We assume that the training mainly takes the shape of experience-sharing in seminar formats, and that the focus is on both knowledge and skills. We stipulate that the faculty consists of senior and possibly retired diplomats, as well as specialists from fields like international affairs, management and human resources, plus scholars. The program may cover: first, a dialogue with the architects of contemporary national goals and policies—to give the ambassador identity with home objectives. Second, an issue-oriented analysis of international affairs, including relations with key countries and the way these impact on the country or region where the envoy is based. Third, an understanding of the objectives of the line ministries and departments engaged in foreign affairs, plus the interconnections between the different functional areas as seen by these agencies. Fourth, contemporary management techniques, and technology, as relevant to the optimal running of the mission, and fifth, public diplomacy skills, plus contacts with the domestic foreign affairs community, especially its non-official segments, and the concerns of these stakeholders.

In the armed forces, the appointment to flag rank is preceded by an attendance at a war college or an equivalent institution, i.e. mandatory training in higher command, through lectures, seminars and simulation exercises. A limited training opportunity is given to other civil service officials in mid-career and senior-level training programs, organized by their own training institutions. But unlike in the armed forces, most civil services do not treat management training as an essential precondition to holding responsibility at apex levels.

Some countries, such as France, Germany, Japan, Russia, and the UK among others, rely on a part-substitute—an annual conference of all ambassadors, convened in the capital, usually coinciding with annual leave so as to economize on travel costs. This gathering is used for two-way communication, and if handled well, becomes a major learning and knowledge transmission event for the ambassadors, as also for the senior hierarchy of foreign ministry officials who attend. The ambassadors also receive high-level directives on policy goals, and briefings on all relevant aspects of the country's economy and the like. The German Foreign Office structures its conference in the shape of committees that examine particular issues, and produce recommendations for the entire system.

An alternative to jumbo gatherings of all ambassadors is the regional conference, convened at opportune times and locations, for instance coinciding with a major visit abroad by the president or prime minister, or by the foreign minister, provided that event gives time to accommodate such a conference. For instance, India sometimes holds such meetings under the chairmanship of the External Affairs Minister or a minister of state, for envoys in say Central Asia, or Latin America, in the midst of a foreign tour. This ad hoc device signals interest in a relatively neglected region. The high dignitary who nominally chairs the meeting cannot always give it sufficient attention, in the midst of his bilateral visit or regional conference.[3] Nor is there a sustained follow-up of decisions. In contrast, the countries that have institutionalized the annual conference generally devise a mechanism for the implementation of decisions that flow from it.[4]

The bulk of developing countries do not use the annual conference method, for reasons of cost. For all but the very smallest diplomatic services this is false economy, because if it is worthwhile to expend resources on a network of resident missions abroad, it is even more vital to derive full value from them. If ambassadors are not kept fully abreast of home developments, they cannot function effectively. To cope with the changing requirements of diplomacy, broad-based and continuous training is imperative. Annual or periodic conferences of all ambassadors are a partial substitute.[5]

Personal Qualities

In ancient India, emissaries were routinely sent on temporary missions by kings and princes; resident ambassadors were unknown. The *Arthashastra* (see Introduction), declares: 'Envoys are the mouthpieces of kings. They must carry out their own instructions and it would be wrong to put them to death, even if they were outcastes.'[6] The Laws of Manu, a commentary that emerged some centuries later, states: 'An ambassador should be versed in all the sciences; he should understand hints, questions and expressions of the face; he should be honest, skillful and of good family.'[7] Comparable admonitions are to be found in the ancient texts of other civilizations that deal with the dispatch of envoys.

What are the qualities traditionally sought in the resident envoy? Harold Nicolson's pre-World War II definition is timeless:

A man of experience, integrity and intelligence, a man of resources, good temper and courage, a man above all who is not swayed by emotion or prejudice, who is profoundly modest in all his dealings, who is guided by a sense of public duty, and who understands the perils of cleverness and the virtues of reason, moderation, discretion, patience and tact.[8]

A classic nostrum of diplomacy has been Talleyrand's advice: 'Above all, avoid an excess of enthusiasm.' It suited the age of the stiff upper lip and of detached reserve that was often admired in the envoy. Today one might misinterpret that advice to mean passivity, or an aversion to proactive methods, which misses the point. Zeal is good, when tempered by good judgment. Consider Benjamin Franklin's enduring advice: 'Sleepless tact, unmovable calmness, and a patience no folly, provocation or blunders may shake.'[9]

Changed times mean transformed working conditions, and this naturally affects the skill-sets needed. Life was simple, more predictable when the ambassador operated within narrow, intimate circles of fellow-professionals of the host country with whom values, style and dialogue syntax were shared. This was also true of the diplomatic corps, which too offered stronger shared bonds than today. The ambassador must today confidently deal with regional and local politicians outside the capital, or others whom he may find boorish, as also with supercilious academics, reclusive scientists, and suspicious, self-styled representatives of 'civil society', many of whom have their own antipathy to officials of any kind. In place of reticence and aloofness, he must practice the common touch, reaching out to new non-state partners. Promotion obligations also require salesmanship. This calls for an open attitude, as well as flexibility, shifting from one style to another, as needed.

Yet, completely unchanged is the cardinal need for integrity, personal honesty and a personality that evokes confidence, combined with sound communication skills. The envoy needs a telegenic personality, to be as Raymond Cohen has observed 'also a TV performer!'[10] This adds up to a formidable list, that we seek a paragon of virtue and talent. Is this a realistic set of demands? Yes, if we acknowledge that the pursuit of excellence is a necessity at the apex of any profession.

Consider the issue of honesty. The old witticism of Sir Henry Wotton, the honest man sent to lie abroad for the country's good, deserves but an endnote.[11] In real life, the ambassador does face moral dilemmas in situations where the complete truth may not sit well with the country's interest and his instructions. The pragmatic middle path then is to 'economize' with the truth; confining oneself to a narration of the points that support one's own case. But it is counter-productive to deliberately engage in an untruthful démarche. The envoy loses credibility and effectiveness if he is found out. Such a compromise may sound contrived, but it is aligned with the simple advice proffered by the Indian sage Manu, two millennia back: 'Speak the truth but not the unpleasant; speak the pleasant but not the untruth.' As one interviewed ambassador observed, the outcome of a diplomatic démarche may hinge on the interlocutor's subjective decision: do I take a risk and act as the envoy demands? The envoy's chances for success improve greatly if he is believed, in a relationship of trust.[12]

Professional Skills

One reason that diplomacy practitioners are insufficiently recognized as professionals is that their skills and expertise are 'soft', not sharply etched. Moreover, diplomacy makes no claim to uniqueness in its core expertise; those same skills are applicable to other activities as well. A lawyer or a chartered accountant does not face a similar problem, since his skill possesses a distinctiveness. The diplomat's defining expertise is a broad compendium of knowledge, craft and skills, none of which are arcane or hard to access. But as we see below, it is this complete collection that is the profession's unique hallmark.

Let us examine this in terms of the new skills the ambassadors will need in the 21st century. From the perspective of adaptation to the working environment, the diplomat should master three skill sets, whatever be his or her job assignment. These are political diplomacy, economic diplomacy and media-image-public diplomacy, intertwined together as integrated diplomacy. First, with an expanded range of topics entering diplomatic exchanges, the ambassador will need a breadth of knowledge, plus a native curiosity to inquire into new subjects, together with an awareness of his own limitations. He should be able to deal with diverse experts, relating their knowledge to his holistic goal—managing and building country relationships. Some corporate leaders call this requirement, also applicable in work sectors, a 'broad-band' ability.[13] Second, the ambassador needs to comprehend the societal processes in his home country. The blurring of the internal–external boundary makes this essential. This includes the envoy's extensive travel and contact-building in the home country.[14] But more is needed, such as the 'senior fellowship' programs of the US State Department, where high-ranking foreign service officers spend a year working on a study of their choice, related to developments within the country, and traveling to meet domestic constituents. A similar result is achieved through assigning diplomats to attend senior civil service and defense college training programs, interacting with domestic counterparts. All these activities should receive a stronger impetus. Third, an understanding of economics is already a *sine qua non* for the profession. The ambassador needs to understand the national and international macro-economic forces that shape his country's agenda. For instance, he must comprehend the impact of globalization on his country, as also the WTO process and the operation of the World Bank and the IMF, since they impact on bilateral diplomacy almost as much as on multilateral economic diplomacy. He must master the operational methodology of economic promotion, in order to assume a personal leadership of this activity. Fourth, media skills have long featured in the ambassador's répertoire; they gain in importance. The envoy is required to proactively 'exploit' the media of the country of assignment as an instrument to access and to engender favorable opinion. Equally vital are image-building skills, and the methods of public diplomacy. Fifth, thinking skills are often taken for granted. The French with their superb *'Grandes Écoles'* system that produces the bulk of civil servants and diplomats, might argue that this ability is built into their system. Other countries, like Singapore and South Africa, rely on self-development and motivation gurus like Edward de Bono of 'lateral thinking' fame, and Stephen Covey, of *The Seven Habits of Highly Effective People*, and others. Innovative thinking is a professional requirement for the ambassador, more than ever before.[15]

Underlying all these is a mindset of cross-cultural openness, a sharp awareness of one's environment, and an interest in the dynamics of societal change. Of course, a fascination with international affairs is taken for granted.

Language and Other Expertise

Like diplomats, the ambassador who knows the local language carries an inherent advantage. The extent of gain depends on the language culture in that country. For instance, an ignorance of the French language would be a serious handicap in Paris, while at The Hague, the inability to speak Dutch may matter less because local officials and others are not culturally averse to using English, and most of the people one will encounter speak English well. Then there are countries such as Italy or Germany, where English can be understood reasonably well, but without a comprehension of Italian or German, the envoy will be at sea in following the TV, and have virtually no access to the print media. Nor can this envoy follow speeches at the many public functions that he is required to attend, where customarily no interpretation or post-event translation is provided. The situation in countries with strong language differentiation like China, Japan, Russia, or in the Arab world, is more difficult.[16] Even in Third World countries where English or another international link language predominates, it is the local language that gives access to the regional media and to wide contacts.[17]

With language ability goes country or regional expertise. Typically a diplomat-linguist will have spent one or two substantive assignments at an early part of his career in his area of specialization. This produces insight and background knowledge that is always an asset. It becomes a vehicle for connections with people, in that country and in diplomacy-related fraternities (diplomats, journalists, scholars and businessmen). Consequently, major diplomatic services require new entrants to learn one major foreign language, and thereafter to maintain their language skills.[18] Through such a system, the diplomatic system provides itself with a range of officials at varying levels of seniority, covering all major and regional languages, relevant to its context.[19]

Not all career ambassadors are linguists in their assignment country, but in selecting the envoy, such an expertise would be a strong desirable, though not an imperative. Large, well-run services have a language pool for selection. Mid-sized services, especially those with a high ratio of embassies, in relation to total personnel, cannot afford to rigidly apply the language requirement. Small services do not have the manpower to apply this criterion.

In the mid-1990s, Japan saw an unusual language 'reward' formula, an informal grouping of about a dozen Japanese-speaking ambassadors stationed in Tokyo. Named '*Heisei-kai*', it was constituted by the ambassadors themselves, with the encouragement of the Foreign Ministry.[20] Meeting in social gatherings several times a year, they got access to members of the royal family and were taken on special outings, ostensibly to practice their language skills. The Japanese establishment indirectly signals that such an inner circle also improves access to the distinctive Japanese culture. A leading Japanese daily commented: '...The dispatch of Japanese-speaking ambassadors shows the stance of these countries to place importance on their relations with Japan.'[21] The author is not aware of a comparable language encouragement system, but it merits cautious emulation.[22]

The foreign ministry has the option of giving intensive language training to ambassadors, whether or not they come from the career track. Using intensive 'immersion' methods, working knowledge of a language can be acquired in three or four months, if the individual is sufficiently motivated. Major Western services and others like the Chinese and the Russians use this option, but most other diplomatic services do not offer language training, partly on the ground that senior personalities do not have time for full-time training. Nor do they routinely pay for such courses, even if an individual envoy wishes to join one.

There is also the functional expertise that a diplomatic service needs in its ambassadors. For instance, there are assignments where the requirement of economic diplomacy is particularly strong, be it of the bilateral genre (as in the capital of a major economic partner) or of the multilateral variety (e.g. at Brussels). There may be other special skills that are needed for particular assignments, like expertise in disarmament and security affairs, WTO affairs, environmental negotiations and the like. No individual can master all these, but via career planning and focused skill developments, the service as a whole builds up its collection of such experts at all levels.

Most diplomatic systems debated whether their officials should be 'generalists' or specialists. The broad consensus today is that the era of the pure generalist, with no particular expertise of his own, is over. At the other extreme, dividing up the system into separate, self-contained sub-groups of 'kremlinologists', 'sinologists' and 'arabists' (customary among major Western services until some 40 years back), no longer works. China was the last bastion of fairly rigid area specialization, up to the mid-1990s. It now routinely rotates all diplomats, including ambassadors, to regions outside their base speciality, to broaden experience.[23] In contrast, the mid-sized and small services could never afford over-specialization, and have always practiced flexible deployment.

The net conclusion is that today's envoy is a hybrid, a kind of 'generalist–specialist', possessing broad-spectrum skills that cover most professional subjects, but also rooted in his individual base of language, regional and functional expertise. We have seen earlier that he combines a knowledge of bilateral diplomacy with multilateral skills, and is equally familiar with work at the foreign ministry, and the field. In particular he needs the leadership skills as directly relevant to this profession, including the ability to work with specialists, and to find interconnections and bridges between different functional areas as they affect external relationships. He offers living proof of diplomacy as a true profession with its specific skills and craftsmanship.

Career Management

At a career diplomat's first head of mission appointment, diverse strands of experience come together, including some seemingly routine activities of the early years—like protocol, consular and report-drafting jobs. His knowledge base is built through training, observation, work participation, plus assimilation from mentors. The early years are formative. Those fortunate to have served with good ambassadors start with a distinct advantage; the lessons of the first appointment, positive or negative, endure through the individual's career. That is one more reason for foreign ministries to send trainees to the very best heads of missions.

'Career planning' involves more than charting a future path in the way it suits the individual official. Well-managed diplomatic services devote sustained attention to this task. By the time an official has completed the first two or three appointments, with a service record of 7 to 10 years, a tentative outline of future potential is discernible, like that official's points of strength, special ability and aptitudes. With this, it becomes feasible to guide his or her career along tracks that are best suited to the full development of that potential, plus optimal HR utilization for the service as a whole. Some examples illustrate this.

Singapore uses an assessment system called 'Current Estimated Potential' to identify the likely level that each official will reach around the age of 40 to 49, that is, after roughly 20 years of service. The result of this annual confidential exercise is not communicated to the official. It identifies what that service calls his or her 'helicopter potential', and places the best on a fast career track. They are sent on skill-enhancing assignments, preparing them for higher responsibility. The diplomatic service accepts the method as dispassionate and fair, given the strong efficiency-oriented, elite-driven ethos of the island state.

In Germany, for the first ten years of service, a 'cohort' of a particular year moves together, with promotions to the rank of first secretary coming almost simultaneously. By this time, the potential high flyers have identified themselves, first by opting to work at the Foreign Office, and second by positioning themselves in highly demanding assignments that attract notice, like the staff of the minister or a state secretary. The fast track operates quite rapidly thereafter, and by the end of the 20th year of service, the very brightest may be abroad serving as ambassadors in the highest of the ranks available, that of *Ministerialdirektor*, or at the Foreign Office in the higher rung of state secretary.[24] In contrast, the laggards of that same cohort may still be at the rank of counselor, holding that level for the rest of their career.

The Indian system is a complete contrast, owing to the distrust of the entire civil service in 'merit' as a promotion criterion.[25] Consequently, promotion depends on seniority.[26] Selectivity is applied only within the 'batch' or cohort, and even here, seniority is the leading factor. Those officials that are identified as having reached the limits of potential are not promoted, but in practice barely 15 or 20 % are left out, at the final two rungs. Where real selectivity comes into play is in the assignments for ambassadors. India appoints ambassadors in three grades, equivalent to the ranks in the central administration of: secretary to the government, additional secretary and joint secretary.[27] In recent years, a few heads of missions appointed to key assignments like Beijing, Dacca and Islamabad have belonged to the lowest of the ambassadorial grades, on the eve of their next promotion. This is possible because grade seniority is not attached to posts. Flexibility in small services is fine, but it undermines morale when relatively junior ambassadors are sent to the most sensitive posts.[28] In 2003 there has been public discussion about the entire civil service shifting to merit-determined promotions, but this is unlikely to see early implementation.[29]

There is one serious limitation in systems that identify potential ambassadors at an early stage, giving them a fast promotion track. Different assignments provide varying degrees of 'visibility', i.e. an opportunity to impress high officials. This leads to a bias favoring those who serve at prominent locations, like the permanent mission in New York or the staff of high personalities. It is essential to cast a wide net, paying equal attention to talented individuals at other places, even the boondocks. If they are ignored, the fast track becomes a source of internal friction and demoralization, as has been the experience of some advanced countries.[30]

Diplomatic services are self-contained and do not permit easy lateral movement to another home service. Consequently, they have a problem in deploying individuals who have reached the limit of their potential, and cannot be promoted. Foreign ministries have a few jobs where an awkward individual can be tucked away, in a kind of limbo. But there is a finite limit to those that can be so accommodated. Other methods are used to deal with what amounts to surplus middle-senior level staff. Examples: placing individuals on 'administrative leave'; sending off a few to academic institutions that are willing to receive them as 'ambassadors in residence' (often with the tab picked up by the foreign ministry); and imaginatively creating temporary jobs outside the foreign ministry (dispatch to subsidiary offices or on deputations to other agencies). The US and some others have an 'up-or-out' system, with a limit on the number of years that one may spend in a middle grade; thereafter, non-promotion leads to compulsory retirement. Some services implement a 'golden handshake' formula from time to time, to get rid of deadweight.[31] In many countries, social conditions rule out such methods.

Most foreign ministries have in their portfolio ambassadorial assignments to places of peripheral importance. Career diplomats who have been passed over for promotion are often sent to such places. These grace appointments occur in most large services. In mid-sized services with an extensive network of missions, such appointments of 'unpromotable' officials may occur even at early career stages. Since these officials are unsuitable for work in the foreign ministry, they rotate from one 'minor' ambassadorship to another. Of course, this is inefficient and potentially dangerous. Even places of tertiary importance may suddenly become prominent, in our volatile world. A lack of promotion selectivity is at the root of the problem.

The Ethical Dimension

Writing on the genesis of the diplomatic corps, G.R. Berridge has noted that diplomats had 'professional interests that united them as professionals, as well as political and commercial interests that divided them'.[32] Do these professional interests include a higher, professional morality that unites them, beyond their responsibilities as representatives of their own countries? Is this particularly true of the multilateral envoy?

Like any civil servant, the ambassador owes a high, overriding loyalty to the state, and is subject to its disciplinary system. At appointment, or on joining the public service, officials customarily swear an oath of loyalty and secrecy. The ambassador's Letter of Commission charges him with upholding the country's interests.

This responsibility cannot be lightly cast aside. The question arises, is he just an agent of the state? Does he sustain any other higher, or concurrent, responsibility?

Diplomacy guru Harold Nicolson evoked the values of another age in his classic work *Diplomacy*:

> The professional diplomatist is governed by several different, and at times conflicting loyalties. He owes a loyalty to his own sovereign, government, minister and foreign office; he owes loyalty to his own staff; he owes a form of loyalty to the diplomatic body in the capital where he resides; he owes loyalty to the local expatriate community and to its commercial interests; and he owes another form of loyalty to the government to which he is accredited and to the minister with whom he negotiates.[33]

An ambassador working in the circumstances of the 21st century would probably find difficult the notion of 'a form of loyalty' to either the host government or the diplomatic corps of which he is a member. There is no gainsaying the *professional obligations* that he holds towards both the entities, of course each of different shape and texture. These obligations center on his need to sustain credibility with the receiving state and his fellow envoys. They can also be seen as essential conditions that facilitate his work, framing the environment within which he operates. But they do not constitute 'loyalty', however broadly one might define the word; they cannot compare, substantively or figuratively, with his permanent commitment to his own country and people. Internationalists and cosmopolitan idealists may dispute this assertion, but diplomacy practitioners would surely see the practical logic.

A possible exception is diplomats whose specialized work makes them members of an epistemic community, i.e. a network of those sharing professional interests that advance national interests, for instance, multilateralists such as permanent representatives and other diplomats that work on EU affairs, or those engaged on functional specialities like international environmental negotiations. It has been observed that such envoys, while representing countries, also work to advance other concurrent interests, such as those of the unification process within Europe.[34] These instances indicate that the pursuit of what may look like extra-national 'obligations' is in fact a long-perspective national interest promotion, with no cross-cutting clash of loyalties.

Abba Eban graphically sketched a different professional dilemma of the ambassador:

> Since the ambassador is often alienated from his [or her] country and thrown into close contact with people from other lands, he tends to develop a closer affinity with his professional colleagues than with his fellow citizens at home. He is very vulnerable. On the one hand he is the articulate champion of his country's interests. Indeed his basic function is to get as much as possible for his country while giving as little as possible in return. But he is more obliged than any other public servant to perceive the limitations of national attitudes and seek legitimacy for his positions in terms of a broader public ideal.[35]

The communication channels at the envoy's disposal, especially the widely distributed cipher message, ensure that his advice reaches the highest decision-makers. Let us keep in mind also the fact that counterparts in the home civil or defense services, who may confront similar agony over the moral dimensions of the actions of their governments, seldom have comparable means of registering their disagreement directly to the highest authorities of the country. We may view the ambassador's professional grievance channels as a special privilege offered to the personal representative of the head of state. But as noted earlier, the cipher message or other communication addressed to the high authorities are two-edged, and can easily hurt the sender, when used unwisely. Governments and their leaders do not take kindly to advice that runs counter to their own predilections, however well meant. The dissenting envoy walks on a razor's edge, and must act with prudence and long-term calculation

The fact that instances of ambassadors resigning from their posts are rare, even in times of foreign affairs crisis that divides the home public, indicates that in reality such dilemmas are few and far between. One should proceed from this pragmatic fact, and not overstate the ethical problem. The ambassador does not have to wear his patriotism on his sleeve, but like all public officials, he has a natural inclination to defend his country's interests.

An envoy representing a failing state, one that faces collapse, or one ruled by an autocratic regime that has come to the end of the road, be it Iraq in early 2003 or the North Korean regime in our times, faces a personal dilemma, where professional and family obligations present stark choices. Each situation of this nature is unique and leads to its own dénouement. One can only sympathize with the ambassador and his staff who must choose in the midst of conflicting obligations, compounded by gross uncertainty.

Rogue Ambassadors

Every diplomatic service has its skeletons in the closet, which include willful misdeeds by its ambassadors. Foreign ministries invest much effort to keep such incidents out of public scrutiny, even after internal inquiries are held, and punishment dispensed. Numbers are misleading as only a few emerge in the public eye. Such cases are of two kinds: misdemeanors of a personal character, and those that involve professional misconduct. The former generate salacious interest, but it is the latter that produce a more serious impact. An example: in the 1970s, a Western ambassador in the former German Democratic Republic was caught handing over sensitive official documents to a local intelligence agency. In the acute phase of the Cold War there would have been other incidents of a similar nature, often involving 'honey traps' that were hushed up.

There is something about the isolation of command—again the analogy with the ship's captain is apt—that sometimes leads ambassadors into actions that are patently wrong, in terms of financial impropriety or personal conduct that may involve individuals under their charge, behavior in the country of assignment and financial wrongdoing. Rarely, personal and professional misconduct are blended together.[36]

Personal indiscretions may be of several different kinds. First, there are the romantic liaisons, often the result of isolation and frequent family separation. For local observers in any capital, the diplomatic corps resembles a glass fish bowl, and indiscretions by ambassadors or their spouses become the talk of the town, till the next happening. Second, there are financial scandals, often involving property deals or corruption over business deals where the envoy has been paid a commission. Such incidents used to be rare, but with the closer engagement of diplomats in business, the temptations have increased. Third, there are incidents of indiscipline, sometimes involving the ambassador in confrontation with embassy colleagues, or the foreign ministry at home. Fourth, there are security lapses, rarely of a willful nature, but often involving blackmail by agencies of the receiving state that may have entrapped the envoy in compromising circumstances. This was especially common in the days of the communist regimes in East Europe. Fifth, there are local indiscretions, such as drunken behavior in public places, or major traffic incidents that may be alcohol-related. There are also incidents of indebtedness, ranging from the failure to pay shopping bills to non-payment of rent, or other property disputes, where the envoy invokes immunity to escape the judicial process.

Such incidents surface from time to time in many capitals, and the worst the envoy suffers often is recall home. This was the fate of the Senegalese Ambassador to Delhi in May 2003 following an alleged physical altercation between the envoy's adult son and the Indian flag-car chauffeur at a hotel reception, in which the chauffeur was killed. The police filed a case of involuntary manslaughter, but the Ambassador refused to waive the immunity that extended to his son as a member of his family. After some weeks, despite public demonstrations by relatives and friends of the deceased and critical newspaper comment, the envoy was recalled home.[37]

In parts of the world, local shortages or other market conditions offer temptations. Galbraith has written of the early 1960s in New Delhi, when imported alcohol and gold were two items commanding high local prices; he mentions one ambassador 'accredited to several countries in this area [who] is said to be deeply involved in the black market'.[38] Galbraith narrates another story of an Arab envoy whose baggage burst open at the airport, spilling gold all over the place, and adds: 'He was disaccredited and returned home after a total term of around ten days.'[39] New Delhi remains an assignment where the demand for imported alcohol remains temptingly high, though the illicit gold market has withered away after import liberalization. Alcohol is also a high-risk commodity in countries where local governments impose abstemious policies. Some three decades back, a repackaging industry thrived in the Lebanon, where gin would be repacked as a tin of orange juice, and vodka as a tin labeled pineapple chunks; foreign embassies in some Arab capitals routinely ordered supplies of the banned booty in the name of diplomats close to completion of tenure, so that if anything went wrong, that diplomat could be withdrawn with a minimum of disruption. A story, surely apocryphal, tells of a US ambassador in a major regional capital who received a phone call from the Chief of Protocol that the ambassador's upright piano had arrived and was at the docks. The ambassador thanked him for taking the trouble to call personally, at which the local worthy responded plaintively: 'Please have it collected urgently, Mr Ambassador, since it is leaking badly!'[40]

Any serious incident eventually leads to a recall by the sending state, sometimes at the unofficial prompting of the receiving state. This is typical when the event leads to local publicity, or comment in the home media—foreign ministries are much more sensitive to the latter. It is rare for the receiving state to invoke the ultimate sanction of declaring an ambassador *persona non grata* over a personal incident, unless there is an aggrieved local citizen or enterprise that can exert a great deal of pressure.

Then there is another kind of situation, where the receiving state demands the withdrawal of the foreign envoy on account of a political offence, like direct interference in the domestic affairs of the country. The usual course is to advise the sending state that a particular ambassador is no longer welcome and he should be withdrawn by a set date. Some years back, a Western envoy in an African capital went too far in criticizing the internal policy of the receiving state. After locally delivered gentle warnings did not work, this was eventually brought to the notice of the foreign ministry of the sending state at a high level, accompanied by evidence; the ambassador was quietly withdrawn, without publicity.[41] In such cases, the state initiating the action should be ready for the eventuality of reciprocal action by the other side. An open *persona non grata* declaration involving an ambassador is very rare. Handling such a demand, and avoiding reciprocal fallout becomes a matter of good communication and diplomacy.

Professional indiscretion of a more subtle kind occurs when an ambassador wilfully violates instructions, or exceeds the brief given to him by his government. This is relatively rare and happens if an envoy believes that he is acting in conformity with some higher values, or believes that he knows better than MFA colleagues where the country's real interests lie. Such behavior can seldom be justified. For any envoy, or any other civil servant, who is in profound disagreement with his government's policy or the instructions given, the only legitimate action is to resign from his post. This occurs rarely in diplomatic services; the resignations that take place usually involve more personal grievances than policy discord. A rare instance that comes to mind is the resignation of the British Ambassador to Israel, Sir Terence Garvey in the early 1980s, when he found himself opposed to his government's policy on the Arab–Israel dispute.

We should also take account of the less overt professional misconduct that shades into incompetence. Often such cases are not detected, nor even recognized by the diplomatic system, without hard scrutiny at its own systemic parameters.

First, there is the deliberate mis-reportage by ambassadors, which can happen for reasons as innocent as seeking better light for oneself than justified by facts, while reporting on a diplomatic conversation. Or one may 'shade' a little bit an oral response given to one's démarche. This can happen when the envoy does not want to be the bearer of bad tidings. Most career diplomats encounter situations where a draft discussion record that they have prepared, as a 'note-taker', covering a meeting with a foreign dignitary, is amended by the principal, for such cosmetic reasons. By themselves, such alterations have little impact, but they can have cumulative impact, or produce serious distortions during a crisis. We can imagine, for instance, that sycophantic reportage by its ambassadors may well have contributed to the Iraq regime decision in 1990 to invade Kuwait, when it grossly miscalculated the reaction of the international community. We also know from subsequent reports that the US envoy in Baghdad may have also acted contrary to instructions in dialogue with that regime, further contributing to that miscalculation. India's miscalculation in its 1996 contest for an elected seat at the UN Security Council (when it lost to Japan) partly resulted from similar inaccuracies by its ambassadors and special emissaries in reports covering its vote-canvassing around the globe.[42]

A second kind of professional misconduct arises if an ambassador does not act on the instructions given, or follows them half-heartedly. For instance, he may believe that the démarche will not yield results, or he may question its content. In such situations, body language or tone may signal a message that runs counter to the démarche. Such actions are hard to monitor. A third kind of misconduct occurs if the ambassador, through lethargy or disinterest, fails to act on an opportunity to advance the national interests. This is hard to identify, even if the foreign ministry at home is aware that its envoy at a particular location has lost interest or gone into hibernation. A fourth and more frequent 'misdemeanor'—stretching this term—is professional incompetence, either through a lack of ability to handle an assignment, or a deficiency in personal behavior. A former head of the Indian diplomatic service has written of the quality of representation in the neighboring Himalayan kingdom of Bhutan. Praising the envoys that have been exceptionally sensitive in handling this key job, he adds: 'We have also had ambassadors adopting a superior big-brotherly attitude and creating a chasm in relations, which then took years to bridge.'[43] He observes that within the entire diplomatic network, it is at the capitals of contiguous small neighbors that 'the personalities of the ambassador and his wife...make such a crucial difference'.

Much of the creative work of an envoy is discretionary. Besides dealing with the inevitable cases of misconduct, a permanent challenge to the diplomatic system is to motivate its personnel and enhance their professionalism.

Reward and Sanction

In the UK, it is customary to confer knighthoods on several ambassadors each year, in parallel with similar awards to other British civil servants. Most Western states have a finely graded system of national awards; rare is the senior European or Japanese envoy that does not sport in his lapel a rosette of some kind, proof of such recognition. There are comparable practices in Latin America, francophone Africa,[44] and in some Arab states. In contrast, in many other countries, ambassadors rarely qualify for national awards.[45] It seems shortsighted not to operate a graded system of national awards, with a broad coverage of all societal segments.

The US State Department has its own awards for outstanding diplomats. One of these is an award given for the best economic promotion work in the field, and besides the one chosen, several other ambassadors and other diplomats deemed to have performed well are named, with some details of their achievements. This form of peer recognition is of value in any system, as a means of encouraging high performance. Another way of doing this is to have a recognized body, such as an association of retired ambassadors, name a serving envoy as a 'diplomat of the year'.

Ambassadors necessarily consort with foreign governments; one sensitive issue is whether an envoy should accept an award from a foreign country. In the 17th century, Queen Elizabeth I put this in a pithy idiom: 'I do not want my dog to wear a foreign collar'.[46] Notwithstanding such wisdom, most Western countries allow envoys to accept foreign awards, after formal permission from home. But many developing countries, including China and India, do not permit their envoys to accept foreign awards, save in very exceptional circumstances.[47] The rationale is that the prospect of an award may lead the envoy to misjudgment, however marginal, in dealings with the sending country, or in asserting home country interests. Some might deny this to be a real problem, but situations do arise where envoys allow local popularity to shade their stand.

Sanctions imposed on rogue ambassadors usually follow civil service procedures, unless there is a special law governing the diplomatic service. They range from peremptory removal from a post abroad to suspension from the service, formal inquiry, and finally, dismissal. Criminal proceedings are extremely rare. In terms of frequency of occurrence, while an ambassador's premature recall from an assignment happens once in a while, dismissals are very rare in most services.[48] On the other side of the coin, instances arise where ambassadors, who find themselves aggrieved, be it over promotion or other matters, take recourse to judicial appeal, in consonance with the procedures in that country. In India, most such cases first go to a Civil Administrative Tribunal; subsequent appeal is possible to high courts and the Supreme Court. Foreign ministries invariably exert their utmost to keep personnel cases out of the public domain, often seeking a compromise to avoid a legal dispute.

In Retirement

What about ambassadors at the end their careers? Should they withdraw from public activity, pursue chosen vocations, or is there a need for the systemic use of their accumulated experience? The author is not aware of any broad-based study of an issue that should be of interest, at least to diplomatic services and their members.

Retirement benefits for envoys parallel what other civil servants in their country obtain, such as monthly pensions, and other facilities. In a few countries, often in Africa, special privileges are given, like the tax-exempt import of an automobile.[49] Whatever the obligatory retirement age (ranging from 55, 58, 60, to 65), an increasing trend is that the end of a professional career does not lead to hibernation. Most individuals handle this life change as the commencement of new activities. Varied options emerge.

Retired ambassadors come together in associations and groups for episodic activities such as social gatherings, lectures and seminars, preserving a link with their areas of interest, often with the support of the foreign ministry. Some, like the 'Association of Retired Ambassadors' in Beijing, apply themselves to the continuing study of international issues. In New Delhi, an 'Association of Indian Diplomats' operates programs of lectures, besides an annual award for the best young entrant to the diplomatic service. Some retired envoys involve themselves with the training activities, either collectively or through personal effort. Many individuals choose to settle at the country's international activity locus, the national capital, at least for the first several years, thereafter moving away to other towns and areas of retreat.

Academic activity is a frequent choice as a second career, focused on international relations and diplomatic education. The proliferation in think tanks and research institutes that we witness in many countries provides an abundance of opportunities. The

British have a charming practice of appointing a few retired ambassadors as 'masters', heading colleges at Cambridge and Oxford, which mobilizes the administrative skills of outstanding individuals, especially their networking talent at a time when institutions are compelled to seek new funding sources.

A political career is rare in Western countries, perhaps because entry thresholds are high; such as the US re-election rate among congressmen at around 97%! France is the singular exception in Europe where the elite graduates of the *Grandes Écoles* use the revolving door for themselves at all career stages, covering diplomacy and the civil service, business and politics. But this is not replicated in other European countries. India has seen several former envoys contesting elections to the national parliament, who have gone on to assume offices as ministers in the central government, and governors of states. K.R. Narayanan, President of India from 1997 to 2002, is a career diplomat who served as an ambassador in several countries, Turkey, Thailand, China and the US. In other countries, career ambassadors have gone on to become foreign ministers, notably in South Korea and Burma.

Business consultancy is an option that a good number of retired ambassadors pursue. In the UK, city directorships are offered to some who have maintained the right kind of contacts. In Germany, in contrast, very few retired ambassadors (or civil servants) are to be found on boards of management or in the senior echelons of companies. In the US, some become lobbyists or join law firms, but not nearly as many as those who turn to academia and think tanks. In Japan, many high-ranking former ambassadors are appointed as advisers to major corporations, at lucrative emoluments and prerequisites. In some countries, there are a hardy few that open their own consultancy enterprises, but rather few are successful on their own.

The Republic of Korea has used retired ambassadors in an innovative way, starting in the early years of its internationalization program some two decades back. The foreign ministry encourages former envoys to join a cooperative consultancy enterprise (created with the help of that ministry), that offers expertise to Korean companies looking for information and contacts in foreign countries.

This creates a win-win situation, deploying the accumulated expertise of the envoys, and creating value for the companies that use them as well. In this age of globalization, this is a model that deserves emulation, especially by other developing countries that need to expand the external reach of domestic business enterprises.[50]

The UK has a unit in the Foreign Office that helps with the placement of retired envoys, including those seeking an early change of career. This is a method that others could borrow, the more so when it becomes essential to offer options to public servants forced to look outside the service under the 'up-or-out' formulas that some apply to thin out numbers at high age levels.

The US makes the best public use of former envoys, thanks to its 'revolving door system' and an extensive network of grace and favor appointments that the federal government operates, with many different kinds of advisory bodies, committees and special appointments that are available. Washington DC's 100-odd think tanks and foundations form an unparalleled network that uses retired ambassadors and others who have served in the administration. Japan has a system of appointing a number of advisers, some to the foreign minister and others, ranked even higher, 'to the government'. They are used as special emissaries from time to time, but for most it is an honorific title. China also now makes good use of its outstanding envoys by appointing them to an advisory group—there is flexibility in that system by virtue of the fact that beyond the formal institution of ministries and departments, there are networks of 'small groups', task forces and other advisory bodies that are accountable to both the Communist Party and the State Council. This provides a pragmatic mechanism for the sustained use of talent and experience. Since 2000, India has established a 'National Security Advisory Board' where some retired ambassadors have been appointed to one or two-year terms. Finally, leaders in many countries use former envoys for informal advice.

As a rule, informal consultation processes are subject to the vagaries of circumstance, plus a kind of unstated resentment from those who are in office at any point in time, towards those who have retired. Where such a mindset exists, it blocks the optimal use of embedded knowledge in civil services. Consequently, institutionalized methods for consulting retired envoys and other civil servants are superior to those that depend on subjective or episodic arrangements.

Many retired ambassadors turn to writing, often in the shape of memoirs that relive the halcyon days. Newspaper columns are another attraction. One observes a relative absence of major writing efforts by former envoys of developing countries, visible in the relative scarcity of published material. A recent development in China is the emergence of 'pen clubs', which link former envoys writing their memoirs or about particular incidents; a strong public demand has encouraged this movement. Oral history projects are a recent innovation, starting in the US and now spreading to the UK and other places. We may regard these as a form of data collection that adds to collective memory, and indirectly, even public accountability.

Beyond these alternatives, the majority are content to fade gracefully, surrounded by their extended family and memorabilia, or immersed in personal vocations such as social work, recreation and spiritual quest.

8

◆

THE FUTURE

Do we foresee a day when the system of resident ambassadors will end? Might changes in the international system, or technology, or other developments radically transform the way envoys are deployed abroad?

No state has seriously considered replacing the ambassador as the prime, permanent channel of contact and relationship promotion with foreign countries. This institution remains the first instrument for advancing external interests. Some scholars assert that the resident envoy is a major constituent of the international system. In today's prolific community of states and their incessant, pluri-issue multiple-level international dialogue, this institution has undergone a continuous adaptation. Therefore, we should focus on a likely evolution, rather than build artificial scenarios of extinction. These changes cover the structures, functioning, and training needs covered in earlier chapters.

EU Experience

The European Union's political engineering—the continuing 'deepening' of unification exemplified in the proposed constitution, plus the dramatic 'widening' from 15 members to 25 in 2004, and more around the corner—extends also to the diplomatic system and its methods. In foreign affairs, the implementation of the 'Common Foreign and Security Policy' (CFSP), and the appointment of the 'EU Foreign Policy Chief' in 2001, have been visible signs of this process. How does this affect the role of the ambassador?

The German Paschke Report of 2000 has had some influence on other EU states—which have endorsed its conclusion that the European unification process has changed the responsibilities of EU ambassadors and led to the emergence of 'a new type of European diplomacy with its own functions and characteristics'. An academic study of foreign ministries in EU countries published in 2002 concludes that while trends in the countries studied are not altogether clear, the notion that MFAs are in irreversible decline ignores their considerable adaptive capacity, and the most agile of them are shifting to a new role as 'spanners of boundaries', providing renewed value.[1] The study examines particularly the MFA's situation in the member countries in intra-government interactions, and in Brussels in terms of the role of the permanent representatives heading the mammoth missions that each EU state maintains at the EU headquarters. But we await an EU-wide study of the ambassador system, as also of the operation of the global system of EU diplomatic representation.

A concept often discussed in Europe but yet to see the light of day is the 'joint embassy'—one envoy representing multiple states. It would save resources, financial and human, and enable wider diplomatic coverage around the world. It would also be a unique demonstration of mutual trust and cooperation. One might have expected that the European Union, a unified entity in which states have partly pooled their sovereignty, might be an early mover. Yet, the small Caribbean island states are the only ones to have put this into practice, e.g. through an ambassador at Ottawa who represents eight 'Caricom' states.[2]

One problem has been the concept that the ambassador represents the head of state of a sovereign nation. Germany has been the first with a law that permits such joint representation. Other EU states are in the process of passing the enabling legislation, but the formula is difficult for constitutional monarchies. The first of the joint EU ambassadors will probably represent those countries that are ready to try it, as one more act of variable geometry. Clearly, joint ambassadors may be feasible in places where the interests of participating states are limited, and where none perceives special connections—it would be hard to imagine a joint EU ambassador with French participation in francophone Africa.

One should also look at the current formula of the EU Representative as exists in some 70 countries outside the EU. Bearing the title of 'ambassador', these representatives belong to the EU's burgeoning diplomatic service and act as administrators of EU aid, and as coordinators of EU activities in the receiving country. Might they serve as joint envoys for the EU at remote locations? Possible, but again the concept would come up against the particular interests of major European states, e.g. in the commercial arena.

Even the limited formula of 'co-location', placing missions of several countries together, to share services, has produced limited results. It was tried at Abuja, the new Nigerian capital, but the result was inconclusive. Against what was to be a single complex housing all 15 EU states, several opted for their own locations of choice, and only 6 were left in the joint complex. Germany, an advocate of joint action, is engaged in around a dozen co-location projects around the world, with one or more EU partners;[3] the UK, France and the Nordics are also strong advocates. The other form in which joint EU action takes place is at the micro level, with embassies in foreign capitals coming together to write joint reports, and exchanging diplomats to work in one another's embassies—which matches similar personnel exchanges at the EU capitals.

In all these moves, a collective EU entity takes more substantive shape, in a progressive and measured manner. A 'Europe of States', where a number of member-states are unwilling to pool sovereignty beyond the point where their identity is threatened, is unlikely to abandon the national system of diplomatic representation. And there is no other large regional or collective entity that is at the stage of comprehensive replacement of the ambassador representing the sovereign state.

The Entrepreneur-Ambassador

One of the attributes of an entrepreneur is to generate and manage innovation within an existing set of circumstances. That core entrepreneurial function is as applicable in public affairs as it is to business. One way of understanding excellence and leadership in diplomacy is through this model. Four entrepreneur-envoy cases from the establishment best known to the author, the Indian Foreign Service, are offered. Each has involved blending political, economic and other forms of public interest entrepreneurship, guided by an individual's perception of advancing national interests.

N. Krishnan:[4] He was the permanent representative in Geneva in 1967–71 when the emerging global scourge of man-made drugs, the 'psychotropic substances'[5] was first debated at the UN Narcotics Commission. In 1967, when the global spread of these substances was detected, the shared position of the major powers, influenced by their pharmaceutical industry, was that international regulation was unnecessary; it should be left to each country to decide on its control regime. Sweden vehemently opposed such *laissez faire*. India had no brief on the issue, nor was it then a national problem, but Krishnan and delegation leader D.P. Anand[6] crafted their own brief, also persuading the Ghana delegate to join. For the next several years, these three counters argued the case for unified action, through the customary meanderings of multilateral diplomacy, when the big powers preferred procrastination. Eventually, the changing contours of the drug problem in their countries, plus the shifting public mood post-1968, forced a change from within each. Subsequent negotiations culminated in the UN Convention on Psychotropic Substances signed in Vienna in 1974. At that time, international NGO power did not exist and public consciousness of such issues was muted. Idealism and practical diplomacy won out.

Ranjit Gupta:[7] As Ambassador to Oman in 1989–94, he vigorously championed several ambitious joint venture projects, including a one billion dollar fertilizer project (which achieved financial closure in 2002 and is under execution), two refineries which were later abandoned, and a planned undersea gas pipeline across the Arabian Sea that never took off, later abandoned as unviable owing to cost and technical hurdles, because of the deep sea-bed to be traversed. He has subsequently explained to the author his rationale for pushing this proposal, in terms of a political need to project the Indian eco-political reach in the Gulf, as also to encourage Iran and other

Gulf states of the potential for bold actions. Later, as Ambassador to Thailand (1994–98) he co-authored with Thailand a proposal for trans-regional economic cooperation, BIMST-EC, pushing a reluctant home bureaucracy into acceptance, after gaining high level endorsement in New Delhi. The concept has gathered strength over the years; the leaders of Bangladesh, India, Myanmar, Sri Lanka and Thailand, plus new entrants Bhutan and Nepal, are to hold their first summit in early 2004.

Shiv Shankar Menon:[8] He has been a master of quiet political diplomacy, with an unassuming style. Both in Sri Lanka (1997–2000) and China (2001–03), he played a critical role in building external and internal consensus in favor of reworked bilateral ties, a model of quiet political outreach. Continuing his exceptional experience with high diplomacy, he has been High Commissioner in Pakistan since July 2003. At each of these three countries, his assignment has coincided with a remarkable, evolutionary transformation in bilateral relations. While a serving official's contribution in a complex political process is hard to pinpoint from outside, he surely meets Napoleon's norm of that desirable 'lucky general'.

Leela Ponappa:[9] Another serving official, she is known to be persuasive, combining high integrity with a low profile. She crafted the pioneering India–Thailand Free Trade Agreement (FTA) that was signed in October 2003, utilizing her experience with India's first FTA with Sri Lanka in 1998–99, when she headed the territorial division in the Ministry of External Affairs in New Delhi. She has been especially skillful at networking diplomacy, reconciling inter-ministerial interests in New Delhi, showing also that all too often the hardest negotiation task can be at home!

The 'public entrepreneur' envoys described here, and their counterparts that exist in other countries, blend proactivism with judgment and persuasive skills to implement their goals. They import into their work the methods, the mindset and the tools of a good business entrepreneur. In particular, they confront near-identical calculations of risk and gain. But unlike entrepreneur-owners in the business world, they are not autonomous. In this respect too, the envoy resembles a trans-national corporation chief executive heading a country subsidiary, who enjoys a considerable latitude of action, but remains answerable to higher management.

What are the effective envoy's operational parameters? First, he retains a significant latitude for local initiative. The headquarters sets the goals, and provides the resources, but the local environment is for the envoy to comprehend and master. He looks for windows of opportunity, makes connections between disparate issues, and works to both short-term and long-term priorities, to sustain, build, diversify, deepen and embellish relationships in the country of assignment, in pursuit of national objectives. Often, opportunities have to be developed through local actions. He needs to discern the actions he can undertake on his own and the others where he needs the prior approval of headquarters. Second, he deals in public goods and services. Some of these are tangible, be they exports from home, the mobilization of investments in either direction, or the creation of cultural, scientific, educational or other connections. Others, like improved political understanding or a more positive country image are less concrete, hard to measure. But they are all amenable to entrepreneurial action. Third, he depends on proactive methods, asserting leadership over both those under his direct charge, and others whom he can influence or motivate, both in the country of assignment and at home. If anything, he pursues a wider model of leadership behavior than might apply to a business leader, but quite similar to leadership in public life. Fourth, economic and public diplomacy are particularly amenable to entrepreneurial methods, though that spirit applies to the other activity areas as well. In particular, openness to new ideas and innovation are a unifying common thread. Fifth, the ambassador takes personal responsibility for the mission's performance, taking both credit and blame as merited. The instructions that he receives from his headquarters, plus its consultation–decision mechanism to which he has access at most times, help him, but do not provide a valid alibi if things go wrong. Sixth, as in business, public service entrepreneurship involves rising above the difficulties as they exist in a given situation, and stretching the envelope of the possible, not wasting energy on the unattainable, or awaiting change in the framework conditions.

Applying such a business model reveals one vital aspect of diplomacy—the inherent trade-off between risk and potential gain.

Any new initiative or pursuit of opportunity involves both advantage and potential for failure. Judgment and good decisions come from knowledge, training and experience. Of course, the ambassador is not alone in shouldering risk; he works within a support system that assists, checks, and evaluates. He has the foreign ministry and the full machinery of the government, to guide and advise in circumstances of doubt. But there are many situations where the envoy has to sponsor a proposal or to act, where an entrepreneurial mindset is rather appropriate.

It is dangerous to pursue the comparison too far. Balance and good judgment, the indispensable allies of the envoy, temper his entrepreneurial spirit. A static environment may offer no opportunity for proactivism. If conditions in the receiving state are adverse, obviously new initiatives have to wait, and the ambassador may have his hands full with containing the situation. Further, if one's private agenda supplants the public interest, the envoy would come to resemble the businessman in ways that are far from desirable. This has become a real risk with the contemporary growth of economic diplomacy, in which the promotional activities, and advocacy of business interests of home country enterprises, expose all diplomats in the field, especially the ambassador, to temptations that could scarcely have been imagined a generation earlier.

Power and Influence

'Power is the ability to obtain the outcomes one wants', (Joseph S. Nye Jr.).[10] What real power does today's ambassador enjoy? On the surface he does not measure up to the envoys of the past who were real plenipotentiaries, and seemed to shape events abroad and influence international affairs. But examined closely, quasi-autonomous ambassadorial authority passed into history long back, as soon as national capitals discovered instant communication, initially via the telegraph, and subsequently in all its technological derivatives. Even during the inter-War years of 1919–39, marked by complex inter-state moves in Europe and at the League of Nations, now seen as a classic era of diplomacy, the envoy played a circumscribed role.¹¹ Today's ambassador is a civil servant in all respects, even if some countries bestow personal ranks like 'cabinet status' on non-career envoys. Such frills mean nothing in substantive international contacts, and do not lead to power.¹² It is more instructive to examine the envoy's *influence*, his ability to induce or to function with others towards the outcomes he attempts to promote. In terms of hard power, the ambassador has but little at his disposal.

In gauging the envoy's influence, we may summarize the narrative of earlier chapters. First, he is a contributor to the shaping of policy, besides his larger role as the field agent implementing that policy. In the increasingly plural diplomatic process, he has competitors, but the evolution of communications technology has unexpectedly led to his capacity for integration into the decision and policy formulation chain. The extent to which this actually happens depends on the country's diplomatic system and the willingness of that system to harness the latent possibility of using the envoy in a way that overcomes most of the barriers of geography. How far can the envoy assert his viewpoint? It depends on the country and circumstances; we know of instances where individuals have exerted an unusual degree of influence, virtually shaping the policy towards a particular foreign country.

Second, plurality, multiplicity and complexity in international discourse—in players, issues and processes—makes the resident ambassador the country's single best resource on the assigned country. The same is true of the multilateral envoy in relation to the international organization to which he is accredited. Again, this is a capacity that has to be exercised within the working structure and environment of the diplomatic system. If this is not handled with adroitness and balance, the potential remains unexploited.

Third, everything hinges on the individual. Not all ambassadors are able to deliver on the potential. It should logically follow that countries deploy their best talent at the capitals that truly matter to them, but all too often, this does not happen. The inhibiting factors can be a mix of poor HR deployment, defective systems of promotion and motivation, or simply poor governance of the diplomatic process. For any diplomatic service, it is vital to celebrate the role models, not so much for the recognition that they merit, but for the influence these models exercise on others, raising both expectations and capabilities.

So, how influential is the envoy? Fairly influential, especially in his capacity to do good and to deliver on exploiting the beneficial potential of a bilateral relationship. But he can function to his capacity only if the entire system and its processes are optimized.

Globalized Diplomacy

G.R. Berridge writes: 'A diplomatic service that is well resourced and above all well staffed can give a state a significant increment of power and influence.'[13] This simple truth needs better recognition in different parts of the world, especially in the global South. It also underscores the importance of the study of the diplomatic process, as a force multiplier in international affairs.

The conclusions of this study are summarized below.

First, *we observe the salience of the ambassador as an institution*. The present state of world politics requires countries to practice globalized diplomacy. Its characteristics are: it is *intensive*, in that the engagement with high priority partners is deep, growing continually to exploit the full potential of mutually beneficial cooperation (example: The EU has become an aspiration model for other regional organizations, be it ASEAN or the OAU, for the manner in which the voluntary pooling of sovereignty can produce mutual benefit.) It is *extensive*, in that each country reaches out to distant regions to forge new partnerships (example: In 2002, Brazil, India and South Africa, as three large countries in different continents, decided to intensify economic and other exchanges, to forge new political linkages; one manifestation was their joint action at the September 2003 WTO Ministerial Meeting, Cancun.) It is *innovative*, seeking out-of-the-box solutions to festering problems, or to isolate these, unblocking other initiatives (example: The Anglo-Irish Good Friday Accord of 1998, which leaves open the future status of Northern Ireland, within a framework safeguarding the vital interests of each state and all its constituencies.) It is *regional* in that the cultivation of one's neighborhood is always the high priority (example: With the regional body SAARC in paralysis owing to seemingly intractable India–Pakistan differences, the smaller South Asian countries are turning to other bilateral and cross-regional options like bilateral free trade agreements and 'Ganga-Mekong Basin' concepts).[14]

The institution of the ambassador is shaped by a wide matrix of factors, as they interact with one another. The envoy is the prime instrument of outreach and promotion in relationship building in bilateral diplomacy and the permanent negotiator in multilateral diplomacy. He also plays a vital role in the public–private networks that operate in the different functional areas of international dialogue, supplementing the work of the foreign ministry as the external affairs coordinator.

An expanded role for the envoy valorizes also the concept that he serves the entire system of government, not excluding the non-state actors. The foreign ministry, in nurturing the envoy as a value-provider for the full national system, also improves his capacity for direct and indirect service to all these constituents. In turn, the ambassador contributes to the discharge of the MFA's expanding obligations to them, whether we call this external affairs coordination or 'boundary-spanning'.[15]

Second, *maximizing value out of the ambassador system should be a national goal*. The action remit and responsibility of the ambassador has become larger, even while he is more tightly integrated into the foreign affairs structure. Some of his autonomy—more notional than real anyway—has been traded, in return he has gained involvement in a wider range of issues. For instance, he cedes negotiation competence, in areas other than political, to the functional experts, but needs to master greater complexity. He must adapt his vision to be able to view both the trees and the forest.

In the future, we should expect harder calculations by countries in determining external priorities, extending to the distribution and density of the diplomatic network. This may lead to a scaling back in the number of embassies abroad and a thinning down of staff for most. 'Status competition', among great and lesser powers has surely contributed to a situation where many maintain resident ambassadors in countries of peripheral interest. The crunch of financial resources and governance rationalization will help this process. So will information and communication technology. New possibilities include: non-resident ambassadors, 'virtual' envoys, and micro-embassies and sub-offices—some staffed entirely by local personnel—as noted earlier. This is underway in some countries (e.g. Italy has reduced its embassy strength from 124 in 1994 to 118 in 2000). Japan, in the midst of major diplomatic structural reforms is also set to cut back on the number of missions. Such moves always face resistance from entrenched diplomatic services, quite acute in some countries.[16] Technology also facilitates leaner embassies, much of consular work and some commercial work shifted to back-offices at home, visible in some systems.

We noted earlier German efforts in adapting procedures to the present international environment. Others like Australia, France, New Zealand, Singapore and the UK have also pursued innovative methods. Several have thinned out their foreign representation, closing marginal embassies, or cutting back sharply on home-based personnel at places where interests can be handled in different ways. In parallel, there is a consistent shift to a more intensive use of locally recruited staff.

One possibility is the 'regional ambassador' who may be based in a large country in a particular region, to supervise small 'satellite embassies' in neighboring countries which could be headed by resident chargé d'affaires (this is different from the concurrent accreditation formula, where there is no physical presence in the second capital covered by the envoy). This idea comes up from time to time in some countries. The drawback in this concept is that the regional envoy becomes an intermediate level between the mission on the ground and the foreign ministry, which would surely create more problems than it solves.[17]

Some countries will probably deploy more multilateral envoys, dictated especially by expanding economic and other functional tasks, be it at WTO in Geneva, or at the other specialized agencies that dominate international affairs. The management of multilateral diplomacy is expected to remain in the hands of MFA professionals, while specialists handle the negotiation of technical issues.[18] Regional diplomacy would also command increased attention, with professionals remaining in the driving seat. At the same time, in the mix of work handled by foreign ministries, a swing back to bilateral diplomacy is overdue, revalued in its own right, without taking anything away from multilaterals.[19]

Third, *improvements in the diplomacy process must be viewed as a public good*. Producing optimal value from ambassadors, today and tomorrow, demands changes in the ways they are utilized by the diplomatic system. Traditionally, the ambassador was seen by the MFA as 'their man' providing inputs into a decision-making process that valued his contributions, but did not directly include him in the policy chain. Different diplomatic services can attest to the 'us-and-them' mindsets that often prevail at headquarters, despite the fact that the same officials serve in embassies and MFAs. As detailed earlier, there are good reasons for treating the ambassador and his team more integrally. First, he and his team are the very best information source on his country of assignment, unmatched by anyone at headquarters. Second, the envoy has the capacity to find interconnections between different areas of activity, of the non-obvious kind, yielding leverages and trade-off possibilities. Third, the communications revolution has eroded distance as a conditioning factor and now lets the diplomatic system use him as an integral team member in the decision process.[20] A citation from the German Paschke Report offered in Chapter 5 underscores this.

Is the process described above actually happening anywhere? Only in part. One reason may be that the 'relationship manager role' is a consequence of a gradual, dynamic process, not a sudden event, and for that reason has not attracted sharper notice. An experienced German diplomat, Berndt von Staden, had commented some years back:

The ambassador is increasingly becoming the head of a 'service enterprise' responsible for preparing and carrying out...direct intercourse between his government and that of the host country...Most of the negotiation functions that once devolved upon the ambassador have disappeared. But at the same time the tasks of persuasion and interpretation have grown to an equal or greater extent.[21]

In an interview, a Western ambassador agreed with the author's analysis, but was skeptical if foreign ministries would allow this kind of intrusion on what was perceived as their area of jurisdiction; he felt that a competent ambassador should manage to get himself involved in the decision process, but this may not happen as a matter of right.[22] A couple of the contributors to a 2002 study on EU foreign ministries have forcefully asserted that embassies are more actively integrated with the MFA; in the concluding essay, co-editor Brian Hocking notes that this is facilitated by contemporary information and communications technology and adds: 'The general verdict is that embassies are increasingly involved in the shaping as well as interpretation of policy.'[23] The German Foreign Office has implemented this aspect of the Paschke Report, to the point where the computer networks in the ministry and missions are integrated. Ambassadors and their teams interface seamlessly with ministry counterparts, with documents and comments exchanged continually. The same is true of the US, where the direct message from the envoy to home official becomes a new communication device, since it is not circulated to others, unlike cipher messages.

Fourth, *better recognition of the diplomatist as a professional is worthwhile*. The professionalism of the diplomatic system has grown in response to changed functions, in a process that is also linked with the tighter integration of the entire machine with the other stakeholders in external affairs. When it works well, it becomes a virtuous circle, providing feedback into the process itself. The extent to which this happens hinges, partly, on the ambassador system delivering stronger value, as perceived by domestic partners, state and non-state.

This also demands revitalized training, constantly adapting it in line with an evolution in functional needs. With a porous domestic–external divide, the envoy needs exposure to the domestic governance process, and an inclusion in the dialogue that foreign ministries undertake with the home constituencies relevant to his work. Instituting a regular training program for ambassadors, where officials of other external-oriented ministries and non-state constituencies also join, is the most efficient method for pulling together the diverse themes that should be covered in such programs.

Fifth, *a transformation process is underway in well-managed foreign ministries*. The management of the diplomatic machine has emerged as a major challenge. Several interlocking factors are responsible for this. First, governments all over the world confront a demand for better efficiency and value-for-money from public services. Optimizing the way external relations are handled is one of many parallel concerns. Second, new management techniques have permeated all fields of activity, starting with the corporate domain and extending to social institutions, the voluntary sector and the public agencies. The techniques themselves have undergone rapid evolution and refinement. Third, we see the diplomatic process with new eyes, and begin to recognize that it is intertwined with policy in a way that defies simple differentiation. Reform of the foreign ministry process gathers momentum in capitals as different as Berlin and Beijing. Fourth, it is slowly understood that the gap between productive diplomatic systems and those marked by stasis and inefficiency is largely one of management—plus training— and not resources. A few developing countries have understood this truth, and this has, hopefully, a cascading effect.

How else should foreign ministries adapt themselves? Knowledge management is increasingly vital for organizations. One task is to tap the knowledge and learning that reside in the organization, and institutionalize the process through which these are harvested. The profusion of reports and dispatches that ambassadors submit should be archived digitally, and through use of hypertext and keyword search, should be accessible across the headquarters and embassies abroad. (The practical obstacle is the security of such system-wide IT networks.) Most diplomatic systems do not as yet treat knowledge management as a core function. The rapid evolution in the external environment makes this especially vital. Another priority should be the study of other systems, to identify best practices and to benchmark one's system against the peer services. This is beginning to take place and should gain further momentum in the years ahead.[24] Improved communication with domestic publics on foreign policy goals, and frequent, comprehensive dialogue with the foreign affairs community is another requirement, as a form of public diplomacy at home. The ambassador is a cog in all these activities.

Reform in foreign ministries and in the diplomatic systems that they manage, is taking place in many countries. The international environment and the velocity of transformation in global affairs make it essential for foreign ministries to build change management into the system.

Finally, *high performance by ambassadors hinges on empowering individuals.* The foreign ministry and the rest of the government party create the environment that regulates the diplomatic machine. The techniques of performance management and human resource management animate the system, encouraging officials and building an enabling environment. But the ambassador depends on self-initiative to deliver his best in the kaleidoscopic, multilayered environment where he functions. The incubation of entrepreneurship is a human process, not a matter of rules and supervision—even while these create the vital conditions where the envoy can function creatively in pursuit of the country's external interests. The evolution taking place in the operation of the ambassador system gives the possibility of integrating the field and the center, into a near-seamless entity, working to a higher efficiency than before.

The best diplomatic systems produce exemplars that inspire the entire system. The uniqueness of the environment in each foreign country, the very personal way in which envoys go about building trust, reaching out to external and domestic constituencies, gives this profession its craft character, where almost no work is routine or mechanical, or capable of being reduced to set formulae. It is a profession that celebrates individuality. The challenge for the diplomatic system is to build excellence into its genetic code, and to uplift the performance of the entire system as well. At stake is nothing less than enlarging the international power and influence of one's nation.

NOTES

Introduction

1. An extract from an informal note given to me by the Ministry of Foreign Affairs, Thailand.
2. A few other instances: in UK the top decision-making body at the Foreign and Commonwealth Office is called the 'Board of Management'; business management principles are also applied to the operation of important projects such as 'Invest Britain' that represent the cutting edge of the country's economic diplomacy. New Zealand calls the head of the foreign ministry 'chief executive officer' and applies a series of other business methods to the management of performance and human resources.
3. L.N. Rangarajan, *The Arthashastra* (Penguin, New Delhi, 1992). This is an excellent work of translation and rearrangement, accompanied by an introduction that makes this classic work easily accessible.
4. Rangarajan, *The Arthashastra*, p. 576–8.
5. Abraham de Wicquefort, *The Embassador and his Functions*, 1681, translated by Digby in 1716 (facsimile edition, University of Leicester, 1997).
6. While serving in the Canadian diplomatic service, Justin Robertson edited the collection *Foreign Ministries in Developing Countries and Emerging Market Economies* (Halifax, *International Insights: Dalhousie Journal of International Affairs*, Volume 14, Summer, 1998). It focuses on the experience of countries that do not often figure in comparative international studies.

7. Distinguished US economist, who served as President Kennedy's envoy to India in 1961–63.
8. Served as US Permanent Representative to the UN in 1991–94 before becoming Secretary of State.
9. Confidential interview, May 2001.
10. This has been the situation in India, and the experience in many African countries is no different. In the early 1980s when India's dependence on foreign aid was acute, the finance ministry virtually dictated the policy towards Western countries.
11. For instance, in Germany the Foreign Office (AA) plays an overall coordinating role, but all gut issues on foreign economic cooperation, plus policies regarding the World Bank, are decided by the Ministry of Economic Cooperation (BMZ) and foreign embassies deal directly and exclusively with the latter on aid matters.
12. Brian Hocking, ed., *Foreign Ministries: Change and Adaptation* (Macmillan, London, 1999).
13. Robertson, *Foreign Ministries in Developing Countries and Emerging Market Economies*.
14. Martin F. Herz, ed., *The Modern Ambassador: The Challenge and the Search*, (Institute for the Study of Diplomacy, Georgetown University, Washington DC, 1983).
15. Hocking, *Foreign Ministries*.
16. Hocking, Brian, *Diplomacy of Image and Memory: Swiss Bankers and Nazi Gold* (Diplomatic Studies Program Discussion Paper No. 64, University of Leicester, April 2000).
17. Japan is one major exception, and business delegations never accompany their leaders, on the curious argument that Japan does not mix politics with business. And yet Japan is the one country that goes the furthest in support of its businessmen, as a matter of normal diplomatic practice by their ambassadors abroad.
18. A more graphic instance of business engaging in political diplomacy, to overcome the sanctions that the US applied to India after its nuclear tests of May 1998 is narrated in Kishan S. Rana, *Bilateral Diplomacy*.
19. For developing countries, this is one more arena where the playing field is uneven. Western NGOs with an international vocation have the resources to impose their own agendas in other countries through the NGO subsidiaries they sponsor and finance. US-based economist Deepak Lal has called this a new from of 'imperialism'.

20. Paul Sharp, *Making Sense of Citizen Diplomats* (Center for the Study of Diplomacy, Leicester, 2001) This gives an excellent analysis of peoples diplomacy, also giving its long pedigree; President Eisenhower had endorsed citizen diplomacy in 1956 as a means for reducing global tensions.
21. A real-life instance is narrated in Kishan S. Rana, *Inside Diplomacy* (Manas, New Delhi, 2000; revised paperback edition, Manas, 2002), pp. 370–3.
22. Confidential interview, January 2001.
23. LTV Washington Seminar, 1980, quoted in Abba Eban, *Diplomacy for the New Century* (Yale University Press, New Haven, 1998).
24. Concrete example furnished during a confidential interview, April 2001.
25. Essay by Egidio Ortona, former Italian Permanent Representative to the UN and former Secretary General in the MFA, published in Herz, ed., *The Modern Ambassador*.
26. Gail Scott, *Diplomatic Dance* (Fulcrum Publishing, Golden, Colorado, 1999). Written by a journalist, this is a racy account of some of the leading ambassadors on the Washington DC circuit.
27. I witnessed this in Namibia in late 2000.
28. *FCO—Department Report on the Government Expenditure Plans, 2000–01 to 2001–01*, (HM Stationery Office, London, April 2000).
29. Essay in the book *The Modern Ambassador*, ed. Herz.
30. Confidential interview, February 2001.
31. Major developed countries use the most advanced MFA–mission communications systems. But improvements proceed at such a fast pace that small countries too have the option of catching up. For instance Botswana with 10 missions abroad runs its own intranet.
32. Confidential interviews, 2001–2.
33. Robert Wolfe, ed., *Diplomatic Missions: The Ambassador in Canadian Foreign Policy* (McGill and Queen's University Press, Ottawa, 1998).
34. Herz, *The Modern Ambassador*.
35. The author's research covering India, Thailand, Japan and observations of the situation in some other countries bears this out as well.
36. Australian High Commissioner Penelope Wensley at a seminar 'The Changing Contours of Diplomacy' at New Delhi on 29 November 2002.
37. In January 2001, India appointed its first woman as the head of the

Foreign Service, when Chokila Iyer took over as Foreign Secretary, the civil service head of the Ministry of External Affairs, New Delhi. This is yet to happen in any other major diplomatic services.

Chapter 1: The Transformed Plenipotentiary

1. K.P.S. Menon, *Many Worlds: An Autobiography* (Oxford University Press, Bombay, 1965).
2. K.P.S. Menon narrates (*Many Worlds*) a small incident that captures the flavor of the time. In 1949, Prime Minister Nehru had invited the Turkish Ambassador and his wife to dinner at his home at a mixed gathering where he was the only foreign envoy present. A day later, the Ambassador's deputy informed Foreign Secretary Menon that the seating at the dinner did not give due weight to the Ambassador's status. Nehru sent him a charming note, mentioning that his years in the independence struggle did not educate him in the niceties of protocol, and he regretted any inadvertent offence!
3. Late Dr S.M. Patil, longtime chief executive of Hindustan Machine Tools and the father of the Indian machine tool industry, frequently recounted the story of the first consignment of Indian manufactured machine tools that arrived at Rotterdam in the mid-1960s. Proud at that achievement, he approached the Indian Ambassador to request him to preside over a small ceremony at the dockside, only to be told that ambassadors did not engage in such work of traders! Similar stories of disdain for economic activity are part of the diplomatic legends of most countries.
4. Karl Th. Paschke, *Report of the Special Inspection of 14 German Embassies in the Countries of the European Union* (German Federal Foreign Office, Berlin, September 2000). Though not published officially, this report has been debated in the Bundestag and the German media; an English translation was made available to the author. It is available at the website *www.diplomacy.edu*.
5. An authoritative account of the contemporary scene in Europe is given in Brian Hocking, and David Spence, eds, *Foreign Ministries in the European Union: Integrating Diplomats* (Palgrave Macmillan, Basingstoke, 2002)
6. Examples: a Danish TV series in 2002 on the theme 'Our expensive diplomacy'; a strong article on 28 June 2003 by the editor of a prominent daily *Indian Express*, 'Indian Fossil Service' (archives at *www.indianexpress.com*).

7. Atlantic Monthly, September 1996, cited in Mary Locke and Casimir A. Yost, eds, *Who Needs Embassies? How US Missions Abroad Help Shape Our World* (Institute for the Study of Diplomacy, Washington DC, Georgetown University).
8. Former Consul in Moscow Thomas Hutson.
9. Cited extensively in works like Herz, *The Modern Ambassador*, and Robert V. Keeley, ed., *First Line of Defense: Ambassadors, Embassies and American Interests Abroad* (American Academy of Diplomacy, Washington DC, 2000)
10. L.A. Times, 15 February 1977.
11. Berridge, G.R. and James, Alan, *A Dictionary of Diplomacy* (Palgrave, London, 2001).
12. One of the outstanding instances of such egregious largess took place in New Delhi in the early 1950s, mainly at the behest of Prime Minister Nehru. Vast swathes of choice land were given away to foreign countries to set up new embassies in the 'diplomatic enclave' at peppercorn rent on 100-year leases. The US and China took over 20 hectares each, while the UK and Germany took 10 hectares (and Germany returned 5 hectares as this was seen surplus to needs!). Some 30 other countries took smaller parcels, and a common feature of neglect in each of the acts of grace was the absence of mention of reciprocity for India's own needs in the foreign capitals concerned. (See Rana, *Inside Diplomacy*, Chapter 15).
13. This is a thesis argued in my book *Bilateral Diplomacy*, that the craft techniques of building relations are often taken for granted.
14. The classic **bilateral ambassador** represents one country in another. In July 2002, UN membership stood at 192 (including Switzerland whose population had earlier rejected membership in many referenda, and then accepted the proposition in February 2002, and the newest member East Timor which became independent in May 2002). This total of 192 nation states gives a theoretical maximum of 36,864 pairs of relationships between different countries. Not all of them exist in practice. Thus, an Afghanistan just relieved from the Taliban yoke may have little to do with Uruguay, or Vanuatu with Albania. Nor may Burma have much to do with Zaire, though they surely recognize one another. On a rough estimate, some 25,000 to 30,000 pairs of nations maintain diplomatic relations with one another. In many cases resident embassies are not established, and the relationship is without substance. Such diplomatic communication or dialogue that takes place is episodic. Sometimes the UN Headquarters at New York is

the setting for bilateral contact, for reasons of mutual convenience. The total number of resident bilateral ambassadors is about 7700 (source: *Europa Yearbook*, 2000). Add to this some 500 to 600 full-time multilateral ambassadors, to make up a grand total of some 8300 ambassadors. The country with the widest international network is the US, maintaining resident ambassadors in 150 countries, while France, Europe's leading diplomatic power has envoys in about 140 states. At the other end of the spectrum, Kenya has 38 resident ambassadors, Botswana has 11 ambassadors, and there are very small diplomatic capitals with just three or four, or even two, resident ambassadors.

High Commissioners are the ambassadors exchanged between countries that belong to the Commonwealth, the cluster of 54 countries that have historical connections with UK. They function in exactly the same manner as ambassadors, but the special nomenclature symbolizes a closer relationship between these countries. In this book, in keeping with contemporary practice, the generic term 'ambassador' includes the high commissioners as well.

Concurrently accredited ambassadors are those bilateral envoys who reside in one foreign capital but additionally represent their country in another country, visiting it from time to time. It is an economical representation device.

Multilateral ambassadors are the heads of missions to the UN and other agencies, with a concurrent title of 'permanent representative' (PR) to that agency. The largest cluster is at the UN in New York, followed by the UN's Europe headquarters at Geneva. Countries with large 'permanent missions' might have two or even four officials carrying the title 'ambassador'. This is a gesture of courtesy; they may handle different committees or subjects, but the mission can have only one head. Ambassadors/PRs are also accredited to the EU, NATO, OECD, and the like. At places like Nairobi, Rome and Vienna, bilateral ambassadors often concurrently represent their countries to the UN agencies headquartered there. A Western country may, in contrast, have even four missions at a place like Brussels, a bilateral embassy accredited to Belgium, plus permanent missions to EU, NATO and even to the West European Union (WEU).

Non-resident ambassadors live in the sending country capital, covering one or more countries from there. A measure of economy, it provides nominal representation, and has been used effectively by Singapore, Malta and some other small countries. Others have resorted to this device when conditions of insecurity or severe hardship have made it unattractive to maintain a resident mission. With the advent of the Internet, it is possible to develop this into a 'virtual' ambassador.

Other examples: The **ambassador-at-large** is a device used by a few countries, most notably the US, entrusting a public figure or official with a special function, like helping in the Middle East dialogue, highlighting the situation in the Great Lakes region in Africa, or handling an issue like wider adherence to the rule of law. These had proliferated under the Clinton administration and in March 2001, newly appointed Secretary of State Colin Powell abolished 23 of the 55 appointments. Other countries use the term **roving ambassador**, often charging them with diplomatic explorations for resolving a problem, usually between other countries. Japan gives the title of Ambassador and Adviser to senior diplomats after retirement. In France, 'Ambassador of France' is an honorific given to a select few. Similarly, under US law, the President, subject to Senate confirmation, gives the title of 'Career Ambassador' to a handful of select professionals who have served with special distinction. There is also an international Convention on Special Missions that covers the appointment of 'Special Ambassadors' to deal with specific problems, but this device is rarely used.

There are also disguised envoys, **ambassadors-in-all-but-name**. When relations have been diplomatically broken following a crisis of some kind, the work of protecting interests is often (but not always) entrusted to a friendly power, and it is not unusual to find a senior diplomat of the country that does not maintain relations installed inside such an 'interests section', maintaining discreet contacts. Similarly, liaison offices or trade offices are used as the contact vehicle, when it is not possible to have diplomatic links. For example, many countries maintain such offices in Taiwan, many headed by senior diplomats detached for short duty with national chambers of commerce that nominally run the offices, since they cannot have official links with that entity owing to China's insistence on a 'One China' policy.

There is a new aberration that is recent, the grant of **personal rank** of ambassador, in situations where there is another accredited ambassador in that country. A few countries use this as a device to confer higher status on the Deputy Chief of Mission (DCM). This is especially inappropriate at a bilateral post, but at a multilateral mission it does not matter very much since the key designation there is of permanent representative; at a conference or a committee; the title of ambassador is viewed as an honorific with no substantial meaning.

Another recent American innovation is the title **Deputy Ambassador**. It is used in common parlance to refer to the Deputy Chief of Mission, but it has no formal standing.

15. Washington DC is the world's largest diplomatic capital, with 173 resident embassies, followed by Brussels (especially as headquarters of EU): 162; Paris: 155; London: 149; Berlin: 147; Moscow: 140; Beijing: 130; Rome: 127; Tokyo: 123; and Cairo: 117 (*Europa Yearbook*, 2000).
16. This issue is examined further in Chapter 6.
17. The 'realists' and 'neo-realists', postulate that the basic global condition is one of anarchy and the state's primary concern is to assure its own survival. Even when the state deals with issues other than its security, security remains the underlying goal. The contemporary ambassador may well believe that the security and well-being of his nation is at the root of his diplomacy goals. But the concept offers little by way of practical diplomacy guidance. The 'liberals' and 'neo-liberals' focus on the pursuit of cooperation and harmony among states as the dominant task of external relations. On the basis of his professional experience, the ambassador may appreciate the comprehension shown by liberals of his myriad tasks, in building networks of political, economic, cultural and other relationships. A third dominant theory of international relations, Marxism, stands devalued now, but the ambassador may view with favor the notion advanced by their cousins, the 'institutionalists', that it is the structure and manner of functioning of institutions and agencies that determines nature and content of external relations. For one thing, these objective factors impose the parameters within which he is able to function. Yet, our ambassador may not share with the votaries of this school a completely deterministic view of the situation, i.e. that structure determines all. In the real world, the envelope of action can always be stretched with astute foreign policy and with agile diplomacy.
18. An article by Donna Lee of Birmingham University eloquently argues this point: 'The Old and New Significance of Political Economy in Diplomacy', being published in *Review of International Studies*, Volume 30, Number 3, July 2004.
19. Abba Eban, *Diplomacy for the New Century* (Yale University Press, New Haven, 1998).

20. Richard Langhorne, *Who are the Diplomats Now?* (HMSO, London, 1996).
21. Keith Hamilton and Richard Langhorne, *The Practice of Diplomacy: Its Evolution, Theory and Administration* (Routledge, London, 1995).
22. An instance of this inquiry is *Still Lying Abroad? On the Institution of the Resident Ambassador* by Robert Wolfe (Leicester: Diplomatic Studies Program, Paper No. 33, University of Leicester, 1997). The author mounts a robust defense of the ambassadors' continuing relevance.
23. Wolfe, *Still Lying Abroad?*
24. G.R. Berridge, *Diplomacy: Theory and Practice* (Prentice Hall, London, 1995).
25. A couple of examples. Keeley, Robert V., ed., *First Line of Defense: Ambassadors, Embassies and American Interests Abroad* (American Academy of Diplomacy, Washington DC, 2000). American Foreign Service Association, *Inside a US Embassy*, 2nd edition (Washington DC, 1996).
26. As a compromise in what was a very close vote, it was agreed that the main structures of several federal ministries would remain in Bonn, but that compromise formula is unlikely to endure beyond a few more years, simply because of difficulties in managing the divided system of governance.
27. By early 2003 some 30 foreign embassies, mainly representing small African countries, are still in Bonn. The fact that the Federal Economic Cooperation Ministry has stayed back in Bonn has helped them, but down the road they have little choice but to move to Berlin. It also remains to be seen how long the divided location of Federal agencies works endures.
28. Mary Locke and Casmir A. Yost, eds, *Who Needs Embassies? How US Missions Abroad Help Shape Our World*. This book catalogues other cuts carried out in US missions abroad.
29. Paschke report, executive summary.
30. An outstanding account of some of the Western exemplars of diplomacy is found in Gordon A. Craig and Francis L. Lowenheim, *The Diplomats: 1939–1979*, (Princeton University Press, Princeton, 1994).
31. This particular appointment was made during the short tenure of V.P. Singh as Prime Minister. If may have been a deliberate act of policy, but the consequences it produced were surely beyond anyone's calculation.
32. John E. Esterline, and Robert B. Black, *Inside Foreign Policy* (Mayfield, New York, 1975).

33. I have advanced this hypothesis in both my earlier books; *Inside Diplomacy* was completed in August 1999. When I read the Paschke Report for the first time in May 2002 via an English translation very kindly provided by the German Embassy in New Delhi, it was a pleasant surprise to find that most of the conclusions of this report were in parallel to my ideas.
34. Rana, *Inside Diplomacy*.
35. Jan Melissen, ed., *Innovation in Diplomatic Practice* (Macmillan, London, 1999).
36. US Senate Foreign Relations Committee Report of 1981.
37. Source: *Europa Yearbook 2000*.
38. For example, Egypt, Israel, and South Africa, have two separate ambassadors at Brussels, while India manages with one envoy, who also concurrently covers Luxembourg).

Chapter 2: Ritual and Form

1. Alan Gotlieb, in *I'll be with you in a Minute Mr Ambassador*, is particularly emphatic on the drawing power of the ambassador's social entertainment.
2. Berridge and James, *Dictionary of Diplomacy*.
3. Example: the elaborate customs, now almost extinct, of sending visiting cards with penciled notations to indicate if it was to felicitate an ambassador on the national day, or to thank him for a dinner. A corner turned up indicated that it was in lieu of a personal call. Such visiting cards carried only the envoy's name and designation; a phone numbers or addresses were deemed too trivial. Today, most even include email particulars!
4. One instance is the Philippines. The envoy may need to explain to a delegation from home the reasons for his own high ranking, when he is placed above the permanent secretary from the foreign ministry!
5. For example, Prime Minister Indira Gandhi personally approved the seating plan for every formal function she hosted, and made frequent changes to the guest list as well. That list often came back to the Chief of Protocol with the comment that more 'interesting' names should be included, drawn from diverse walks of life. As for the table seating plan she might remark that x and y 'had very little to say to each other' and should be separated! Her special concern was to ensure that her foreign guests felt comfortable in congenial company. Source: author's experience on her staff in 1981–82.

6. Elmer Plischke, ed., *Modern Diplomacy: The Art and The Artisans* (American Enterprise Institute, Washington DC, 1979).
7. The formal system of ambassadors' instructions, developed by the French, and the variations others have developed on this are narrated in *Bilateral Diplomacy*, pp. 242–3.
8. This was my own experience with the instructions given by Prime Minister Indira Gandhi in September 1975, before I went to Algiers, when she instructed me to focus on building stronger economic relations. In like fashion, I noted at the commissioning ceremony in Namibia (n.12 below) that the distilled political advice from Namibian President Sam Nujoma to his outbound envoy came not in the prepared speech he read out (clearly a collection of standard homilies drafted by someone else), but during the impromptu champagne toast he proposed to the ambassador.
9. In some diplomatic services *all* officials are required to undertake such familiarization tours before taking up any assignment abroad. It is a device worthy of wide emulation.
10. Tan Koon San, *Excellency: Journal of a Diplomat* (The Other Press, Kuala Lumpur, 2000).
11. Confidential interview, November 2002.
12. I witnessed the commissioning ceremony of Ambassador Eddy Amkongo at the State House, Windhoek in October 2000, prior to his departure as the Namibian envoy to the Democratic Republic of Congo. The elaborateness of the ritual even outshone credential ceremonies in some other countries! A remarkable sight at the buffet reception that followed was President Sam Nujoma personally supervising the buffet table, also greeting each guest. After all the guests had helped themselves, the army band that had played the national anthem at the start and end of the ceremonial, came and helped themselves—again a fine demonstration of African egalitarianism.
13. There are instances when an ambassador has been forced to seek the cancellation of a scheduled credential ceremony because the papers had not reached him, on account of a processing delay at home, the late arrival of a diplomatic bag, or a similar problem. There are stories in different diplomatic services of empty envelopes having been handed over, to fulfill requirements of ritual—after all, the head of state does not personally examine them! While such stories persist, the author has not been able to verify any.
14. The writing of such documents as a means of transmitting the accumulated knowledge is customary even in the corporate world.

A good handing over note may run to even a hundred pages. I learnt with some surprise that the Australian diplomatic service does not employ this method; one would have thought that the innovative 'benchmarking' exercise that the Australian foreign ministry carried out in 2000 would have brought home the value of such handing over notes. Norway is now considering this too.

15. Among Commonwealth countries, this takes the shape of a 'Letter of Commission', as distinct from the usual 'Letter of Credence'. Commonwealth countries that retain the Queen as their head of state exchange 'Letters of Introduction' and their high commissioners are accredited technically to the receiving government and not to their shared head of state. These technicalities apart, the ambassador and the high commissioner function in the same manner.

16. There are exceptions. At my first ambassadorship in Algeria (1975–79) the Chief of Protocol was one Boudjakji, singularly reclusive and idiosyncratic. When I asked to call on him on arrival in September 1975, he sent back a verbal message to the effect that 'of course' I could not meet him, as I had not presented credentials. As it turned out I called on his deputy, and in the course of four years, never met him. Later, I told a senior official at the Algerian MFA that Boudjakji probably was a mythical creation of some genius, as someone to be blamed by foreign envoys when they could not get satisfaction from the ministry.

17. The full text of the interesting protocol guidance note used in Malaysia is given in Tan, *Excellency*.

18. There is a hoary collection of credentials' presentation stories in each diplomatic service, some apocryphal. A good one relates to Addis Ababa in the days of Emperor Haile Salase, whose palace had a collection of fairly domesticated lions. A frequent ploy by court officials was to leave the ambassador-designate by himself in one of the waiting salons for a while, and send in one of the big cats, and then watch the reaction! An Indian ambassador of the old school probably found out about this in advance and braced himself for the encounter, and did not react visibly when the massive male lion padded in. Later after the credentials, the Emperor asked him with a twinkle in his eye that he seemed to have handled well the standard ploy of his staff, not reacting to the lion. Replied the ambassador: 'What lion, Your Majesty? The palace has only the Lion of Judah!' This delighted the Emperor, since the ambassador had used one of his formal titles, and he remarked that here was one envoy who had delivered to his courtiers their comeuppance.

19. Most capitals these days process a batch of ambassadors at a time, to save time. Between three to five is a customary number, but there are capitals that use 'lean production' assembly line techniques and handle even seven or eight, when hard pressed!
20. In late 1975, I enjoyed a brief tenure as a concurrently accredited envoy to Mauritania, before the political dispute in the region over West Sahara made it impractical to handle this work out of Algiers. In November 1975, arrangements were worked out for me to travel to Nouakchott to present credentials, reaching there on the Air Algérie flight that went on to Dakar, a day before the Independence Anniversary. I was met at the airport by the Chief of Protocol who took me straight to a spacious but unpretentious villa that was the actual residence of President Mouktar Ould Daddah. After a short wait, I was ushered in, presented my papers, and was seated on the verandah for a short conversation with the President, when I heard the Air Algérie flight take off for Dakar. The thought crossed my mind that if I had moved a bit faster, I might even have caught that flight and established a record of sorts by completing the procedure in the midst of the aircraft transit halt! A little later when the Chief of Protocol graciously accompanied me to my hotel, I asked him as to the disposal of the initialed copies of the credential papers. He reflected a bit, and with a straight face remarked: 'You should keep them, carefully'!
21. It was noted in New Delhi in September 2001 that the new US envoy, Ambassador Robert Blackwill, reached his post at the end of July, and was fully operational a few weeks later, even escorting the visiting US trade negotiator to a meeting with the Indian Prime Minister, without having presented credentials, a ceremony that was held up on account of the indisposition of the Indian President.
22. The tradition of the special diplomatic uniform is now retained only by some European nations. Immediately after the Bolshevik Revolution in 1917, the Soviet Union broke away from custom, and decided to abandon most of the old forms and courtesies. But in the early 1920s many of these were reintroduced, including an elaborate special uniform, which continues now in Russia. In contrast, countries of the Third World have opted for traditional attire or morning/evening cutaway coats and white tie (also known affectionately as 'penguin outfits'). There are other countries that accept dark suits as formal attire.
23. *In Different Saddles* (Asia, Bombay, 1967).
24. There are Asian countries where the ambassador's spouse joins the audience with the head of state, together with the latter's spouse.

25. Many envoys at such solitary encounters rely on memory to prepare their record of discussion. But when the interlocutor is accompanied by note-takers, often more than one in number, it is not inappropriate to scribble on a piece of paper some key words from the statement made by the interlocutor. Many envoys use this technique, of course with discretion and in a way that does not hinder the envoy's primary role of communication with the interlocutor.
26. Based on the author's observations and personal experience, June 1986.
27. Since the early 1990s there is some change; several career envoys, either on the verge of retirement or just retired, have been sent to London, Moscow and Washington DC. This is tacit acknowledgment that professionals do these jobs better than others.
28. According to press reports in 2003, one of the proposals doing the rounds in Tokyo is for a 20% quota for non-MFA officials, set off against appointments in other ministries for Japanese diplomatic service officials.
29. According to one source, in mid-2003 another four ambassadorial appointments were promised to career officials.
30. Clare Booth Luce, *Foreign Affairs*, October 1957.
31. Laurence H. Silberman, *Foreign Affairs*, Spring 1979.
32. Plischke, ed., *Modern Diplomacy*.
33. George Crile, *Harper's Magazine*, October, 1974.
34. Silberman, *Foreign Affairs*.
35. Toon's essay, Hertz, ed., *The Modern Ambassador*.
36. In March 1992, I was at the end of my assignment in Mauritius, a country of special linkages for India (mainly because 70% of its population is of Indian origin). Hearing that a political appointment was under consideration as my successor, I sent a personal communication to Prime Minister P.V. Narasimha Rao, urging that in the complex and delicate ethnic and religious mix of the island-state, a professional would do better justice to the advancement of Indian interests. This advice was based on the experience of Mauritius that some Indian politicians tended to view the island's complex ethnic equations from a domestic Indian perspective, quite inappropriate for that country. In the event, an outstanding diplomat, Shyam Saran was sent as my successor, and subsequent appointments too have been from the ranks of professionals.
37. In 2002, India decided to appoint an Indian academic living in the US, Bhishma Agnihotri, as Ambassador-at-Large for Indians overseas, in effect undercutting the Indian Ambassador in Washington DC, who

had traditionally handled overseas Indians living in the US. The US State Department initially refused diplomatic status for Agnihotri on the grounds that he was an Indian national holding a Green Card. It seems that the issue was resolved by Agnihotri giving up his Green Card, at which point the State Department turned down his nominal appointment as 'special adviser' to the Indian Ambassador, pointing out that such a rank was not recognized under the Vienna convention. In the end, Agnihotri was appointed as special adviser within the Indian Permanent Mission in the UN, with 'Ambassador status'. According to a report in *India Today*, 6 October 2003, he enjoys 'diplomatic privileges' but no 'diplomatic immunity'. Other Indian press reports have referred to the large budget enjoyed by Agnihotri, with the right to travel around the world, in fulfilment of his nominal duties. The episode ill serves Indian diplomacy.

38. Sometimes the term is used to refer to the members of the diplomatic service, but this is semantically inaccurate. There is a similar Consular Corps, consisting of consuls general and their officials.
39. The 1815 Congress of Vienna had stipulated that the Papal Nuncio should always head the Corps, but this Eurocentric practice is now to be found only in some West European countries and in Latin America.
40. Rana, *Inside Diplomacy*. In Germany in the early 1990s, the Asia-Pacific Group (in itself an unusual regional group cluster, encompassing countries from Pakistan to Mongolia, Japan, and New Zealand, and everything in between), carried out joint visits to federal states and to cities, soliciting invitations from them, mainly for economic promotion. It became the envy of other groups.
41. In Nairobi, during my first call on a Western ambassador, he told me that local officials were unreliable guests; some would not show up at a sit-down dinner without any explanation or notice, and a few might even turn up with their friends! So he had stopped inviting Kenyans to his dinners, surely in breach of his principal function of cultivating influential persons. It had not occurred to this ambassador that the simple solution was to switch to buffet dinners, where any dropout or unexpected arrival of guests hardly mattered.
42. Prem Budhwar, *Many Lands Many Peoples* (Konark, New Delhi, 2002).
43. Abba Eban, *The New Diplomacy* (Weidenfeld & Nicolson, London, 1988).
44. L.N. Rangarajan, edited, rearranged, translated and introduced, *The Arthashastra* (Penguin, New Delhi, 1987), pp. 577.

45. Abraham de Wicquefort, *The Embassador and his Functions* (1681; Leicester University, Leicester, 1997), pp. 265.
46. In May 2003 the press reported an incident of alleged involuntary homicide in New Delhi, involving the Senegal Ambassador's son, aged about 24. At a hotel reception he was seen beating up his driver, and the latter suffered a head injury in a fall, causing his death. Diplomatic immunity was claimed for the son, as a dependent, and the police could take no action against him. Small public demonstrations were held for a couple of days. In the end, the ambassador was withdrawn by his government. A year later, Senegal paid the equivalent of $100,000 as compensation.
47. Interestingly, it is countries like the US and other rich states that are especially adept at enforcing such reciprocity.
48. The majority of diplomatic services use the 3-year rotation formula for all their diplomatic personnel, but there are a few that extend this to 4 years, partly on grounds of economizing on transfer costs. This applies to ambassadors as well.
49. The Jackson Committee of the Senate.
50. As narrated in *Inside Diplomacy*, in ten assignments abroad in 35 years, five as an ambassador and one as a consul general, I stayed the longest period, four years and one month, in Algiers in the late 1970s. In many ways it was the most satisfying of jobs, and in the fourth year I enjoyed access and an action arena that were the product of the unusual length of that assignment. In the Indian system, the average assignment is well short of three years.
51. Confidential interview, December 2000.
52. In an interesting essay, Maldives diplomat Ali Naseer Mohamed has shown that major powers tend not to reciprocate with resident missions, in dealings with micro-states (*The Diplomacy of Micro-states*, Clingendael Discussion Paper No. 78, January 2002).
53. Source: *Europa Yearbook 2000* for the figures of foreign embassies in different capitals, while the numbers of great power embassies abroad come from Andrea Cascone, *Comparing Diplomatic Services: Structures, Networks and Resources of the Ministries of Foreign Affairs of EU and G8 Member States* (Diplo, Malta, 2002).
54. Another major instance of the withdrawal of ambassadors becoming a point of blockage was India's decision in 1961 to withdraw its ambassador from Beijing (with China retaliating), on the eve of war on the border the following year. The return of envoys became a

sensitive symbol of the normalization process, and ambassadors returned only in 1976.
55. An excellent narration of the stages in such a downward spiral in relations is given in Berridge, *Diplomacy*, 2nd edition.
56. Confidential interview, July 2003.
57. I witnessed this first hand in January–February 1972, where I served as a first secretary in the Indian Embassy at Beijing. Ambassador Kaiser, who had ably served Pakistan in the tense lead-up to the 1971 War, was among the several officials who opted for Bangladesh, in what turned out to be a smooth operation, where we provided logistic support and facilitated their initial contact with their new government.
58. This was my personal experience at Nairobi, San Francisco, Mauritius and Bonn, immediately after the 1984 crisis in Punjab over the misguided militancy movement launched by Sikh dissidents, after the assassination of Prime Minister Indira Gandhi and the ensuing anti-Sikh riots in Delhi. Personal threats, and acts of minor violence against the mission took place in 1984–89 in Nairobi and San Francisco, but there was no serious incident. That period of internal violence in India and terrorist acts abroad peaked in some years, and ended a decade later.

Chapter 3: Partners and Techniques

1. In *Inside Diplomacy* I had offered the definition 'outreach, feedback, management and servicing' (pp. 28–30). In *Bilateral Diplomacy*, 'promotion', which had been subsumed earlier in the word 'outreach', was added (pp. 24–9). 'Negotiation' was left out on the basis that its importance had reduced for professional diplomats, in bilateral diplomacy, even while it was the lifeblood of multilateral diplomacy. Clearly that was inadequate.
2. Article 3 of the 1961 Vienna Convention states: 'The functions of a diplomatic mission consist *inter alia* in: (a) representing the sending State in the receiving State; (b) protecting in the receiving State the interests of the sending State and of its nationals, within the limits permitted by international law; (c) negotiation with the Government of the receiving State; (d) ascertaining by all lawful means conditions and developments in the receiving State, and reporting thereon to the Government of the sending State; (e) promoting friendly relations

between the sending State and the receiving State, and developing their economic, cultural, and scientific relations.'
3. Keith Hamilton and Robert Langhorne, *The Practice of Diplomacy: Its Evolution, Theory and Administration* (Routledge, London, 1995), pp. 234.
4. Confidential interview, April 2001.
5. Brian Hocking, ed., *Foreign Ministries: Change and Adaptation* (Macmillan, London, 1999).
6. Situations of breakdown in relations between an ambassador and the foreign ministry's territorial unit sometimes arise; almost invariably the foreign envoy is the loser, because the system in the receiving country will seldom adapt itself to suit the envoy. I encountered situations in New Delhi and at other places where a foreign envoy accused the MFA counterpart of prejudice, or broke off contact with the territorial head, or tried to bypass the territorial head. None of this works.
7. Andrea Cascone, *Comparing Diplomatic Services: Structures, Networks and Resources of the Ministries of Foreign Affairs of EU and G8 Member States* (DiploFoundation, Malta, 2002). The four organized on a functional basis (the survey was conducted in 1999–2000): Austria, Greece, Ireland and Luxembourg.
8. In the unique US system, the identification of the 'political' and the 'bureaucracy' levels is complicated by the fact that all appointments at and above assistant state secretaries need Senate approval, and therefore represent a political choice. Despite this, typically the Secretary of State and the Deputy Secretary of State are equated with political levels in other countries; the Under Secretary for Political Affairs is regarded as the counterpart to the civil service heads of other MFAs.
9. In most foreign ministries, high officials have small secretariats of their own, with one or two diplomats as their aides; a communication delivered to them (say via a junior diplomat) will reach the dignitary concerned with a minimum of delay.
10. In *Inside Diplomacy*, I narrated the baleful practice that Germany's Hans Dietrich Genscher established towards the end of his record tenure; he simply stopped receiving ambassadors, even for the customary first call. Of course he remained accessible to the envoys of major powers. His successor Klaus Kinkel, a former civil servant, continued with this method during the years I served there (1992–95), p. 320.

11. Such escort duties provide the ambassador with a unique opportunity to develop personal connections with the visiting ministers and their team.
12. When then Algerian Foreign Minister Bouteflika (who became President in 2000) visited India in 1973, he was escorted by one of the MFA Directors, whose younger brother was the Chargé d'Affaires in New Delhi. During the meeting with Prime Minister Indira Gandhi, a master of the subtle signal, she told Bouteflika that the Chargé had kept India well informed of developments. Later, while relaxing in the hotel pool, Bouteflika turned to the Director and remarked: 'Not bad, she even calls our man by his first name!'
13. An example: when Indian Prime Minister P.V. Narasimha Rao visited Germany in February 1994, the half-full day of official talks was to be followed by a working lunch hosted by Chancellor Helmut Kohl with just 6 from each side. I submitted a suggested list, placing the Indian Foreign Secretary at the last available place. The Prime Minister saw that the German Ambassador was on their list and added my name, dropping the Foreign Secretary. He told his staff that the Foreign Secretary would understand that this did not lower his status, but it was important to convey the 'right signal' about our Ambassador.
14. John G.H. Halstead, essay in *The Modern Ambassador*, Herz ed.
15. During three years in Germany, I had just one occasion to meet Chancellor Helmut Kohl, accompanying an Indian dignitary, but I frequently met the ministers of state in the Federal Chancellery, in productive dialogue.
16. At a major European capital, an ambassador fluent in the language, who had served earlier in the country, used friendships built 15 years earlier to advance his country's interests in an exceptional manner. At his departure, exceptionally, the President wanted to host a dinner for him. Rigid protocol was circumvented: the Ambassador 'happened' to be in a restaurant that the President visited one evening, and was invited to join him at his table! In *Inside Diplomacy* I have narrated my experience with back-channel contacts in Kenya, pp. 62–3.
17. Most successful envoys have their stories on contact building. A Western envoy in a major 'closed' capital used golf as his point of access, having figured out that a high dignitary favored a particular course for his golf lessons. A former Indian envoy to an Arab country recounted in an interview how by chance he found a connection to a powerful, inaccessible high personality through a local businessman that no one had bothered to cultivate.

18. Confidential interview, March 2001. This manner of activism sometimes leads to local problems. One is a frequent shortage of interlocutors, since a small MFA may not have more than a couple of personalities that match the directive on 'highest levels'. It may also trivialize the contacts, or engender local resentment, especially in contrast to other foreign envoys that are not as active.
19. *Diplomacy for the New Century* (Yale University Press, New Haven, 1998).
20. John Kenneth Galbraith, *A Life in Our Times* (Houghton Mifflin, London, 1981) pp. 391.
21. John Kenneth Galbraith, *Ambassador's Journal* (Houghton Mifflin, Boston, 1969).
22. Hocking, *Foreign Ministries*.
23. *The Making of China's Foreign and Security Policy in the Era of Economic Reform* (Stanford University, Stanford, 2001).
24. Confidential interview, August 2001.
25. Robert V. Keeley, ed., *First Line of Defense: Ambassadors, Embassies and American Interests Abroad* (American Academy of Diplomacy, Washington DC, 2000).
26. Ibid., pp. 90–3.
27. It is a sign of the times that a communication can be sent by a cabinet level official, addressed to a foreign head of state, and the ambassador allowed the ingenuity to find a local solution.
28. Keely, ed. *First Line of Defense*, pp. 38–42.
29. Another method: the cultural wing, or the embassy's cultural center, can establish a running schedule of visiting cultural artistes, essentially as an information exchange, listing anticipated events over a horizon of 10 or 12 months, placing this on a website. This reaches out to other potential culture multipliers, like friendship associations that host cultural events or lectures.
30. Such bilateral eminent persons' groups consist of non-officials, supported by the governments, with a handful of official members who provide 'backstopping'. Typically meeting once or twice a year, they are charged with producing practical, actionable suggestions to intensify bilateral relations. The working of the Indo-German Consultative Group, active since 1992, is narrated in Rana, *Inside Diplomacy*, pp. 66–8.
31. Based on my experience at several assignments and observations of similar actions by other envoys.
32. Overseas Indians are often called Non Resident Indians (NRIs) and

Persons of Indian Origin (PIOs). The Indian government addresses them through a series of official initiatives, such as the annual *'Pravasi Bharati'* conferences organized in New Delhi since 2003. See also Rana, *Inside Diplomacy*, Chapter 18.
33. Prime Minister Indira Gandhi was especially interested in such meetings; we devoted considerable energy in planning these during the year I spent on her staff, 1981–82. See also Rana, *Inside Diplomacy*, p. 238.
34. Harold Nicolson, *Diplomacy* (Institute for the Study of Diplomacy, Georgetown, 1958).
35. In 15 years as a head of mission, I recall only three occasions when I handled negotiations involving an agreement. In one instance the last small bit of reconciliation of divergence was handled over the phone!
36. There are situations where if a pro forma representation is to be made, or the issue is not vital, a routine response to the MFA division or department will produce a predictable response. But where an affirmative response is important the ambassador will pull out the stops and approach senior officials in the office of the head of government or state. The envoy realizes that these channels cannot be overused. Confidential interview, March 2001.
37. Sad but true, there are many envoys who clutter such messages with details of the case they argued, overlooking that this rehashes familiar ground for the MFA receiving such messages from different embassies; author's observation.
38. Confidential interviews, March–April 2001.
39. Confidential interview, February 2001.
40. Keith Hamilton and Robert Langhorne, *The Practice of Diplomacy: Its Evolution, Theory and Administration* (Routledge, London, 1995).
41. Example: While I was High Commissioner in Mauritius, a thriving democracy with a wide spectrum of political opinion based partly on ethnicity, on the eve of national elections in 1991, the leaders of the opposition complained to a visiting Indian dignitary that I had been partisan in 'excessive' support to the government in power. I replied that diplomatic missions dealt primarily with the government, but I had accepted all opportunities for open contact with the opposition as well. The unstated sub-text was that one of them wanted clandestine contacts; my response was to invite him to an open meeting, which he refused!
42. Confidential interview, April 2001.

43. Confidential interview, November 2000. The direct and transparent method used here would not work at many places, and it is quite rare for an MFA to expose to an embassy its internal decision chain.
44. Comments from some confidential interviews, plus personal experience confirm this.
45. Interview, September 2001.
46. Canada, 10 July 2000, Vol. 156, No. 2. *Recasting the role of the ambassador*, by Stephen Handleman.
47. *Businessworld*, New Delhi, 25 February 2002.
48. Confidential interview, November 2000.
49. Some personal examples are given in Rana *Inside Diplomacy*, Chapter 4, 'Economics in Command'.
50. Alan Gotlieb, *I'll be with you in a Minute Mr Ambassador: The Education of a Canadian Diplomat in Washington* (Routledge, London, 1995). Gotlieb has given instances of temporary alliances of convenience that he joined, to defeat adverse actions in the US Congress.
51. Council on Foreign Relations/CSIS Report, January 2001; this was headed by former Defense Secretary and National Security Adviser Frank Carlucci.
52. A comprehensive new study on pubic diplomacy, edited by Jan Melissen is under preparation.
53. G.R. Berridge and Alan James, *A Dictionary of Diplomacy* (Palgrave, London, 2001).
54. *Paschke Report*, September 2000.
55. Evan H. Potter, *Canada and the New Public Diplomacy* (Netherlands Institute of International Relations, Clingendael, July 2002), Discussion Papers in Diplomacy No. 81.
56. These activities have been led by public relations specialists. UK's 'Cool Britannia' initiative of has been seen as a successful campaign. In 2003 Germany launched a 're-branding' campaign to present a more updated image to the EU and the rest of the world.
57. *A Journey Through the Cold War* (Brookings, Washington DC, 2001).
58. Confidential interview, February, 2001.
59. In some systems, all reports from the embassy go in the name of the ambassador. This is an old-fashioned practice, which lacks in flexibility, and detracts from the benefits of multi-level correspondence between the embassy and its home partners.
60. Cipher messages rank in a hierarchy of security classification, from 'top secret', to 'secret' and 'confidential', in usage that is standard in the UK and countries that have a British legacy. The US uses different

terminologies, as do others, but the systems are comparable. The phrase 'cipher telegram' is a hangover from the past when these were indeed sent via telegraph systems, before the telex, the fax and the Internet-based intranets.
61. Robert V. Keeley, ed., *First Line of Defense: Ambassadors, Embassies and American Interests Abroad* (American Academy of Diplomacy, Washington DC, 2000).
62. Confidential interview, May 2002.
63. This well-documented story was narrated to the author in 1999 by the Chairman of a major travel company who added that he had stood in the queue to verify for himself the way the system worked.
64. India, a source of illegal migration to the West, also faces an inflow from neighboring Bangladesh, again driven by comparative economics.

Chapter 4: The Multilateral Ambassador

1. G.R. Berridge and Alan James, *A Dictionary of Diplomacy* (Palgrave: Basingstoke, 2001).
2. The present situation in almost every UN agency and in the other international organizations as well is one of very considerable power of the secretariats, some of which actively practice their own brand of diplomacy *vis-à-vis* member governments. For instance, ILO plays off governments against the labor and business representatives in its unique tripartite structure. Elsewhere too, one result of subject complexity and interconnection has been the growth in the relative strength of secretariats.
3. Monteagle Stearns, *Talking to Strangers: Improving American Diplomacy at Home and Abroad* (Princeton University Press, Princeton, 1996).
4. This conclusion is based on an informal, unscientific poll, covering ambassadors as well as young diplomats.
5. This information emerges from my ongoing study covering the foreign ministries of some Asian countries: China, Japan, India, Singapore and Thailand.
6. Michael Dobbs, *Madeleine Albright* (Holt, New York, 1999).
7. The ceremony at the UN specialized agencies is similar. The permanent representative at the European Union actually hands over two sets of letters, one each for the President of the European

Commission and to the President of the Council of Ministers, the two governing arms of the EU.
8. A personal example: at the UN Conference on Women that met at Nairobi in 1985, I quickly found that the 15-member official delegation led by a Minister of State from New Delhi (including parliamentarians, social activists, academics, a movie star and the wife of a senior official) was more than a handful. The daily delegation meeting at the start of the day produced minor drama, some days centered on the urge of some delegates 'to do something useful', which in practice meant launching personal initiatives and delivering speeches on own hobby-horses, not part of the official brief. It took all the combined skills of my mission colleagues and officials from home to keep our delegates sufficiently occupied and out of mischief!
9. J.N. Dixit, *Across Borders: 50 Years of India's Foreign Policy* (Picus, New Delhi, 1998).
10. A few countries that were left out did question the basis on which G-15 was created, but did not press their criticism to any extent. The group recently decided to admit some more members, without changing its name.
11. A third instance of promotional activity in a multilateral setting is of a different character, relating to the UN Narcotics Commission in the years 1967–70, and is narrated in Chapter 8.
12. Nicolson's words are memorable: 'Diplomacy is not the art of conversation, it is the craft of negotiation of agreements in precise and ratifiable form.' *Diplomacy* (Institute for the Study of Diplomacy, Georgetown, 1958).
13. For right-wing US opinion that exclusion from the Human Rights Commission has rankled as a failure caused by a culture of 'process, politeness and accommodation', Newt Gingrich, *Rogue State Department*, Foreign Policy, July–August 2003.
14. Rana, *Inside Diplomacy*, pp. 89–90.
15. Diplomatic services have their own legends of intensive lobbying efforts, when there is a tight contest for an elected appointment such as to the International Court of Justice at The Hague, or for some relatively lucrative UN office that may be open to an individual. Usually countries include the prospective candidate in their delegation to the particular UN General Assembly session that is to vote on such appointments. One Indian candidate became so involved that he viewed each minor committee vote in terms of adding or subtracting from his likely election support tally; he was finally told by the PR

that there were a few other agenda issues that India had to pursue, and that he should keep his cool and not interfere in every issue!
16. In *Bilateral Diplomacy*, I have written about the changing educational background of new recruits in Germany and elsewhere; economics is replacing law as the tertiary educational subject of a majority of new entrants.
17. Confidential interview, January 2002.
18. Monteagle Stearns, *Talking to Strangers: Improving American Diplomacy at Home and Abroad* (Princeton University Press, Princeton, 1996).
19. Confidential interview, July 2003.
20. For a comprehensive account see Hocking and Spence, eds, *Foreign Ministries in the European Union*.
21. Ibid.
22. Other regional organizations have their own practices. Sub-regional bodies in Africa, like SADC and ECOWAS do not use the PR system. Nor does MERCOSUR of Latin America. The regional bodies of the UN, like ESCAP based in Bangkok, have PRs from several countries, distinct from the ambassadors accredited to Thailand.
23. A refinement added in the past year is that the joint EU démarches now go only in the name of the EU, modifying the earlier phrase 'the EU and member-states'.
24. Stearns, *Talking to Strangers*.
25. Rana, *Inside Diplomacy*, p. 218.
26. In the case of India, out of eight permanent representatives in New York in the past 25 years, all but two moved to UN jobs directly from their assignments. A similar pattern is visible with other countries, but in smaller numbers.

Chapter 5: The Domestic Dimension

1. Andrew Cooper, ed., *Niche Diplomacy* (Macmillan, London, 1999).
2. Confidential interview, January 2002.
3. During a workshop at the Brookings Institution in mid-2001, when I offered an outline of this book before a select audience, an Indian colleague who had served in the office of high personalities in New Delhi remarked that sometimes our own ambassadors behave as spokesmen of the other country's viewpoint. This happens, but the more frequent situation is the inability to listen to a perspective different from one's own. This is a typical problem for the envoy.

4. Confidential interview, November 2000.
5. Confidential interview, May 2003.
6. Two instances: in the late 1990s, the German Ambassador in India was criticized in his home media, unfairly, for doing too little to help business enterprises. In 2002 criticism surfaced in the US over the management style of Ambassador Blackwill vis-à-vis his embassy colleagues in New Delhi.
7. This expression is borrowed from Richard Faber, *A Chain of Cities: Diplomacy at the Edge of Empire* (The Radcliffe Press, London, 2000).
8. A personal example: In 1994 the Indian Embassy faced a problem in Germany when an important delegation from a business organization decided to postpone their journey, barely five weeks before it was to commence, unmindful of the preparatory work carried out by the German partners. This was their second postponement and would have represented a general loss of credibility for us. I telephoned the Foreign Secretary and sought his help; he had the means to speak more forcefully than I could have done and the visit was maintained, with another person leading the delegation.
9. In the course of my assignments as a head of mission or post, there was one instance when the Indian Ministry of External Affairs expressly forbade me from endorsing messages on a specific topic to the external intelligence agency R&AW. I felt that my responsibilities were not limited to MEA, and my right to offer feedback or suggestions to other agencies of the government could not be curtailed, but prudence dictated acceptance of the MEA directive.
10. One US ambassador reported that when efforts to lift sanctions imposed by the US Congress on a country in Latin America were under way, he personally lobbied over 100 congressmen in Washington DC. Cited in Smith Simpson, and Margery Botchel, eds, *Education in Diplomacy* (Rowman and Littlefield, New York, 1987).
11. The media, increasingly using investigative techniques, look closely at the conduct of envoys, as visible in the Indian print media and in other countries.
12. Many European countries are the source of old migration, most notably Ireland, Italy and Spain to the New World. For instance, gauged in terms of the size of its Italian population, Buenos Aires equals Venice in size. For small states like Malta, and even Ireland, the size of the overseas community is several times the size of the nation's population. All this involves the overseas ethnic groups into

domestic affairs, and forces the envoy to develop a sensitivity to their linkages with domestic political forces.
13. There are credible accounts of ethnic community leaders and major Indian businessmen arranging meetings for visiting Indian ministers at 10, Downing Street, London, and with important congressional and administration leaders in Washington DC.
14. My experience in the cultural and ethnic arena in Mauritius is narrated in *Inside Diplomacy*, pp. 155–7.
15. This incident and its impact on bilateral relations was the subject of a newspaper article that I wrote, *Indian Express*, 7 June 2003 (also reproduced in the Mauritius daily *L'Express*, 11 June 2003).
16. In London and in the US, Indian envoys have confronted such situations, and the same is true of the other envoys from South Asia. We can call this a form of domestic politics played out in the foreign capital.
17. Confidential interview, November 2001.
18. The guidance I received at a short but purposeful meeting with Prime Minister Indira Gandhi in September 1975, before my first ambassadorship in Algeria was simple and powerful. She pointed to the fact that bilateral political relations were excellent, and added: 'that is good as far as it goes'; my task would be to give commensurate economic content to the relationship. This became a guiding compass for action.
19. This is the result of a system of periodic consultation among EU members on administrative issues concerning foreign ministries, which came into existence in 2000. It has generated a great deal of cross-fertilization.
20. Confidential interview, August 2001. Given the intensive consultations needed for implementing new activities in Germany, where lengthy inter-ministry coordination is involved, it is not easy to apply in full the French concept.
21. For a more detailed survey of performance monitoring issues, including personal experience with writing one's own start of mission objectives, see: Rana, *Inside Diplomacy*, pp. 79–83 and Rana, *Bilateral Diplomacy*, pp. 243–5.
22. US embassies are also required to report on performance, under the terms of the Government Performance Results Act that applies to all federal agencies. One official interviewed remarked that this is not always taken very seriously, confidential interview, 2003.

23. The UK's system of objectives and targets is elaborated in an expenditure plan document that the Foreign and Commonwealth Office publishes every two years. It is a model of transparency of the foreign affairs governance process.
24. Singapore's monthly report format has three parts: the mission reports on the major activity undertaken (it may range from a commercial event to weeding out old records or visits to regions); a listing of the major dispatches sent by each embassy diplomat; and details of new contacts established with influential local personalities. It is a method worthy of emulation.
25. Confidential interview, October 1999.
26. In the US inspections are mandatory at a maximum interval of 3 years. This means that about 50 embassies (besides consulates) have to be inspected each year; (some inspection reports are publicly available on the State Department's website, a degree of transparency that has no other emulator as yet). Many others opt for inspections once in around five years. The Germans have a particularly rigorous system. See Rana, *Bilateral Diplomacy*, pp. 240–1.
27. Examples are Austria and Germany; the latter entrusted the task to their largest consultancy enterprise, Roland Berger and Partner, which produced a report in 1996 that ran to over 1000 pages (Hocking and Spence, *Foreign Ministries in the European Union*).
28. The actual figures are available in an Italian Foreign Ministry monograph by Andrea Cascone, *Comparing Diplomatic Services: Structures, Networks and Resources of the Ministries of Foreign Affairs of EU and G8 Member States* (DiploFoundation, Malta, 2002). The conclusion on an optimum level for the efficient operation of the diplomatic system is based on this analysis and the author's studies; Rana, *Bilateral Diplomacy*, p. 121.
29. This is the case with India with a ratio of 1 to 3; that personnel shortage at headquarters is at the root of many of its problems. At the end of 2003, an effort is reportedly under way to expand manpower and redress the imbalance.
30. The ranking of ambassadors, relative to the permanent head of the MFA is a subject on which practice varies greatly. There are countries such as Thailand and Turkey where ambassadors are appointed in a single rank, placed just below the permanent secretary. This, as noted in Chapter 7, leads to inflexibility in personnel management. In Germany, the two career State Secretaries in the Foreign Office outrank all career officials; as and when they are sent

out abroad as ambassadors, they step back in rank, to the next level, that of *Ministerialdirektor*.
31. The problem is compounded in some countries when non-career ambassadors are given additional notional status, like 'ranks' equivalent to cabinet ministers, ministers of state, or even of provincial governors (this happens in India). These are gestures intended to assuage the egos of politicians who may have held such offices, but mean nothing in the receiving country. They give an inflated notion to the incumbents in relation to their dialogue at home.
32. These elementary lessons in domestic diplomacy are learnt through observation, when working at the foreign ministry in a junior capacity.
33. One observed consequence of the use of intranets is that officials carrying their laptop computers have a tendency to check incoming mail several times a day, which changes the quality of contacts.
34. Paschke Report, 2000.
35. Speech by Steffen Rudolph, Director-General of Central Services, entitled 'Foreign Service Reform', 19 June 2001: 'We want to empower our missions: it never ceases to surprise me to what extend we still consider it necessary to prescribe, regulate and control in minute detail from Berlin the inner workings of our missions. This is wasteful and violates the common sense rule that the people on the spot know best...'
36. Confidential interviews, January 2000 and January 2001.
37. I am obliged to one of the participants from a developed country in one of the internet-based courses I teach at the DiploFoundation for a graphic perspective, as seen from outside the MFA, on the value of improved collaboration of this nature. This has confirmed to me once again how much this is a rarity, despite all the lip service paid to the theme.
38. For the envoy it means a special effort, placing himself in the shoes of the agency that needs assistance, and going beyond just the minimum work obligations. A personal example: In Germany we worked hard on a particular defense project. On the eve of Prime Minister Narasimha Rao's official visit in February 1994, the Secretary of the Department of Defense Production paid a rare, even unprecedented compliment, to my team and myself at a meeting chaired by the PM, stating that we had played a vital role in obtaining German approval on the project.
39. In the US, a demand has surfaced from time to time for stronger presidential control of the State Department, e.g. Laurence H. Silberman's article in *Foreign Affairs*, Spring, 1979 and Newt Gingrich

in *Foreign Policy*, July–August 2003 calling for 'long overdue transformation', that would include 'loyalty to the president'. In other government systems, such as Germany, the Chancellor as executive head of government has limited powers to intervene in the affairs of the Foreign Office, though he retains primacy of initiative in external affairs.

40. I witnessed this during the time I worked on the staff of Prime Minister Indira Gandhi, 1981–82. The frequency of such direct communication between leaders has grown since then.
41. Monteagle Stearns, *Talking to Strangers: Improving American Diplomacy at Home and Abroad* (Princeton University Press, Princeton, 1996).
42. Episodic evidence indicates that transcripts of this nature are not maintained in countries that do not have strong institutional systems.
43. *Mission to Iran* (New York, 1981). This lack of access surely contributed to the manner in which this ambassador's advice on the events in Teheran was ignored in Washington DC.
44. My four years in Algeria (September 1975 to November1979), saw a major political change at home, first in March 1977 when Indira Gandhi lost the national elections, and again in mid-1979 when the Janata government changed prime ministers. Algerian interlocutors found it hard to understand that the same envoy could represent a new government. The notion of an apolitical civil service was novel for them, since they had not seen any change in the ruling FLN party, other than Boumedienne's coup of 1965 that overthrew the Ben Bella regime.
45. Based on personal observations in Germany and elsewhere. Sometimes stories also surface in the press about efforts of envoys to get out of unattractive assignments (e.g. two stories in *Indian Express*, July 2003)
46. At several assignments I found that recommendations from business enterprises and other non-officials on useful persons to cultivate in the target country enriched our networking reach. In one case in Germany, when I suggested to embassy colleagues that I had been advised to call on a particular office-holder, they countered that this contact was unnecessary at the level of the ambassador. He became a useful ally and one of our strong assets in that country.
47. Ambassadors also need mindset changes in such dealings. The CEO of an Indian public sector enterprise told me that while visiting a European capital to sign a major contract, he called on the ambassador to apprise him. The latter demanded a written brief from him, and the CEO, peeved at what he saw as a bureaucratic attitude, ended the

meeting, dropping his idea of inviting him to the signing ceremony and the dinner that was to follow, where the envoy might have expanded his circle of contacts.

48. In Germany we found this out by accident, when we remonstrated local hosts that they had not informed us of visits by some Indian journalists. Thereafter, we made it a point to keep track of incoming visitors as best as we could, and invariably invited them to a meal or some other social function, at the Residence or at the home of one of the diplomats. It led to a situation where journalists opted on their own to come to the embassy, for mutually useful exchanges.
49. Confidential interview, November 2000.
50. Ibid.
51. The experience in Germany in 1992–95, dealing with NGOs on the Narmada water project which was under discussion with the World Bank at that time, has been narrated in *Inside Diplomacy* (pp. 370–3). We lost that particular battle, and the German decision to abstain from supporting India on this project was an element that contributed to the Indian decision to forgo further World Bank aid. The lesson I learnt, and tried to implement subsequently, was that one should not initiate dialogue with sensitive actors like NGOs in times of crisis. One needs channels of communication with them in good times, to prevent the crisis from occurring.
52. One instance is the campaign by the NGO 'PETA' against the cruel treatment of animals in poor countries, that takes the form of boycott against imports of leather products produced in these countries. African countries find some of the development NGOs to be a powerful source of lobbying and funding.
53. Badr-Ud-Din Tyabji, *Memories of an Egoist* (Roli, New Delhi, 1988).
54. Jan Melissen, ed., *Innovation in Diplomatic Practice* (Macmillan, Basingstoke, 1999).
55. In the Canadian diplomatic service, one of the four core values that is propagated is innovation, which is deemed to be one of the essential principles that the service is enjoined to advance, for the public good.

Chapter 6: Leadership in the Embassy

1. The myth of extraterritoriality, even if it has no hard basis in international law (e.g. the 1961 Vienna Convention), reinforces this image.
2. In 1966, at the height of China's Cultural Revolution, Chinese non-diplomatic personnel working as embassy chauffeurs, cooks and

service staff brought the embassies to a standstill by refusing to carry out orders. The fact that Chinese embassies in the West do not employ any locally recruited staff compounded the problem.
3. Until the 19th century, the embassy staff were called the ambassadors 'official family'. In cultures like those of Africa or Asia, where professional and personal life are not separated into watertight compartments, and where paternalist behavior is a norm, not a pejorative, it is easier to deal with such personnel issues, than in cultures where a sharp distinction is made between the different spheres, and it becomes harder to deal with problems that arise from stress, separation or personal difficulty.
4. Cited by Katie Hickman, *Daughters of Britannia* (Flamingo, London, 1999).
5. Elmer Plischke, *Modern Diplomacy: The Art and the Artisans* (American Enterprise Institute, Washington DC, 1979).
6. Relations between ethnic communities and 'their' diplomatic representatives are a rich area for social research. While there is a growing body of Indian diaspora studies, there is little published material on this subject. For example, stories surface from time to time in the Indian press on the problems faced by Indian envoys in dealing with fragmented Indian communities. The Indian High Commissioner in London has always had a hard time in steering his way between such local rivalries, and there have been times when some businessmen enjoying special proximity to the powers in New Delhi have virtually functioned as parallel, unofficial envoys.
7. At a seminar organized by the Quakers on the outskirts of Geneva that I attended in 1967, a psychologist made the point that diplomats compensate for the continuous dislocation of their life by cherishing the friendships formed at their first assignment. Empirical evidence, and my experience, tend to confirm this.
8. In some diplomatic services, and in some legal systems, the ambassador's power to conduct marriages is curtailed, but generally such power is available. In 1963 my sister was married at the Indian Embassy in Bonn, at a time when my brother-in-law was studying in Germany.
9. Some of the smaller countries in Africa and Latin America follow the practice of giving diplomatic rank, of second and third secretary or attaché, to all home-based staff. Their missions are too small to make this a problem for the receiving country, which sometimes imposes a limit on the size of embassies.
10. In practice, well-connected political appointees might get the privilege

of selecting a deputy. It is only the ambassadors at the largest missions that get a diplomat-level official to work as a personal assistant.
11. John E. Esterline and Robert B. Black, *Inside Foreign Policy* (Mayfield, New York, 1975).
12. CFP-CSIS Report, January 2001.
13. Dana Priest, *The Mission: Waging War and Keeping Peace with America's Military* (Norton, New York, 2003).
14. *Foreign Service Journal*, May 2001.
15. Author's personal experience in two situations abroad.
16. In some diplomatic services, it has become routine to designate the second-ranking official in even small embassies as the DCM. This is a misnomer, because the term implies that the individual is of senior rank.
17. J.K. Galbraith, *Ambassador's Journal* (Houghton Mifflin, Boston, 1969).
18. The diplomatic services that have a single civil service rank for ambassadors do not have this flexibility, since in such systems, an individual who has served once as ambassador cannot go abroad as a deputy. Besides creating rigidity, this is also unrealistic, since the job that a deputy has to handle say at Washington DC or New York is far more challenging than an ambassadorship in a distant outpost.
19. In *Inside Diplomacy*, I have narrated my experience with the breaking down of rigid work allocations, and other aspects of the working of Indian embassies, pp. 311–41.
20. These covert officials are different from 'declared' intelligence and security agencies' representatives, who work openly as liaison and communication channels with host counterparts. They play a vital role in the war against global terrorism and crime.
21. Monteagle Stearns, *Talking to Strangers: Improving American Diplomacy at Home and Abroad* (Princeton University Press, Princeton, 1996).
22. Esterline and Black, *Inside Foreign Policy*.
23. A former British envoy publicly commented in the UK media in October 2003 on the way some of the reports by intelligence officials in embassies are lifted from the media or echo common gossip. Diplomats who have served at politically important posts can testify to the uncommon keenness of their intelligence colleagues to get hold of political reports written by others.
24. J.N. Dixit, *Mission Colombo* (Konarak, New Delhi, 1998).
25. Confidential interview, April 2001.
26. One indicator of the sensitivity of the work of the defense attachés is that they are the only embassy officials whose appointment is subject to an *agrément* procedure, as with the ambassador.

27. An exception to this was encountered by the author in a very small mission headed by an ambassador of abrasive temperament. Visiting this ambassador in his office, I asked about the other officials under his charge, and he responded that the only diplomatic level official was an assistant military attaché. I suggested that we call him in to join our informal conversation; the ambassador declined, telling me that he was not on talking terms with him!
28. A personal example will illustrate this. In the Indian system, the chiefs of the armed force services have a fixed 'quota' of foreign visits, and each visit has to be cleared by the Defense Ministry. I encountered a situation in Germany where the armed service attachés in the embassy made soundings, without my knowledge, with the local counterparts 'in anticipation' of final approval by the Indian Defense Ministry—only to find that the latter did not approve of a visit that the Germans had accepted! This embarrassment led me to insist with my colleagues and New Delhi that the embassy would not begin the process of seeking local approvals until all the procedures at the Indian end had been completed.
29. The difference between a consulate and a consulate general is simply one of rank of the official heading the 'post'—as these are called, distinguished from the embassy (or high commission, or permanent mission, for which the appellation 'mission' is utilized.)
30. Based on personal experience as a consul general (at San Francisco, covering 18 states) and as an ambassador with three subsidiary offices in Germany (Berlin, Frankfurt and Hamburg) plus two honorary consuls general (in Munich and Stuttgart).
31. A system of regular meetings was started in the US in the late 1980s during my time in San Francisco. I followed a similar method of biannual meetings in Germany in 1992–95.
32. Diplomatic law and practice do not offer much shelter to such subsidiary offices, but they are used to gain a foothold in cities of economic importance that have not been opened by the host country for consulates. One Indian example is Ahmedabad and Hyderabad where no consulates exist, but a few countries have set up their own small trade offices, headed by Indians.
33. In my career, I dealt with honorary consuls at two places, first from San Francisco where as a career consul general I dealt with our honorary consul at Hawaii, a businessman of exceptional grace who passed away during my tenure, and was replaced by his wife. The second place was Germany, where we initially had an honorary consul general

at Stuttgart, and then established a new honorary consulate at Munich. Both gave excellent results.
34. Example: When the Sri Lankan envoy in Germany joined the group excursions of Asia Pacific ambassadors, he often added to the program his own set of bilateral visits organized by his honorary consul.
35. In *Bilateral Diplomacy* I have narrated an incident where I was at the receiving end of such a lobbying effort (p. 144). In recent years, several European countries have tightened procedures of granting permission for new honorary consulates and the selection of individuals.
36. For over a decade, India had an exceptional person as its honorary consul general in Stuttgart, a leading businessman named Helmut Nanz. At a dinner in his honor in Bonn in 1994, to thank him for all that he had done, he declared in his after-dinner speech that no previous ambassador had made him work as hard!
37. Thailand uses the same term, as a work responsibility for its 'CEO ambassadors' in a formula developed in 2003.
38. An example: In 1986, as a consul general I encouraged the local branch of an Indian bank in San Francisco to hold monthly meetings of leading Indian businessmen and technocrats to discuss economic issues and meet interesting visitors from home. Supported by that success, a group of young electronic engineers decided in 1987 to create a forum for business dialogue, 'The Silicon Valley Indian Professionals Association' (SIPA), that survives to the present. That in turn indirectly prompted the creation of 'The Indus Entrepreneurs' (TiE) in 1992, which now has a global network of branches and has played a role in assisting new ventures in high technology by technocrats from South Asia.
39. Brian Hocking and David Spence, eds, *Foreign Ministries in the European Union: Integrating Diplomats* (Palgrave Macmillan, Basingstoke, 2002).
40. Andrea Cascone, *Comparing Diplomatic Services: Structures, Networks and Resources of the Ministries of Foreign Affairs of EU and G8 Member States* (DiploFoundation, Malta, 2002), p. 8.
41. Galbraith, *Ambassador's Journal*.
42. Alan Gotlieb, *I'll Be With You in a Minute Mr Ambassador*.
43. Article by Jovan Kurbalija, in Jan Melissen, ed., *Modern Diplomacy* (Mediterranean Academy of Diplomatic Studies, Malta, 1998).
44. Hickman, *Daughters of Britannia*.
45. Ibid.
46. This incident is narrated in Liu Xiaohong, *Chinese Ambassadors: The Rise of Diplomatic Professionalism Since 1949* (Hong Kong University

Press, Hong Kong, 2001). Most of the spouses of the revolutionary cadres of the time had always worked in the pre-1949 organizations, hence their strong reaction to restrictions. Since the 1980s tighter standards are applied, but qualified spouses are allowed to work within the same embassy.

47. In the Indian Foreign Service, couples have been assigned to proximate posts, like Dar-es-Salaam and Nairobi, or Warsaw and Bucharest. But there have also been couples that have served out at places as far apart as Bangladesh and Canada.
48. Chas W. Freeman, *Diplomat's Dictionary* (US Institute of Peace, Washington DC, 1994).
49. The public rooms in the residence are mainly furnished by the foreign ministry, which typically also supplies decorative objects d'art. But there is latitude for the envoy to display personal decorative materials, paintings and the like.
50. For instance, during the years of acute LTTE-sponsored violence in Sri Lanka, many official visitors, including Indian foreign ministers, stayed at the Indian High Commissioner's residence for reasons of security, on the recommendation of the local authorities.
51. These compromise arrangements may include the use of local embassy staff as service personnel at receptions, and sometimes even the use of home-based official junior staff for such purposes, and the use of ethnic community temporary helpers. The envoy's allowances are supposed to contain an element that is to cover such local hire of services, and/or personal staff taken from the home country by the envoy, but this too produces its problems. The net effect is the reduced use of the residence for representational purposes.
52. In Germany in 1992–95, unwilling to abandon the Republic Day reception for which special funds were provided from home (this is customary in most diplomatic services), I added the practice of organizing on that day an open-house music concert featuring a major Indian artiste, in partnership with one of the major radio stations.
53. For instance, this was the theme of a fairly detailed account carried in an Indian journal *The Hindustan Times*, 27 July 2001, which reported that an excessive amount was claimed by many envoys through fudged accounts of social receptions, leading to misuse. A member of parliament was reported to have written to the minister, urging tighter control and reimbursement on actuals, as is the practice in the US and elsewhere.
54. The national day receptions of some EU countries held abroad now have corporate sponsors, as witnessed in New Delhi in 2002. Some

Western countries allow reputed business enterprises to pay for social events at which they provide the bulk of the guest list. In general, developing countries have not adopted these practices, but there is no *a priori* reason that prevents the wider use of such innovative methods.

Chapter 7: Human Resources

1. In services that are too large to accommodate every individual of fair competence to an ambassadorship even at the very end of his or her career (such as those of the US, UK, China, France, Germany, Russia and some others), face an intrinsic morale problem. A pre-retirement appointment as consul general serves as an imperfect substitute for many such officials. Some smaller services have too few ambassador assignments available, plus strong competition from non-career appointees. This reduces the attraction of a diplomatic service, the more so with growing career choices.
2. The Canadian program devotes a week to management methods, starting with a hard presentation by the Inspectors on the kinds of problems that arise in embassies, with ambassadors with previous experience constituting a panel. Time is also devoted to the routine financial scrutiny which the ambassador is expected to exercise. New technology, public diplomacy and human resource management are some of the other issues covered.
3. I have participated in 6 regional or 'selected participant' conferences of ambassadors, two in New Delhi and four abroad, in the course of some 15 years as an ambassador. The most fascinating was in New Delhi in January 1977, chaired by Prime Minister Indira Gandhi, at the end of India's two-year 'Emergency', perceived as a dark era, when some rules of the constitution and democracy were suspended, to protect her regime. The other gathering of selected ambassadors held in the capital in December 1992 was preempted by the demolition of the Babri Masjid and the ensuing political crisis; it was cancelled on the very first day. Envoys were instructed to return immediately to their posts and deal with the international fallout of that event. The four regional gatherings held abroad generally suffered from a lack of attention by the visiting minister who nominally chaired the conference. The few recommendations of each conference were not followed up. But they did provide an update on New Delhi's thinking. India has not held a full conference of envoys.
4. Some foreign ministries resist the formula of collective recommendations from ambassadors' conferences, but this is short sighted,

and neglects the value of brainstorming. This was true of the relatively few conferences organized by the Indian Ministry of External Affairs, but the situation has changed in recent years, and some concrete ideas flow from the meetings.

5. The Chinese now use both the training programs and the annual conference. This is a facet of the rapid reform that the Chinese are carrying out in their diplomatic process.
6. Freeman, *Diplomat's Dictionary* (US Institute of Peace, Washington DC, 1994).
7. Ibid.
8. Harold Nicolson, *Diplomacy* (Institute for the Study of Diplomacy, Georgetown, 1958).
9. Freeman, *Diplomat's Dictionary*,
10. Raymond Cohen, *Theatre of Power: The Art of Diplomatic Signaling* (Longmans, London, 1987).
11. Wotton evidently inscribed this remark in an album at the important commercial town of Augsburg in Bavaria in 1604; when it was reported back to King James I, the monarch was not pleased. Nicolson, *Diplomacy*.
12. Confidential interview, January 2002. The experience of the author and many others also bears this out.
13. This particular term is a favorite of N.K. Narayana Murthy, the head of Infosys Technologies, globally renowned as an outstanding business leader in the software industry.
14. Indian diplomats at all levels are required to undertake these '*Bharat Darshan*' (India pilgrimage) tours each time they are posted abroad, to see first hand the socio-economic developments, and meet with institutions, companies and others that are engaged in activities at the country of assignment. Other countries have similar programs for updating one's own knowledge of the home country.
15. In the value system charter that the Canadian diplomatic service promotes, innovation figures as a specific requirement for improved public service.
16. I learnt this graphically at my first ambassadorship, Algiers (1975–79), with a very limited understanding of French. For a couple of months I went to receptions and other large events, accompanied by the home-based interpreter from the Embassy, but quickly found that this was awkward and inhibited contact. My survival in that linguistic environment forced me to learn French quickly.
17. For instance, India has about 20 major English language dailies, called the 'national press'. But there are also some 1600 dailies in Hindi and other regional languages. With no access to these, even

a selected few, foreign observers miss out on the flavor of opinion in the country's vast regional and non-urban heartland.
18. Typically a system of monetary reward is operated, with a requirement for language knowledge re-qualification every five years or so. Diplomats are also encouraged to learn additional languages. When there is a system of initial language qualification, but no subsequent requirement to re-qualify, nor any reward for those who sustain language ability, as currently in the Indian diplomatic system, many let their language skills atrophy, and the service loses a valuable asset.
19. There is a perpetual debate over the choice of foreign languages to be mastered in a diplomatic service, especially the 'minor' languages, i.e. those spoken often in a single country. If that country happens to be a neighbor, it is useful to have some experts, but a small service finds it hard to sustain narrow expertise.
20. The group is named after the formal name of Emperor Akahito's reign.
21. *Mainichi Shimbun*, 19 April 2001.
22. Serving as ambassador to Czechoslovakia in the early 1980s, I encountered a different kind of an inner group, of envoys who enjoyed hunting, a sport favored by the then Foreign Minister. Possessing more enthusiasm than skill, I joined this group to gain access. It led to a series of excellent excursions into the countryside, and a chance for informal conversation in a convivial environment, plus once by sheer chance a fine wild boar trophy as well!
23. The Chinese diplomatic system continues to lay stress on language expertise, and officials study some 60 languages, besides English, which is now a basic requirement for all. China is also unique in having within the service a large number of interpreter-level specialists.
24. In the German system, the rank of state secretary is available only at home; an official serving at that level steps back one rank if he is assigned abroad.
25. On paper, the Indian system pays lip-service to merit, but in reality, promotion works on an absence of demerit, i.e. as long as one has not committed any misdemeanor or been grossly inefficient, promotion comes almost on the escalator principle, except at the very apex where there are too few posts and selectivity has to be enforced. Yet the Indian armed forces employ modern, effective selection criteria, proving that good HR practices can be enforced.
26. Distrust of the merit principle is mainly because of the fear that those in power would misuse it for the benefit of favorites, not because the principle itself is objectionable. Each time this issue has been discussed

in entities like the Indian Foreign Service Association (which brings together all 'A' branch officials, i.e. those holding diplomatic rank), after long debate, the seniority principle has been deemed as the best of a difficult set of alternatives.
27. The rank of secretary is the highest in the civil service, though there are a few specific appointments (Cabinet Secretary, Principal Secretary to the Prime Minister, Finance Secretary and Chairman of the Railway Board) which are one notch higher.
28. At the same time, the Indian system has done well in one aspect of career planning, by developing experts in areas like disarmament and security affairs, multilateral trade negotiations, and the like. Language and area specialization has worked well for India in Chinese and Russian, but less well in other languages like Arabic or Spanish.
29. India's Constitution-mandated affirmative action, i.e. the policy of 'reservations' or quotas for disadvantaged segments of society, also works as a serious barrier to merit-based promotions. Reservations were designed to favor Scheduled Castes and Scheduled Tribes (expanded in 1990 in favor of other 'backward' groups). This has led to a political demand for reservations in promotions, all the way to the top.
30. Some evidence suggests such a situation of post-modern angst in the Canadian service.
31. The UK has used this method in the past.
32. Berridge, *Diplomacy: Theory and Practice*, 2nd edition.
33. Harold Nicolson, *Diplomacy* (Institute for the Study of Diplomacy, Georgetown University, Washington DC).
34. David Spence, 'The Evolving Role of the Foreign Ministry in the Conduct of European Union Affairs' in Brian Hocking and David Spence, eds, *Foreign Ministries in the European Union: Integrating Diplomats* (Palgrave Macmillan, Basingstoke, 2002).
35. Abba Eban, *Diplomacy for the New Century* (Yale University Press, New Haven, 1998).
36. There was an unusual incident in Algiers in the late 1970s that combined personal malfeasance with professional misconduct. A West European envoy violated financial regulations and was found out towards the end of his term. He then refused to return home, told the local authorities that he remained in charge even after his successor arrived, refused to vacate the embassy residence, and eventually was almost physically removed. Full details did not emerge, but he was dismissed from the service.

37. The Indian press reported some months later that an equivalent of $110,000 was paid as compensation by Senegal.
38. J.K. Galbraith, *Ambassador's Journal* (Houghton Mifflin, Boston, 1969).
39. Ibid.
40. This tale comes from a collection that passed by word of mouth in the diplomatic community. Each place has its own collection of such stories that enliven life in the diplomatic corps.
41. Confidential interview, September 2000.
42. See Rana, *Inside Diplomacy*, pp. 89–90. That election defeat, by a huge 130 to 41 margin, resulted from the unprofessional miscalculation of the response of foreign governments to the Indian diplomatic mobilization effort. One result has been that India has not offered itself for election again since, even though it has a solid claim to a seat on the rotation principle.
43. Jagat S. Mehta (*World Affairs*, New Delhi, April 2002).
44. In the 1970s at Algiers, my French colleague Ambassador Guy de Commynes recounted a delightful story of the time when he happened to visit a provincial town in Chad, where he earlier held concurrent accreditation. At a reception in honor of the visiting 'Emperor' Bokassa, the latter dispensed a clutch of awards to local dignitaries. As the ceremony was ending, he learnt that the French Ambassador was present, and declared: '*Eh bien*, we cannot leave out the Ambassador of France!' He promptly instructed his staff to retrieve one of the decorations already handed out (perhaps with a promise that one would be sent later on!), and conferred it on the French envoy!
45. In India, the '*Padma*' national award (at four distinct levels) is conferred only on some 60 or 70 individuals each year, on the eve of Republic Day. Civil servants, including serving envoys, are seldom nominated, but some retired ambassadors have received these honors, often in the autumn of their lives.
46. These words come from the film *Elizabeth* made in 2000, directed by Shekhar Kapur; other records note that she may have said: 'I do not want my sheep to wear another's brand'.
47. India has made an exception for awards from the neighboring Himalayan kingdom of Bhutan, but even this is after rigorous scrutiny to gauge the merits of each case.
48. In India, one recent alleged incident led to the recall of the Ambassador to Vienna in 2001, amidst press reports on financial irregularity; the official was temporarily suspended from the service.

49. India also offered this special facility for some years, but the privilege ended in the early 1960s.
50. In 1995–96, some of us had explored creating a similar consultancy enterprise in New Delhi. The plan was given up partly because we found at that time that Indian companies appeared averse to such consultants, and paying them for advice. We also realized that the project needed a committed driver, and none of our group was keen to give up his own planned activities.

Chapter 8: The Future

1. Edited by Brian Hocking and David Spence, *Foreign Ministries in the European Union: Integrating Diplomats*, (Palgrave Macmillan, Basingstoke, 2002).
2. Another small state innovation is the appointment of an 'Ambassador for the Environment' and an Ambassador to FAO, in the Bahamas, both based in the home country.
3. Co-location has its critics as well. A Nordic diplomat told the author that in Berlin, the capital of the most important neighbor for that state, it made no sense to have their embassy bundled into a faceless joint Nordic building on Tiergarten Strasse, when they should have an autonomous physical presence.
4. N. Krishnan joined the IFS in 1951, and served as ambassador to Yugoslavia (1977–81), and as permanent representative in Geneva (1967–71) and New York (1981–86), retiring in 1986.
5. The psychotropic substances consist of four sub-groups in terms of their effect: the stimulants, the depressants, the opiates and the hallucinogens. I served as Krishnan's deputy in those years, and played a minor support role. This story is narrated in *Inside Diplomacy*, pp. 314–5.
6. D.P. Aannd, Chairman of the powerful Customs and Excise Board of the Finance Ministry, attended these annual meetings as a perk that flowed from one of his minor charges, the narcotics control administration.
7. Ranjit Gupta joined the IFS in 1964, and was ambassador to Yemen, Venezuela, Oman, Thailand and Spain. He retired after an extension in 2003, as head of the 'unofficial' mission in Taiwan.
8. He joined in 1972, is High Commissioner in Pakistan since July 2003, headed the missions in Beijing, 2000–3, and Colombo, 1997–2000.
9. She joined in 1970, and spent an unusually long time at the Ministry

of External Affairs, New Delhi, from 1982 to 2001, for personal reasons. She has been Ambassador to Thailand since January 2002.
10. 'US Power and Strategy After Iraq', *Foreign Affairs*, July–August, 2003.
11. Gordon Craig and Felix Gilbert, eds, *The Diplomats, 1919–1939* (Princeton University Press, Princeton, 1991).
12. Madeleine Albright, as Permanent Representative to the UN with a seat in the Clinton cabinet, was a rare exception, but she too had her problems with the State Department and the rest of the Washington DC policy management system, Dobbs, *Madeleine Albright*.
13. G.R. Berridge, Maurice Keens-Soper and T.G. Otte, *Diplomatic Theory From Machiavelli to Kissinger* (Pallgrave, Basingstoke, 2001), p. 3.
14. The SAARC summit of January 2004 in Islamabad, and the unfreezing of India–Pakistan relations since the end of 2003 has raised expectations that cooperation in creating a free trade area may move forward. Clearly, the actions taken by India outside the SAARC group have played a role in this evolution.
15. Hocking and Spence, eds, *Foreign Ministries in the European Union*.
16. In India an Expenditure Commission recommended in 2002 a series of economy measures, including the closing of some embassies, but implementation has been slow.
17. In India regional embassies under senior envoys that would supervise junior ambassadors were recommended by the Pillai Committee of 1966. One additional problem is that such supervision flies in the face of the status of the ambassador as the personal representative of the head of state and answerable to him, through the country's government.
18. This conclusion is partly supported by the 2002 study of EU diplomacy, Hocking and Spence, eds, *Foreign Ministries in the European Union*.
19. This is one of the themes of Rana, *Bilateral Diplomacy*.
20. These themes have also been presented in Rana, *Inside Diplomacy* and *Bilateral Diplomacy*.
21. Berndt von Staden, former German Secretary of State and Ambassador to the US; essay in Herz *The Modern Ambassador*.
22. Confidential interview, December 2001.
23. Brian Hocking, and David Spence, eds, *Foreign Ministries in the European Union: Integrating Diplomats* (Palgrave Macmillan, Basingstoke, 2002)
24. In some Asian countries, China, India and Thailand, this is an observed trend. Similar trends are surely under way elsewhere.

SELECT BIBLIOGRAPHY

Adcock, Sir F. and Mosley, D.J., *Diplomacy in Ancient Greece* (Thames & Hudson, London, 1995)

American Foreign Service Association, *Inside a US Embassy*, 2nd edition (Washington DC, 1996)

Barston, R.P., *Modern Diplomacy*, 2nd edition (Longman, London, 1997)

Berridge, G.R. and James, Alan, *A Dictionary of Diplomacy* (Palgrave, Basingstoke, 2001)

Berridge, G.R., *Diplomacy: Theory and Practice*, 2nd edition (Palgrave, Basingstoke, 2001)

Brind, Harry, *Lying Abroad: Diplomatic Memoirs* (The Radcliffe Press, London, 1999)

Caldwell, Dan, and Mckewon, Timothy J., eds, *Diplomacy, Force and Leadership* (Westview Press, Boulder, 1993)

Cascone, Andrea, *Comparing Diplomatic Services: Structures, Networks and Resources of the Ministries of Foreign Affairs of EU and G8 Member States* (Diplo, Malta, 2002)

Cohen, Raymond, *Negotiating Across Cultures* (US Institute of Peace, Washington DC, 1991)

Cohen, Raymond, *The Theater of Power: The Art of Diplomatic Signaling* (1987)

Cohen, Raymond and Westbrook, R., *Amarna Diplomacy* (Johns Hopkins University Press, Baltimore, 2000)

Coles, John, *Making Foreign Policy* (John Murray, London, 2000)

Cooper, Andrew, ed., *Niche Diplomacy: Middle Powers After the Cold War* (Macmillan, London, 1999)

Craig, Gordon A. and Lowenheim, Francis L., *The Diplomats: 1939–1979* (Princeton University Press, Princeton, 1994)
Denza, Eileen, *Diplomatic Law: A Commentary on the Vienna Convention on Diplomatic Relations* (Clarendon Press, Oxford, 1998)
Dobbs, Michael, *Madeleine Albright* (Holt, New York, 1999)
Eban, Abba, *Diplomacy for the New Century* (Yale University Press, New Haven, 1998)
Eban, Abba, *The New Diplomacy* (Weidenfeld & Nicolson, London, 1988)
Edwards, R.D., *True Brits: Inside the Foreign Office* (BBC, London, 1994)
Esterline, John E., and Black, Robert B., *Inside Foreign Policy* (Mayfield, New York, 1975).
Evans, Peter B., Jacobson, Harold K., and Putnam, Robert D., eds, *Double-Edged Diplomacy* (University of California Press, Berkeley, 1993)
Faber, Richard, *A Chain of Cities: Diplomacy at the Edge of Empire* (The Radcliffe Press, London, 2000)
FCO—*Department Report on the Government Expenditure Plans, 2000–01 to 2001–01* (HM Stationery Office, London, April 2000)
Fisher, Roger, *Beyond Machiavelli: Tools For Coping With Conflict* (Penguin, London, 1996)
Foreign Service Training Institute, *The Head of Mission: A Symposium* (FSTI, Ministry of External Affairs, New Delhi, 1991)
Freeman Jr, Chas W., *Diplomat's Dictionary* (US Institute of Peace, Washington DC, 2000)
Galbraith, J.K., *Ambassador's Journal* (Houghton Mifflin, Boston, 1969)
Garthoff, Raymond L., *A Journey Through the Cold War* (Brookings, Washington DC, 2001)
Gotlieb, Alan, *I'll be with you in a Minute Mr Ambassador: The Education of a Canadian Diplomat in Washington* (Routledge, London, 1995)
Haass, Richard and O'Sullivan, Meghan, *Honey and Vinegar: Incentives, Sanctions and Foreign Policy* (Brookings Institution, Washington DC, 2000)
Hain, Peter, *The End of Foreign Policy?* (Royal Institute of International Affairs, London 2001)
Hamilton, Keith and Langhorne, Richard, *The Practice of Diplomacy: Its Evolution, Theory and Administration* (Routledge, London, 1995)
Herz, Martin F., ed., *The Modern Ambassador: The Challenge and the Search* (Institute for the Study of Diplomacy, Georgetown University, Washington DC, 1983)
Hickman, Katie, *Daughters of Britannia: The Lives and Times of Diplomatic Wives* (Harper Collins, London, 1999)

Hocking, Brian, ed., *Foreign Ministries: Change and Adaptation* (Macmillan, London, 1999)

Hocking, Brian, *Diplomacy of Image and Memory: Swiss Bankers and Nazi Gold* (Diplomatic Studies Program Discussion Paper No. 64, University of Leicester, April 2000)

Hocking, Brian and Spence, David, eds, *Foreign Ministries in the European Union: Integrating Diplomats* (Palgrave Macmillan, Basingstoke, 2002)

Jackson, Sir Geoffrey, *Concorde Diplomacy: The Ambassador's Role in the World Today* (Hamish Hamilton, London, 1981)

Keeley, Robert V., ed., *First Line of Defense: Ambassadors, Embassies and American Interests Abroad* (American Academy of Diplomacy, Washington DC, 2000)

Keohone, Robert O. and Nye, Joseph S., *Power and Interdependence* (Harper Collins, 1989)

Kurbalija, Jovan, ed., *Modern Diplomacy* (Mediterranean Academy of Diplomatic Studies, Malta, 1998)

Langhorne, Richard, *Who are the Diplomats Now?* (HMSO, London, 1996)

Liu Xiaohong, *Chinese Ambassadors: The Rise of Diplomatic Professionalism Since 1949* (Hong Kong University Press, Hong Kong, 2001)

Locke, Mary and Yost, Casimir A., eds, *Who Needs Embassies? How US Missions Abroad Help Shape Our World* (Institute for the Study of Diplomacy, Georgetown University, Washington DC, 1997)

Mayer, Martin, *The Diplomats* (Doubleday, New York, 1983)

Mayers, David, *The Ambassadors and America's Soviet Policy* (Oxford University Press, Oxford, 1995)

Melissen, Jan, ed., *Innovation in Diplomatic Practice* (Macmillan, London, 1999)

Miller, Robert Hopkins, *Inside an Embassy: The Political Role of Diplomats Abroad* (Congressional Quarterly, Washington DC)

Moses, Jonathon W., and Knutsen, Torbjorn, *Globalization and the Reorganization of Foreign Affairs Ministries* (Netherlands Institute of International Relations, Clingendael, 2002) Discussion Papers in Diplomacy No. 80.

Nicolson, Harold, *Diplomacy* (Institute for the Study of Diplomacy, Georgetown, 1958).

Paschke, Karl Th., *Report of the Special Inspection of 14 German Embassies in the Countries of the European Union* (German Federal Foreign Office, Berlin, September 2000)

Pearson, Frederick S. and Rochester, J. Martin, *International Relations: The Global Condition in the Late 20th Century*, 3rd edition (McGraw Hill, New York, 1992)

Phillips, Horace, *Envoy Extraordinary: A Most Unlikely Ambassador* (The Radcliffe Press, London, 1995)
Plischke, Elmer, *Modern Diplomacy: The Art and the Artisans* (American Enterprise Institute, Washington DC, 1979)
Potter, Evan H., *Canada and the New Public Diplomacy* (Netherlands Institute of International Relations, Clingendael, July 2002), Discussion Papers in Diplomacy No. 81.
Queller, D.E., *The Office of the Ambassador in the Middle Ages* (Princeton University Press, Princeton, 1967)
Rana, Kishan S., *Inside Diplomacy* (Manas, New Delhi, 2000; revised paperback edition, Manas, New Delhi, 2002)
Rana, Kishan S., *Bilateral Diplomacy* (DiploProjects, Malta, 2002)
Robertson, Justin, ed., *Foreign Ministries in Developing Countries and Emerging Market Economies* (Halifax, International Insights: Dalhousie Journal of International Affairs, Volume 14, Summer, 1998)
San, Tan Koon, *Excellency: Journal of a Diplomat* (The Other Press, Kuala Lumpur, 2000)
Sapin, Burton M., *The Making of US Foreign Policy* (Brookings Institution, Washington DC, 1966)
Scott, Gail, *Diplomatic Dance* (Fulcrum Publishing, Golden, Colorado, 1999)
Seitz, Raymond, *Over Here* (Weidenfeld & Nicholson, London, 1998)
Sharp, Paul, *Making Sense of Citizen Diplomats* (Center for the Study of Diplomacy, Leicester, 2001)
Simpson, Smith, and Botchel, Margery, eds, *Education in Diplomacy* (Rowman and Littlefield, New York, 1987)
Stearns, Monteagle, *Talking to Strangers: Improving American Diplomacy at Home and Abroad* (Princeton University Press, Princeton, 1996)
Stopford, John and Strange, Susan, *Rival States, Rival Firms* (Cambridge University, Cambridge, 1991)
Tyabji, Badr-Ud-Din, *Memories of an Egoist* (Roli, New Delhi, 1988)
Tyabji, Badr-Ud-Din, *More Memories of an Egoist* (Har-Anand, New Delhi, 1994)
Ure, John, *Diplomatic Bag* (John Murray, London, 1994)
Wolfe, Robert, ed., *Diplomatic Missions: The Ambassador in Canadian Foreign Policy* (McGill and Queen's University Press, Ottawa, 1998)
Wolfe, Robert, *Still Lying Abroad? On the Institution of the Resident Ambassador* (Diplomatic Studies Program, Paper No. 33, University of Leicester, 1997)

INDEX

academics, academia, scholars 75–7, 127, 178, 186–7
Africa xx, 79, 87, 156–7, 166, 182
agrément 40–1
Albright, Madeleine 6, 100
Amarna archives 25
ambassador (and), high commissioner, envoy, permanent representative academics 75–7, 127, 186–7; appointment xix–xx, 40–1; assignments xx, 70, 79; best resource 197–8; bilateral 37–8, 58, 64–95, 97–100; career 98, 174–7; catalyst 21, 35; CEO 1; channels 59; children 145, 147; chief executive 36–7; commissioning ceremony, 41–2; conference xxii, 167–8; coordination 146–7; credibility 122–3; deployment 177–8; duration 57–62; embassy team 143–54; empowering 34; entrepreneur 192–6; entertainment 160–4; functional expertise 173–4; generalist-specialist 174; globalized 198–204; golden handshake 178; grades 26, 176; handing over note 42–3; honesty 168–70; indiscretion 6–7, 180–84; initiative 70–1, 78–9, 81–2, 141–2; in residence 178; institution 1, 4–5, 136, 198–9; instructions 183; languages 110–1, 170–4; leadership 93–5; letter of commission 42; *loco parentis* 144–6; loyalty 154, 177–9; manager 91–2; media 56, 77, 82, 84–9, 103–4, 127; misconduct 180–4; multilateral 4, 37–8, 96–120; NGOs 11–2, 79, 101, 126, 140; non-career 35–6, 47–52, 148, 165; non-state partners 74–6; numbers 37; opposition groups 79; personal qualities 168–70; personal rank 24; plenipotentiary 35; policy role 16–7; politicians 126, 136–8, 187; power and influence 194–6; professional indiscretion 183–4; professional skills xix, 6–7, 170–2; reportage 88–91; salesman 81–2; sanction 184–6; scapegoat 127; security 62–3; spouse 143, 158–60; system 199; recall 57–62; regional 112–5, 199–200; regional conference 167–8; relationship manager 201–2; representation 22; residence 60–4; resignation 179; resident 2, 14, 25, 27, 190; retirement 186–

9; reward 184–6; role 5, 23–6, 31, 33–7; rogue 32–3, 180–4; tasks 2, 5, 98–9; taxation 57; training 165–8; under-worked 71; utility 27–8; young diplomats 150; withdrawal 57–62
annual plans 130–1
Ansari, Hamid xvi–ii
APEC 106
archives xviii, 91
armed forces, armed service attaches 153, 167
Arthashastra 2, 55, 168
ASEAN 10, 20, 70, 72, 114
  ASEAN Regional Forum (ARF) 9
ASEM 106
Aung San Suu Kyi 80
Australia
  national day 163; benchmarking 132; performance plans 15

Baig, M.R.A. 45–6
Bajpai, Sir Girija Shankar xiii–iv
Bakula, Kushak 31
BBC 88
Belgium 58
Berridge, G.R. 28, 177, 194
Bhutan 184
BIMST-EC 194
Blackwill, Robert 75
Brazil 59, 198
British Diplomatic Spouses Association 159
Bunker, Ellsworth 16
Butros-Ghali 100

Canada
  ambassadors 68, 82–4; ambassadors training 166; communications 17; DCM training 149; diplomatic tour 55; embassies 58; Foreign Service Institute 149; spouses 159–60
career management 174–7
Caricom 191
Carlucci, Frank 23, 74, 147

Carter, President 137
ceremonial 24, 36, 39–63
chargé d'affaires 60
chef de cabinet 67
chief executive (CEO) 1, 150–1
China, Chinese
  ambassadors 26; Association of Retired Ambassadors 186; Communist Party 188; diplomacy 84; diplomats 19; entertainment 162; Foreign Ministry; Indian Ambassador 194; Indonesia 61; language training 173; Overseas 128; provinces 72; specialization; spouses 160; State Council 128; Training 166; Zhou Enlai 160
cipher messages, telegrams 150, 179
citizen diplomacy 12
CNN 15, 88
Cohen, Raymond 169
Cold War xiv, 1, 8, 21, 28, 151
commercial work 81–2, 84, 94
  e-commerce 94
communication 36, 68–9, 79, 80–1, 103, 134–5, 148–52, 179
  channels 68–9; signals 59–60; speed 36
Confederation of Indian Industry (CII) 81
consular work 92–4
consulates general, consulates, consuls general, consuls 2, 154–6
  honorary 155–6
Contadora Group 70
corporate techniques 132, 164, 194–6
Council on Foreign Relations 85
country image 84–8, 171–2
country team 36, 147, 156–7
Covey, Stephen 171
credentials 43–7
  ceremony 44–6; letter of commission 42, 170; letter of introduction 44, 100
cross-cultural 171
CTBT 104, 118

Cuba 61, 157, 160
culture 21, 86–7
Czechoslovakia 55

de Bono, Edward 171
de Wicquefort, Abraham 3, 55
démarche 70, 78, 81
deputy chief of mission (DCM) 51, 63, 80, 83, 146, 148–50
developing countries (see South)
diplomacy, diplomat, diplomatic, diplomatist
    bilateral 37–8, 58, 64–95; channels 57–62, 66; citizen 12; classic 20; craft 8; definition 64; direct 14; domestic 121–42; economic 81–4, 170–1, 196; high 21; image 171; innovative 171; integrated 87, 170; junior 99; low xx, 7; media 56, 82, 88–9, 170; multilateral 37–8, 96–120; networking 194; political 170; process 3–8, 96, 201; profession 6–7; public 65, 84–8, 103–4, 115, 138–41, 170, 176; public good 201; role of provinces; regional 22, 198–1; renaissance of; risk and gain 196–7; system xix, 1, 4–5, 157, 197; tasks 98–9, 105–8; telephone 137; theorists 27–8; track two 12
diplomatic corps 24, 39, 43–4, 52–5, 66, 146, 158
    dean, doyen 52–3; regional groups 53–4
Dixit, J.N. xviii, 152
Dobrynin, Anatoly 30, 57

East Europe 6, 162, 183
Eban, Abba 27, 55, 71, 179
Eisenhower, President
elites 18
embassy, embassies, missions 143–164
    bilateral 27; co-location 195; heterogeneity 17–8, 101–2; joint 191; lean 157–8; local staff 158, 200; management 149; multilateral 37–8, 96–120; non-diplomatic staff 144, 146; number and distribution 199–200; service personnel 144–6; size 28–9, 157; specialized 104–5; task force 149; tasks 29–30; team 82, 143–54, 156–8
eminent persons group 75
Enron Corporation 83
entertainment (see representational entertainment)
entrepreneur 192–6
envoy (see ambassador)
ethics 177–80
ethnic groups xx–i, 75–6, 127–8, 145–6
European Union 112–3, 190–2
    ambassadors 13; bilateral embassies 29; CFSP 113, 190; CORPER 112; Council of Ministers; European Commission 13, 112–3; foreign policy 32, 192; Parliament 113; regions 73; unification 178

families 158–60
feedback 88–91, 107, 183–4
foreign aid 9–10
foreign minister 67
    chef de cabinet 67
foreign ministry (MFA) 64–74, 132–5
    briefs 91; capacity building 3–4; Chief of Protocol 53, 181; contact channel 9; country director 33; functional expertise 173–4; gatekeeper role 9, 65, 134–5; generalists 174; headquarter-mission ratios 133; human resources 16, 165–89; inspections 164; integration with missions 34–5, 134–5; interlocutor 133–4; knowledge management 203; micro-management 131–2; -mission relations 15, 33–5; process 203; structure 65–6; supervision 132; territorial departments 35, 65–6, 91, 124; transformation 202

foreign policy 1, 3–8, 21, 32, 36–7, 61, 70, 122–8, 203
France
  ambassador's instructions 129–30; chefs 161; diplomatic corps 39; Grandes Écoles 171, 187; ISO 9000 132; Quai d'Orsay 3, 129; performance 16; Secretary General 129

G-15, G-77 xvi, 11, 21, 105–6
G-7, G-8 11
Galbraith, John Kenneth 6, 71, 158, 181
Gandhi, Indira xiv, xv, 30, 68
Gandhi, Mahatma xii
Gandhi, Rajiv xii, 131
Ganga-Mekong 9, 199
Garvey, Sir Terence 183
gender 18–9
Germany
  ambassadors 26; Auswärtiges Amt (AA), foreign office 123–4, 130, 167, 175; Bavaria 72; Baden Württemberg 72; Chancellor 54–5, 68; conferences 167; embassy integration 135; German Democratic Republic 180; image 87; joint ambassador 191; journalists 139–40; language 172; Paschke Report 22, 29–30, 34, 85, 135, 201–2; promotion method 175; shift of capital 28–9; State Secretary 130; Unification 28
Ghosh, Arundhati 104
global South (see South)
globalization 1, 11, 121–2, 171
Gonsalves, Eric xv
Good Friday Agreement 198
governance 6–7, 91
Gulf 193
Gupta, Ranjit 193–4

handing over notes 42–3
head of state (see president)
high commissioner (see ambassador)

high commissions (see embassy)
Hocking, Brian 10, 11
home base 115, 117
human resources 58, 165–89

image (see country image)
immunities, privileges 39, 40, 55–7, 155, 181
India, Indian
  Afro-Asian Conference 141; ambassadors xi–xxiii; 26, 48–9, 52; annual plans 131; archives 91; Association of Indian Diplomats 186; awards 185; Bangladesh war 61–2; colonial period xi–iii; consular work 93; credentials ceremony 45–6; economic diplomacy xvi, 139; economic reforms xvii; Foreign Service 193; languages 116, 172; High Commission, London xi–ii; Ministry of External Affairs xii, xx–ii; multilateral work 111; NRIs, Overseas Indians 75, 127; National Security Advisory Board 188; nuclear tests xvii; Pakistan 60, 151; Peace Keeping Force 153; President 45–6; promotions 175–6; residence 161; Security Council 107, 183–4; spouses 180
Indonesia 61
innovation 141–2, 171, 192–9
instructions 116–20
intelligence work, officials 151–4
International Court of Justice 107
International Labor Organization (ILO) 96, 105
international relations theory 26–7
  agency 26; realist 26–7; theorists 27, 104
Internet 10, 79, 94–5
  intranets 150
interviews for book 8
Iran 41, 153, 193
Iraq, war 12, 61, 118, 183
Israel 128

Italy 4–5
　language 172; resident ambassadors 4–5, 56; Roman Empire 55; study of MFAs 66

Jaipal, Rikhy 31
Japan
　ambassadors 49; chefs 161; *Gaimusho* 9; *Heisei-kai* 173; language 173; Peru 63; Security Council 183–4
Jugnauth, Anerood 74

Kautilya 2, 55
Kennan, George 30
Kenya 30–1, 47, 49, 73
Kenyatta, Jomo 30
Kissinger, Henry 23
Koh, Tommy 31
Krishnan, N. xv, 193

Lall, Arthur 31
language, expertise 110–1, 172–4
Latin America 49, 71, 83, 93, 106, 184
League of Nations xi, 96, 196
Lebanon 182
linkage, leverage 82
lobbying, lobbyists 79
local staff 158, 200
localitis 35

Malaysia 42
Malta 155
management 91–2, 108, 132
　performance (see performance management)
Mansingh, Lalit 93
Manu 168, 170
Mao Tse-Tung xiii
Mauritius 74, 80–1, 127
media 56, 77, 82, 84–9, 103–4, 127
Melissen, Jan 142
Menon, K.P.S. 20
Menon, Krishna xiv
Menon, Shiv Shankar 194
messages 149–50

migrants, migration 92–4
mission (see embassy)
Moi, Daniel arap 47, 73
multilateral diplomacy 37–8, 96–120

Napoleon 160,
Naranayan, K.R. 189
national days 163–4
NATO 8, 49
negotiation 76–7, 96–120
Nehru, Jawaharlal xii–iii, xix
Nepal 161
New Zealand 15, 130
NGOs 11–2, 79, 101, 126, 140
Nicolson, Harold 31, 53, 76, 106, 168, 178
Non Proliferation Treaty (NPT) 118
non-career ambassadors 35–6, 47–52, 148, 165, 193

OAS 114
OAU 114
Oman 193
oral history xviii–xix, 189
outreach 33, 76–88, 105

Pakistan 60–1, 151, 194
Pandit, Vijayalakshmi xiv
Pannikar, K.M. xvi
Pant, Apa Saheb 30–1
parliament, parliamentary 69, 162
Parthasarathi, G. xiv
Paschke Report 22, 29–30, 34, 85, 135, 201–2
Performance, performance management xxiii, 15–6, 128–31
　action plan 130–1; ambassador's instructions 129–30; annual plans 130–1; foreign service inspections 131; ISO 9000 certification 132; outcomes 16; public performance targets 130; targets 16
permanent mission 96–120
permanent representatives (PR) 37–8, 96–120

persona non grata 151, 182
political work 78–81
Ponappa, Leela 194
Portugal 74
Potter, Evan D. 85
Powell, Colin 85
Prem Singh 74
president, head of state 13, 21, 67–9, 136–8
    ambassadors audience 13; credentials 43–7; telephone contacts 13–4, 137
prime minister 67–9
    office 68
privilege (see immunities)
professional skills xix, 6–7, 170–2
promotion 76–88, 105–6, 175–7
    fast-track 175
propaganda 85
protocol 24, 36–7, 39–47
    chief of 43–6, 55, 182; credentials 43–7; initialed copies 43–4; precedence 40
provinces (see sub-state entities)
psychotropic substances 193
public
    attentive to foreign affairs 125; diplomacy 84–8, 92–5, 102–3, 170; interest 197; good 201; -private 11, 164

Queen Elizabeth 44–5
Queen Elizabeth I 185

Ramgoolam, Seewosagur 74
Rasgotra, M.K. xv
Realpolitik 2
recall 57–62
reciprocity 39,40
reportage (see feedback)
representational entertainment 160–4
    grant 162–4
residence 160–4
retirement 186–9
Robertson, Justin 3
rogue ambassadors 180–4

Russia, Soviet Union 8, 20, 28, 30, 57–8, 84, 151, 173

SAARC 114, 199
Saran, Shyam xviii
Scandinavia 14
security 62–3
Senegal 183
serendipity 66
servicing 92–3
Siddique, Tony 30
signals 59–60
Singapore 14
    ambassadors 58; mission size 157; promotion methods 175; team 106; Security Council 107
South Korea 187–8
South, global South, developing, Third World xvi, xx, 87, 92–4, 102–3, 126, 154, 161, 168, 172
    ambassadors 48
sovereignty 192
Soviet Union (see Russia)
specialization, specialists 97–100, 172–4
    functional 173–4
spouse 158–60
Sri Lanka xviii, 153, 155, 194
sub-state entities, provinces 10–1, 72–3
Sweden 193
Switzerland 11, 61

Talleyrand 169
technology 5, 16–7
terrorism 117–8
    9/11 62, 85
Thailand
    anointing ambassadors 41–2; CEO ambassadors 1, 18; FTA 194; ISO 9000 132
The Economist 88
think tanks 76, 127, 140, 187–8
third world (see South)
Tochev, Tocho 30
tourism 86–7
track two dialogue 12

training 165–8, 203
transition countries 6
Truman President 147
Turkey 26, 62, 129
TV 88–9, 104, 122, 125
  24-hour 27, 86, 128
Tyabji, Badr-ud-din 141

Uganda 49
UK
  credentials ceremony 42, 44–5; diplomacy 18; diplomatic corps 39; Foreign Office (FCO) 15; Germany 72–3; Iran 41; knighthoods 184; performance targets 131; Permanent Under Secretary 44; policy goals 15; residence 161; royal family 161; retired ambassadors 187–8; spouses 159; Zimbabwe 60
UN 70, 96–120
  Charter 20; Disarmament Conference 118; ECOSOC 107; General Assembly 13, 102; jobs 119; Narcotics Commission 193; Secretary General 100–1; Security Council 102, 107, 183–4
US
  Ambassadors 26, 35–6, 40, 49–50, 70, 73–4, 79; Awards 185; CIA 152; cipher messages 91; consulates 93; country team 156; credentials ceremony 45; Cuba 61; diplomatic corps 39; ECOSOC 107; embassies, 17; Foreign Service 165; Foreign Service Institute, 165; Kenya 73; lobbying 79; Mission Program Plans 130; National Security Adviser 69; Permanent Mission 80–1; President 42, 103, 137; President's letter 147; professional culture 85; revolving door 188; security 62–3; Senate 57; senior fellowships 171; State Department 10, 33, 165; terrorism 62; unilateralism 118
Uzbekistan 157

Vienna Convention on Diplomatic Relations, 1961 31, 40, 56, 64, 77
Vienna Regulations of 1815 24, 39, 56
visas 92–4
von Standen, Berndt 201

Westphalia, Treaty of 2
Wotton, Sir Henry 169
World Bank 97
World Trade Organization (WTO) xviii, 10, 105, 117, 122, 126, 198

Zimbabwe 60, 73